HANDGUN
COMPETITION

HANDGUN
COMPETITION

a comprehensive sourcebook covering all aspects of modern competitive pistol and revolver shooting

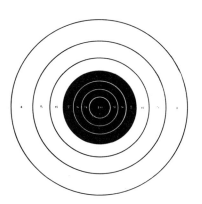

MAJOR GEORGE C. NONTE, JR.

WINCHESTER PRESS

Copyright © 1978 by George C. Nonte, Jr.
All rights reserved

Library of Congress Cataloging in Publication Data

Nonte, George C.
  Handgun competition.

  Includes index.
  1. Pistol shooting.   2.   Shooting.   I.   Title.
GV1175.N65   799.2'02833   77-27417
ISBN 0-87691-253-6

9 8 7 6 5 4 3 2 1

Published by Winchester Press
205 East 42nd Street
New York, N.Y. 10017

WINCHESTER is a Trademark of Olin Corporation used
by Winchester Press, Inc. under authority
and control of the Trademark Proprietor

Printed in the United States of America

Book Design by Marcy J. Katz

Contents

Introduction

There are people who are troubled—even alarmed—by the very notion that a weapon can be used for competitive sport. Or, to be more precise, they are troubled by the use of one particular weapon, a gun. Oddly, the same people who think they discern some mystical contradiction (if not plain bloodlust) in the use of firearms for sport seldom voice such feelings about the hurling of a javelin in the Olympic games. Nor do they find anything bloodthirsty about archery—or even about fencing, which is in essence a body-contact sport that not only involves a weapon but would be quite dangerous if not for the wearing of protective garb and the blunting of the four-sided rapier known as a foil.

The problem, of course, is that the gun is an especially powerful weapon that sends a lethal missile, the bullet, over a long distance; and unlike the other arms mentioned, it is still used for purposes other than sport. Since prehistoric time, man has found it necessary to carry arms, beginning with rocks and clubs, then progressing through knives and swords, bows, javelins, and so on. The most common arm, naturally, was always the best one that contemporary technology could provide. It is only because bows, javelins and swords are so much less effective as personal weapons that they are no longer carried as handguns are. This in no way detracts from the legitimacy of the handgun as a sporting tool. When used for sport, it is as harmless as the javelin or the fencing foil, and it probably requires more skill, more years of practice, before a competitor becomes an International contender.

True, such a weapon cannot be blunted as a foil is, yet statistically it is safer. For that matter, the handgun is statistically far safer than a golf ball or golf club, a hockey stick, a tennis racket, a pair of skis or a gymnastic high bar. I can attest to the validity of the statistics. In 40-odd years of association with handgunning, I have not seen a single report of a death resulting from organized handgun competition.

A few readers may approach this book hesitantly, curious about handgunning but wondering whether target shooting with a handgun is a safe, legitimate sport. I hope I am beginning to persuade them as they read this, and can present the sport well enough in subsequent pages to make them try it for themselves. That alone would be sufficient reward for my months of work on the book. But winning new adherents to this wholesomely competitive game is obviously not my sole objective or even the primary one.

Most readers are likely to be shooters who enjoy hunting, may have done some target shooting with shoulder arms, and perhaps have done some target handgunning, as well. They need no persuasion. What they want is a thorough knowledge of competitive handgun shooting—from facts about the best equipment, its care, maintenance and improvement to facts about the various types of competition and how to participate most effectively. I hope to give them that thorough knowledge. I've tried, in writing this book, to offer information of value to all shooters, from tyros to those with considerable experience in at least some types of competition. If my advice or information improves their shooting, and I believe it will, my primary goal will have been achieved.

One very important chapter in this book—the chapter on handguns and the law—has still another purpose. It explains how a person can pursue the sport of handgunning, particularly competitive handgunning, without violating the law, and without losing his sanity in the effort to learn and obey the host of regulations and restrictions imposed on the use of handguns. As stated at the beginning of that chapter, "no other implement of sport (or defense, for that matter) is subject to even a tiny fraction of the number of laws that affect handguns." Even so simple and innocent a procedure as traveling from home to another city with a handgun in order to participate in a match can be a legal problem—unless the shooter is well informed about the law and how to cope with it. Unfortunately, legal red tape and restrictions have discouraged a great many enthusiastic shooters from using handguns for their sport. If my chapter on the law shows them how to deal with the problem, that alone will make the book worthwhile.

And let's bear in mind that to deal with the legal problems—a manifestly unfair legislative and administrative travesty that interferes with the activities of law-abiding citizens while failing dismally in its intended curtailment of crimes involving firearms—is to do no more than exercise our constitutional right as citizens.

"The right of the people to keep and bear arms shall not be infringed." Our forefathers saw compelling reasons to include that guarantee in the Bill of Rights of our Constitution nearly two centuries ago. They knew that they could not have fought clear of tyranny had the people not been equipped with firearms. And they knew that the people must have the capability to defend themselves against tyranny if it should arise again, as well as to defend themselves from encroachment or invasion by any hostile group or nation. Without weapons, the settlers of America would have been helpless against brigands, against hostile Indians, against the English troops who invaded during the War of 1812, and even against an occasional bear that disputed a man's claim to a cache of meat. Without weapons, for that matter, the settlers would have been unable to procure meat in the first place.

Granted, when those eminent gentlemen of the 18th century wrote our Constitution they could not have envisioned our nation quite as it now exists. Nevertheless, they had good reasons to guarantee in perpetuity that, individually and collectively, the citizens would have the right to be armed. Most other nations had developed from feudal domains where the possession of arms by the common folk (though not by the aristocracy) was forbidden except when those common folk were drafted into an army to fight and die for their ruler. But the United States was to be a republic, not a monarchy. Whereas the purpose of many governments was to deny democracy in order to uphold some form of tyranny, the purpose of ours was to uphold democracy and deny tyranny. The common man, therefore, was to have arms with which to feed and protect himself and his family.

From the beginning, the use of firearms has been part of our way of life. The long and genuine need for arms in the hands of virtually all able-bodied citizens nurtured an affinity for firearms which exists perhaps more strongly in this nation than anywhere else. Secure in the guarantee of the Second Amendment, men and women of virtue, peace and independence have always armed themselves for the defense of home, property and family. Not until very recent years did it ever occur to anyone that this might be considered somehow improper, even illegal. It is true that we no longer need guns in order to procure meat for survival, but there is certainly nothing wrong with using them to provide our own meat occasionally—in strict accordance with the game laws—instead of buying a commodity, the demand for which has resulted in oppressively high pricing and, in some areas, hunger. As to the need for guns as a means of defense, that has not diminished. In my opinion, to deny a law-abiding citizen the right to own an efficient means of defense against criminal activity is not only to deny his Constitutional right; it is also to deny his fundamental right to self-preservation.

But what about the right to use guns merely to hit inanimate targets in a match against other shooters? Perhaps it is a mistake to speak of the right to own *arms;* what may really be at stake is the right to own property. A gun is as much a man's property as, say, an electric drill or an automobile—both of which have enormous potential for criminal use. If pressure groups ever succeed in prohibiting private ownership of one kind of property, they may eventually prohibit ownership of *any* kind of property merely on the basis that there is no real "need" for it. On occasion, while watching the antics of a certain professional athletic team, I've questioned whether a baseball bat has any redeeming social value. No one on that team was able to demonstrate any good use for the thing, and certainly most people have no "need" for a bat, which is occasionally a lethal instrument. Yet it would be absurd to revoke a man's right to play baseball. It is just as absurd to revoke anyone's right to participate in matches with handguns.

There are several means of defense against the tragic absurdities of misguided pressure groups. Most obviously, we can support reasonable legislation and legislators and we can oppose unreasonable legislation and legislators. We can do so both individually and, through our sporting and conservation associations, collectively. We can and must obey the laws already enacted (while working for the repeal of senseless ones) and we can learn how to engage in our sport by coping legally with any obstacles. After all, if the laws really made it ridiculously difficult to be a competitive handgunner, the sport would not be growing at an unprecedented rate, as it is now doing. And finally, we can learn to perform so well in our chosen recreational activity that we impress people strongly with the wholesome excitement—the validity—of our sport. I hope this book helps.

George C. Nonte, Jr.
Major, Ord., Ret.
Peoria, Illinois

1
Handguns and the Law

No other implement of sport (or defense, for that matter) is subject to even a tiny fraction of the number of laws that affect handguns. More than 22,000 federal, state, local and municipal statutes and ordinances govern the manufacture, distribution, sale, purchase, possession and use of firearms. Most of these are directed at handguns. The laws are so numerous, so varied, and change so often that a division of the federal government (Bureau of Alcohol, Tobacco, and Firearms of the U. S. Treasury) is forced to publish an annual compilation. It is worthy of note that in spite of the great resources applied to this compilation, the publishers must include a disclaimer stating, in effect, that they cannot assure the completeness or correctness of the volume, which contained 347 pages in the 1976 edition.

Sometimes a gun owner is unable to determine what laws and ordinances apply to his arms in a given situation. A handgun owner moving into any of numerous cities today cannot ascertain in advance, or often even upon arrival, exactly what laws pertain—unless he procures the services of an attorney. I know of several instances where an individual attempting to determine the pertinent law contacted local police authorities and was given either incomplete or erroneous information. As a result, the gun owner inadvertently ran afoul of the law and had to obtain the services of an attorney—at no small cost—to straighten out matters. In extreme cases, incorrect or incomplete information supplied by law-enforcement agencies has resulted in a violation that led to the arrest of the gun owner.

There is no central source for information on the laws governing possession and use of handguns. The BATF is probably the best informed agency, but its true expertise lies in federal law, which is often interpreted differently by local agents throughout the country. Such differing interpretations have, on more than one occasion, caused an individual to inadvertently violate the "law." Many complaints have been made to the BATF about these differing interpretations, and it is to be hoped that the situation is slowly being cleared up as agents become more experienced and better educated.

The BATF has, however, performed one exceedingly valuable ser-

The author (left) and Bob Hinman, well-known shooting authority, author and outfitter, pore over the latest edition of the BATF's compilation of firearms regulations—the most comprehensive available source of information on gun laws and how a shooter can comply with those laws when moving his residence or traveling to distant matches.

vice. Periodically (more or less annually), it compiles and publishes a thick paperback volume entitled *Firearms Regulations.* Though not entirely up to date by the time it reaches the BATF agents, this is still the most important and extensive single source of information on federal, state and local firearms laws. It contains reprints of the various statutes and ordinances that apply directly or indirectly to possession and use of firearms; and in some instances it reproduces excerpts of broader laws that contain some reference to firearms.

An individual may find it difficult to understand some of the entries without seeking expert advice, but it's the basic reference to which one should turn.

Let's say you are living in St. Paul, Minnesota, and you plan on moving to Columbus, Ohio; you plan to take your handguns (and perhaps other firearms) with you. You certainly do not wish to arrive in Columbus and be immediately in violation of state or local laws. The first step is to contact your local BATF agent (who should be listed under U. S. Government in the phone book as "Treasury, Firearms"). Ask for an appointment to come to his office and examine a copy of *Firearms Regulations.* Agents will usually permit this. If you have a cooperative agent who is not too busy, he may well assist you in locating the proper section of the book and interpreting the provisions of the laws. But don't count on this. Make notes on the titles and sections of those laws that appear to affect you or, even better, try to arrange for copies of the material. All federally-licensed firearms dealers are furnished with this book, so you may also see it at your favorite shop.

With that information in hand, you can protect yourself. Write first to the NRA-affiliated rifle or pistol club in Columbus and ask for assistance. Cite the laws you have found in the BATF reference, and ask if there are any others that bear on the subject. Also ask for information on local interpretation. Don't limit your questions to just the city proper, but to the entire county. Certainly your movements and perhaps even your residence will not be restricted to the city proper. At the same time, it will do no harm to describe the types and numbers of firearms you own as well as the uses to which you normally put them. And it will do your reception there no harm if you ask about joining the club. Certainly you will want to do this eventually, so get started early and make a good impression.

It may well be worthwhile to write a quite similar letter to both the city and county police departments, making it clear that you are a firearms enthusiast and that you are vitally concerned with making certain you do not violate any local laws. Some police departments are so busy they simply cannot respond quickly, if at all, to such outside requests for information. But it's worth trying. And in your letters to the law-enforcement agencies, you might request application forms for any permits, registrations or other documents required by the laws you have read.

You may still encounter problems. Depending on the states and cities through which you plan to drive, it may be unlawful to carry the guns in an automobile with you, even if they are unloaded, locked in cartons or cases, and not readily accessible to any occupants of the automobile. Federal law places no restrictions on a private individual transporting his handguns from one state to another incidental to a change of residence, but state and local laws are confusing and contradictory. If your household will be transported by a commercial carrier, the problem may or may not be solved. Federal law does not prohibit a commercial mover from transporting your firearms as a part of your household effects but, again, such transportation can run afoul of state and local laws. And some commercial movers object to handling firearms or ammunition as part of a household shipment. A somewhat safer alternative is to ship the guns to yourself at your new address. But even if you are thoroughly familiar with the requirements of law at your new residence and intend to comply, the shipment might arrive before all of the preliminary procedures can be approved and completed. This might place you inadvertently in violation of the law.

The best procedure by far is to arrange with a local federally licensed firearms dealer to make the transfer. First, inventory the guns and retain a copy for use at your new residence, then turn the guns over to the dealer. He will enter them on his records in accordance with federal, state and local laws and give you a receipt. Naturally, he will charge a small fee for his effort and for the space the guns will occupy in his establishment until shipment is made. Instruct him to hold the shipment until you advise him to send it. Upon arrival at your new residence, simply comply with all the state and local statutes and ordinances and arrange with a federally licensed firearms dealer there to receive the shipment for you.

A different but related problem is that of traveling to a distant locale to compete in a match. Several years ago, a Midwestern acquaintance of mine attended an invitational shoot in an Eastern city. As he couldn't afford to be away from his business for long, he decided to travel by air. When he made his reservation, he inquired about the airline's policy with regard to the transport of firearms. He was told he could check the gun with any other luggage he had—as long as it was unloaded, with the magazine removed, and secured in a locked case—and it would be carried in the plane's hold, to be delivered to him personally (rather than dumped out on the baggage-claim carousel) when he got to his destination.

However, when he arrived at the check-in counter prior to boarding the plane, he was asked what was in the "odd-looking case." Since honesty usually turns out to be the best policy, he explained that it was a pistol case containing a handgun, ammunition, accessories, and tools for cleaning and maintenance. The clerk told him that it could not be checked through with the baggage, after all, but would be locked in the pilot's cabin and returned to him at the airline's counter when he landed. Regulations hadn't changed, but company policy had. The caution exercised by airlines is understandable in view of the hijacking incidents of the past decade. But, as a rule, handguns can be transported aboard a public carrier if the carrier is informed beforehand and its rules obeyed. Actually, my friend was happier to have his pistol case carried in the captain's cabin than in the luggage compartment, and it was returned to him at the airline counter, promptly and undamaged, as promised.

By prearrangement, he was met at the counter by a member of the host pistol club who happened to be a federally licensed firearms dealer. The reason for this was a wrangle with local authorities, who had been contacted by the club in an effort to comply with municipal restrictions and who had interpreted the city ordinances to mean that no one could have a gun in the city unless it was registered to him by the city—not even for 48 hours and for the sole purpose of competing in an organized match. The authorities relented, but with the proviso that the visitors' guns would be used only on the range and would be transported there by a licensed dealer.

This was an odd case, described here only to illustrate the extremes to which legal interpretation is sometimes carried. Usually, there is no real problem about bringing a gun to a city temporarily, for purposes of competition, if the gun is in a securely locked case and the shooter carries proof of the purpose for which he is bringing it along. The organization that is holding or sponsoring the shoot usually looks into these matters beforehand, helps with any necessary arrangements and informs the visiting participants of required procedures. It's generally up to the police to enforce the local handgun laws, of course, and policemen usually (though not invariably) try to be helpful to an organization holding a match within their jurisdiction. After all, they're shooters themselves, and some of them may be competing in the match. If questions or problems arise, it's therefore a good idea to enlist the aid of the police department.

Federal law has become much more restrictive and much more heavily enforced since the enactment of the infamous Gun Control Act of 1968 (a section of Chapter 44 of 18 U.S.C. as amended by Title 1 of P.L. 90-168). Essentially, the federal gun-control law, as it now stands, contains the following provisions that affect shooters:

- The law prevents transfer to non-residents; that is, you can't buy or sell a gun outside your state of residence. This does not prevent loan or rental for legitimate purposes, or transfer to replace a stolen or inoperative gun being used in organized competition.

- It prevents sale or delivery of a rifle or shotgun, or ammunition for either, to a person under 18 years of age, and the same for a handgun or ammunition to any person under 21.

- It prevents sale or delivery of any firearm when and where same would be in violation of any state or local law.

- It prevents shipment, transportation or receipt in interstate or foreign commerce by a fugitive from justice, unlawful user of drugs or narcotics, adjudicated or committed mentally defective, or anyone under indictment or convicted of a crime punishable by imprisonment for more than one year.

- It requires federal licensing of dealers in firearms (but without clearly defining "dealer").

- It provides for a special federal collector's license to facilitate handling arms and ammunition as relics and curios.

- It allows transfer across the boundaries of contiguous states, *provided* those states have enabling legislation.

- It allows transfer by a dealer *intra*state without personal appearance of the transferee, provided other requirements of the law are met and the transferee supplies a sworn statement that he is not prohibited by law from receiving firearms. The statement must contain the name, address and title of the principal local law-enforcement officer of the area to which the firearm will be shipped; the transferor must send a copy of the statement to that law-enforcement officer, then wait seven days after return receipt of the notification before shipping the firearm.

- It requires a $200 tax be paid on the making or transfer of fully automatic weapons, rifles with barrels shorter than 16 inches, shotguns with barrels shorter than 18 inches, any firearm *made* from a rifle or shotgun whose overall length is less than 26 inches, pistols with detachable stocks whose barrel lengths are less than those just stated, firearms with combination rifle/shotgun barrels less than 12 inches long, mufflers and silencers, and "destructive devices" (except for certain sporting and antique arms and ammunition).

- It requires payment of a $5 transfer tax on pistols or revolvers with a smooth bore (no spiral rifling at all) designed to fire a fixed shotgun shell, firearms with combination rifle/shotgun barrels at least 12 inches long but less than 18 inches, weapons or devices capable of firing a shot and of being concealed, but not of conventional revolver or pistol form (cane guns, pen guns, Stinger, Game Getter, Handy gun). *Making* any of the above requires a special payment of a $200 tax.

- It prevents the importation of handguns which do not meet the weight, size and safety requirements of complex and arbitrary "factoring criteria."

The press has not always been quite accurate in its comments on the Gun Control Act, or GCA '68, as it is widely known. Many readers may therefore be surprised to learn what GCA '68 does *not* do:

- It does not prevent over-the-counter ammunition purchase outside the state of residence.

- It does not prevent transportation interstate for lawful purposes, provided no sale or transfer results.

- It does not include antique guns, muzzle-loaders, or firearms made during or before 1898.

- It does not require a license for handloading for one's own use.

- It does not prevent loan or rental to a non-resident for temporary lawful use.

- It does not prohibit transfer to a non-resident engaged in organized competition to replace a lost, stolen or inoperative arm. (Transferee must certify.)

- It does not prevent purchase in a state contiguous to one's state of residence, provided both states have enacted enabling legislation.

- It does not include shotgun or unprimed non-metallic shotgun cases, black powder, or blank cartridges as ammunition.

- It does not prevent shipment of your firearm to a licensed manufacturer, importer or dealer for repair or customizing.

- It does not apply to air or compressed-gas guns.

- It does not prevent transfer of inherited firearms.

- It does not prevent private sales and transfers intrastate.

- It does not prevent commercial shipment to a new residence in another state.

- It does not prevent you from selling a firearm to a dealer interstate.

- It does not control in any way transfer, shipment or possession of handloading equipment.

- It does not prevent mail-order purchase of a firearm *intra*state.

Unfortunately, any semblance of consistency ends with federal law. At the state level, we have a maze of statutes, ranging from the clean and uncluttered simplicity to be found in Wyoming up through the utter chaos of some Eastern Seaboard states.

Most states require a permit of some sort to carry a handgun openly, though some allow it without a permit while hunting or upon one's own property. Quite a few states—predominantly Western—still allow the carrying of an accessible handgun in an automobile, truck or other vehicle. (Some of those laws have remained unchanged for so long that they still refer to the lawful carrying of a handgun on one's horse or in his saddlebags or wagon.) All states prohibit the carrying of a *concealed* firearm upon one's person, except when licensed or granted a permit by the state or appropriate municipal authority. With very few exceptions, possession of a handgun within one's residence or place of business for the purpose of self-defense is lawful. Again, however, in some states—primarily in the East—this time-honored practice is prohibited without a permit. Where this is allowed, though, the gun may be concealed.

When we get into city and county laws, we encounter a morass of virtually incomprehensible restrictions which appear to serve no useful purpose and which are so inconsistent and contradictory as to defy reason. Some states have recognized this ridiculous situation and by constitutional amendment or pre-emptive legislation have established clear parameters within which local ordinances must be constructed. California is one of the foremost states in pre-emptive legislation to eliminate one of the most confusing and contradictory local-ordinance situations existing in the country. It is to be hoped that other states will follow California's example.

Among the various restrictions I've mentioned, the one prohibiting the carrying of a concealed firearm must be of greatest concern to anyone who is thinking about getting into competitive handgunning. As a general rule, the prohibition doesn't seriously interfere with the need for a competitive shooter to carry his guns to and from the range. Unfortunately, the notion that it's just about impossible to obtain a permit to do so has discouraged many people who might otherwise have become active in match handgunning. But in most states and cities, an unloaded firearm carried in a locked case is not considered an illegally concealed weapon. In many, a permit or license is needed just to *own* a handgun, but once you have obtained your permit no one is going to stop you from engaging in your sport.

2
Gun Selection: the Basic Battery

Elsewhere in this book, you'll find the various types of competition discussed in considerable detail, along with a few comments on appropriate guns. Later, too, I'll discuss the current crop of competitive handgun models in technical detail. But here I want to describe the types of guns in more general terms for the individual just getting started in the game who simply wants to know what makes and models will serve him best without too great an investment and without running afoul of the rules.

In the next few pages, I'll go through the details of assembling a satisfactory battery for each type of competition while keeping the cost as low as is compatible with reaching for master-class scores. Also, without getting into the ultra-sophisticated foreign models and custom-built guns (which sometimes seem to require the advice of a mechanical engineer to understand them).

Standard American, or NRA, competition seems the simplest and most straightforward, but it requires the greatest number of guns. This is due to the fact that there are three categories or classes which require, at the bare minimum, two guns and for which most people consider three a necessity, and some others feel four are needed.

First you will require a target-type .22 rimfire autoloader for the .22 stage of the National Match Course. This gun will be the cheapest to shoot. Quite likely it will fire several times as many shots as any of the others, so you want a thoroughly reliable gun that is exceptionally durable and capable of withstanding many thousands of rounds per year for a long period of time. Fortunately, .22 autoloaders have been highly developed in this country for this specific purpose. At the present time, four major manufacturers provide one or more models,

Ruger's Mark I .22 pistol is the most economical of rimfire autos suitable for target shooting. It lacks some of the refinements found in more costly guns but has the feel and fit, sights and mechanical accuracy that are the vital competitive ingredients and is suitable for someone just getting into match shooting.

ranging in price from about $95 to $200, with extra-cost options sometimes raising the price by 20 to 50 percent. Ruger offers its very basic (and lowest-priced of all) MKI auto, which is simply a target version of the Standard Model .22 auto first introduced in the late 1940's. High Standard offers the most extensive line with several variations based upon its Supermatic design, which was introduced in the early and mid-1950's. All of the High Standard models suitable for National Match use feature interchangeable barrels, and a wide variety of accessories may be obtained for them. Smith & Wesson offers the very fine M41 pistol introduced in the mid-1950's. This gun has long been very highly regarded for National Match use. The S&W line consists of the M41, a variant M46 and sufficient accessories to adapt either to almost any individual and his shooting style. It is the most recent and sophisticated design produced domestically.

Other pistols, manufactured abroad, are suitable for National Match use. Generally speaking, they are of recent and sophisticated design but are available only to a limited extent and are priced quite high ($400 and upward). While in some respects a few of the foreign products may be technically superior to those manufactured here, the average competitive shooter is not capable of using these refinements to improve his scores. Quite frankly, unless one has achieved such a level of proficiency that he is a serious contender for a National Championship, I doubt very much that he would be able to take advantage of the relatively minor superiority of some of the foreign guns.

No one can *buy* the skill necessary to win matches. The most expensive pistol available is only an instrument to be guided by the hand and eye of the shooter, and no matter how precisely it can deliver its bullet (mechanically speaking), that delivery is dependent entirely upon the holding and squeezing skill of the shooter. Almost any of the domestic guns we'll discuss are capable of putting all their shots well inside the X-ring of the 50-yard target from a machine rest with ammunition of match quality. A neophyte marksman most likely will not be able to shoot scores one bit higher with a $500 or $600 foreign pistol than he will with a $95 Ruger MKI.

There are two schools of thought regarding the choice of a first gun. The one school insists on buying the very best (expensive) because that's what you will want eventually and you might as well start with it. The second school favors buying an adequate, low-cost gun to start, then upgrading your guns as your skill progresses. The reasoning is that you aren't good enough in the beginning to know what you'll really want as the ultimate gun anyway. I tend to go along with the second school of thought. Even though you may have done a lot of informal shooting, it will take many thousands of rounds of National Match-type competition under pressure before you really begin to develop valid thoughts and preferences about the gun that will enable you to produce your best scores. You might start with a $500 Walther OSP and then discover that its particular layout, balance and operating characteristics are less desirable for you than other available models. When that happens, you'll have a $500 gun that you dislike; therefore, you probably won't shoot it too well. You'll go through a period of time when you are trying to determine what other gun works best and how you can swap off your Walther for another gun without any great loss.

If you do not have a .22 pistol suitable for match use, I recommend beginning with a basic gun in the $100 range. As this is written, that range is exemplified by the Ruger MKI with its unusual stamped-steel frame, cylindrical receiver and round, enclosed breechbolt. This gun is perfectly capable of producing master-class scores when handled properly, though it does lack many of the refinements found on other more expensive guns—refinements which you'll eventually want. For example, it contains no provision for the attachment or adjustment of weights and balance. There is no provision for trigger-pull adjustment and there is no slide stop to automatically lock the action open after the last shot is fired. On the plus side, in addition to its low cost and durability, it points and balances well; it is functionally quite reliable; the grip shape and angle fits most shooters quite well; and it carries a pretty good set of micrometer-adjustable sights.

Once you feel you've caught up with the capabilities of the Ruger and need a more sophisticated gun, the most logical step is up to the Smith & Wesson M41 or the High-Standard Supermatic Citation with its rear sight on a yoke attached to the frame. The Colt Match Target model is available but, as mentioned, it has not been updated to keep pace with the other two. There are shooters who prefer the guns of a

The Supermatic Citation typifies High Standard's fine line of target autos. It has earned a reputation for excellent performance in American rimfire competition.

Colt's Match Target Woodsman, though less sophisticated than the High Standard and Smith & Wesson designs, is still considered a fine pistol for .22 target shooting.

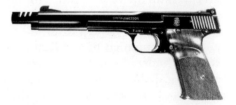

The S&W M41 is generally considered the most sophisticated of domestically produced rimfire target autos. It is very popular among .22 match shooters.

single manufacturer, often because they've gained the most experience with those guns for informal shooting—plinking or hunting. If you're a Colt addict, you'll want the Colt even though it doesn't offer all the refinements of the other two models.

A choice between the S&W or High Standard guns is likely to be almost equally subjective rather than objective. Both guns are capable of superb accuracy and both offer virtually all of the features that you might ever think you need. However, their designs are quite different, their shapes nearly as different, and in appearance they are quite dissimilar. Both offer trigger adjustments, very precise sights whose relationship does not change during firing, adjustable weights, compensators or muzzle brakes, slide stops, interchangeable barrels, etc. A choice between them should not be made upon someone's personal recommendation or upon what you've read about them in shooting periodicals. An intelligent choice can be made only by shooting many times over the course with both guns and then determining which feels and acts best for you. Fortunately, this can usually be accomplished before it is necessary to lay out cold, hard cash for that new gun. Pistol shooters are an accommodating sort, and you'll usually encounter no great difficulty in borrowing different guns on the range so you can give them a try. (A few states prohibit your firing any gun that isn't registered to you, but in most parts of the country you'll have no problem.)

Many old-time shooters have spare guns or guns they no longer use regularly and they are willing to let an upcoming marksman put a few hundred rounds through them to decide which gun he likes best. This doesn't mean you should ignore the advice of more experienced shooters; it should be sought. However, it needs to be tempered with your own shooting experience. The guy who's actively shooting the S&W will most highly recommend it; his neighbor shooting a High Standard will recommend it above all others. Listen to their reasons for their recommendations, consider their shooting abilities, and then, if possible, throw in your own shooting experience before you decide to lay out the money for either.

The second category in the National Matches is centerfire, in which the rules specify a caliber of .32 or greater. This category has caused confusion regarding the choice of a first gun. After all, in .22 events you *must* shoot a .22, and in .45 you *must* shoot a .45. Yet in the more general "centerfire" stage you are forced to make a choice of caliber. In so doing you must weigh the effect of recoil and muzzle jump on your scores. The revolver reigned supreme in centerfire matches before the advent of really good target-type centerfire autoloaders of less than .45 caliber. Only Colt and Smith & Wesson made adequate guns in .32 and .38 caliber, though a few big-bore enthusiasts chose essentially the same guns in .44 or .45.

In the old days, therefore, a shooter had his choice of .32, .38, .44 or .45 revolvers for the centerfire stage. The rules permitted use of the .45 auto, but it was seldom chosen because the state of the art then did not allow it to produce scores quite as good as could be obtained from a first-class revolver.

Today the situation is entirely different. Target-type autoloaders of superb accuracy and reliability are available in .32, .38 and .45 caliber. The superiority of the autoloader over the revolver has long since been proven; therefore, no serious contenders for titles have shot the revolver regularly for some years. A newcomer to this game should not waste time thinking about revolvers and their built-in disadvantages, but concentrate on the autoloader.

For rimfire and centerfire matches, Walther builds the highly developed and expensive OSP and GSP line of pistols (fully described in Chapter 11). An average shooter may have no need of such a gun, but an advanced marksman can benefit from its refinements.

Following my rule about ignoring the very costly and sophisticated guns until you really know you can take advantage of them, we can rule out the .32 auto. At the moment only the Walther GSP is available in this caliber (that is, .32 S&W Long). The GSP is available only in very limited quantities and is priced near the $500 mark. When you begin to shoot high-master scores, it might be a good investment, but not in the beginning.

The only domestically manufactured .38 Special autoloader, the S&W M52, is built for flush-seated wadcutters. It has earned an international reputation for superb accuracy and reliable performance.

In .38 caliber we have one production model, the S&W M52, chambered for the .38 Special wadcutter cartridge. Though the Colt Gold Cup was produced in .38 Special for nearly 15 years, it was discontinued in the mid-1970's. This gun is still widely available on the used market, but its reputation for accuracy and reliability is not quite as good as that of the S&W M52. Among custom guns, we have a wide variety of heavily-modified Colt GM pistols which have been converted to .38 Special and finely accurized for target use. Such guns of fine quality are currently available, but at high prices and usually after a long wait. Thousands of customized Colts may be encountered on the used-gun market; they can present a problem unless one knows their history of performance, and when and by whom they were made. As a general rule, I would recommend against buying a used ".38 conversion" except on very expert advice, no matter how attractive the price.

However, the .45-caliber autoloader is quite acceptable for centerfire matches and has become increasingly popular in recent years. Its popularity is due primarily to two factors. First, by using the .45 auto in centerfire matches, one can meet the requirements for both centerfire and .45 matches with a single gun. This presents an obvious economic advantage. Second, the use of a single gun for both stages trims the total battery down to two guns and thus eliminates the effect of switching from one to another when there are differences between them.

Because of the limited number of guns available for centerfire matches, you really don't have a great deal of choice. The .32 is out, and the .38 is available as a new gun only in the S&W M52. The .45

Colt's MK IV/Series '70 Gold Cup National Match pistol is currently the only American factory-made .45 auto suitable for NRA competition. It can be used in the centerfire matches as well as those that specify .45-caliber only.

is available as a new gun only in the Colt Gold Cup. Both economically and as a practical matter regarding training and practice, the average shooter will be best served by obtaining a Colt Gold Cup .45 auto and using it for both centerfire and .45 matches. There is no low-cost gun in this area; the Gold Cup costs around $300. If later you decide that you want to use a .38 for centerfire matches, then you can always add the S&W M52 or a custom .38 to your battery.

Of course, what I've said above answers the question of which gun you should choose for standard .45 matches; there's only one manufactured currently as a production gun, the Colt Gold Cup. It should be pointed out here that many shooters do not consider the Gold Cup adequate, even though it does produce excellent accuracy. Several of the leading custom gunsmiths do produce their own unique, accurized versions of the Colt Government Model which do usually shoot tighter groups than the production Gold Cup. I'll have more to say about this in the chapter on custom guns and gunsmithing.

The standard Colt Government Model is not only popular as a basis for the building of custom target pistols but is also a favorite for combat matches of the type developed by the International Practical Shooting Confederation.

There is a fourth category of the .45-caliber match known as the National Individual Trophy, and also a team variation thereof. This match is unique, for rules specify that the "Service Pistol" be used. At least until now, this is the U. S. M1911A1 .45 pistol, either the military-contract version manufactured by Colt or another vendor, or the commercial counterpart thereof manufactured by Colt. In years gone by, the term "Service Pistol" meant simply that, a service gun which had not been modified in any visible way. Accurizing by a good custom gunsmith was allowed, but any *visible* alterations, or any affecting safety, were not. Today the rules have been changed a good deal, and many visible alterations are allowed. But no *production* gun takes advantage of the rules to deliver maximum accuracy from the service pistol. Consequently, if you wish to participate in this match, and you must if you ever want that gleaming gold Distinguished Marksman badge, then you have no choice but to go to one of the leading pistol-smiths and have him modify a standard GM .45. Such a gun is usually called a "Hard Ball Gun." The modifications are not cheap, and the cost of a completed gun may well reach $500 or more if the basis is a new commercial model.

Even this does not mean that the tyro shooter must have two .45 autos in his battery. The most practical, economical approach to take is to have a gun made up for the National Trophy Match and also use it in both the .45 and centerfire matches. Thus, a single gun will serve for three matches. Considering the usual match schedule, the gun will see far more use in .45 and centerfire matches than it ever will in National Trophy Matches.

As you can see from the foregoing, a new shooter can compete in the entire range of conventional NRA-sanctioned and regulated matches with only two guns: a .22 autoloader and a .45 auto set up for the National Trophy Matches. On the other hand, if more money is available and one is so inclined, a full battery would consist of a .22 autoloader, a .38 S&W M52, a .45 Colt Gold Cup, and a modified Government Model for the National Individual Trophy. As I've said before, I cannot see any compelling reason for the beginner to feel he must have the full four-gun battery. If he progresses to the point where he consistently shoots high master scores, then it might be to his advantage to obtain the additional guns in the hope of gaining a few more points.

Combat shooting, civilian type, is a relatively new thing that began on the West Coast less than a score of years ago. It is a far less formal kind of shooting than that sanctioned by the NRA, and places fewer restrictions on guns than any other matches. It puts a great premium on speed of fire and efficient gun handling; thus, results are far less dependent upon pure accuracy. Virtually any revolver or autoloader of 9mm/.38 caliber or larger is allowed by the rules, provided that full-charge service-type ammunition is used. Over the years, virtually every type of gun in that category has been used, but the hands-down favorite of top shooters is the .45 auto in its most rudimentary form. Adjustable sights are not needed, additional weights are actually a detriment, fancy target grips only get in the way, and X-ring, 50-yard accuracy is not required. With rare exceptions, a new production-run Colt .45 auto —Government Model, LW Commander or Combat Commander—will deliver adequate accuracy for anyone beginning this game. As one progresses up the ladder, a modest degree of accurizing by a good pistolsmith will probably help.

Choice of a gun for civilian-type combat shooting as promoted by the International Practical Shooting Confederation boils down to a .45

For combat matches, some shooters prefer the Colt Combat Commander (shown here) or the shorter LW Commander.

auto, invariably of Colt manufacture or a military-contract gun of the same type. Any difference between the three models offered by Colt is probably a subjective matter, depending on the individual. Foreign-made .45 autos are available, and if one has sufficient faith in their reliability and accuracy, a few dollars might be saved by using one of them. However, I note that none of the experienced combat shooters use the Llama or Star, both of which are currently available. The .45 H&K P9S hasn't seen enough use for evaluation, and its about-$300 price is high.

Most of the domestically made medium-frame .38 double-action revolvers are quite acceptable for PPC competition. A very well-built example is the Ruger Security-Six.

Police matches are usually called PPC Shoots. The nature of such competition is discussed in detail elsewhere in this book, so I'll only mention here that the rules demand the use of a revolver of .38 caliber or larger and that a premium is placed on double-action accuracy, mostly at short ranges, and on speed in reloading the cylinder. As in the other areas, the beginner need not concern himself with the custom-built PPC guns being turned out by dozens of expert pistolsmiths. These guns are highly refined, suitable for little else except PPC competition, and normally cost several hundred dollars. One may choose a PPC gun from a profusion of standard makes and models. Dan Wesson Arms, Colt, Smith & Wesson and Ruger all produce at least one model each which is well suited for this use. All are classed as medium-frame revolvers and all will produce adequate accuracy for the course.

Of the dozen or so models, the Colt Python is generally considered to have the smoothest double-action pull, while the Dan Wesson M15-2 has the shortest double-action pull. However, neither is as popular among active shooters as the Smith & Wesson K-frame guns. This may be due in part to the fact that the Python sells for well over $300, and the Wesson is a relatively new design by a young company competing against the tradition of Colt and Smith & Wesson.

It is fortunate that the S&W K-frame guns have such a good reputation in PPC competition; they are quite reasonably priced. Of the several variations on this frame, the heavy-barrel K-38 (M14) .38 Special

Guns of the Smith & Wesson K-frame series are most popular for PPC matches. This specimen, a heavy-barreled M10, has been customized for double-action only and is fitted with Pachmayr grips and a Bo-Mar sight rib.

revolver with a six-inch barrel is likely the most desirable as a starting gun. It will produce more than adequate accuracy to shoot perfect scores over the course, leaving the rest of the job up to the shooter— and that is really all the more expensive and sophisticated guns can do. With proper instruction and ammunition, the beginner will do fully as well with a $150 (as this is written) S&W M14 as he will with a Python or custom-built gun costing two or three times as much. In fact, a shooter who can win the National Championship with an expensive gun can probably do so with a heavy-barrel S&W M14.

No organized long-range competitions existed prior to the 1970's. The first International Handgun Silhouette Matches, held in Tucson, Arizona, in September of 1975, generally established the type of targets, the ranges and, to a significant degree, the type of guns and ammunition required to produce top results in this game. Two factors are most significant in choosing a gun and ammunition (*both* are important) for long-range competitive shooting. The first is the fact that even a relatively large target requires superb accuracy if it is to be hit consistently out at 200 meters. The second is the fact that merely *hitting* the target does not produce a score. The heavy, steel-plate, game-silhouette target must be completely knocked off its stand. Doing so requires a heavy, large-caliber bullet moving at relatively high velocity.

These factors combine to require a heavy, large, long-barreled gun chambered for a large-caliber, high-velocity cartridge. Not many such guns are available. Among revolvers, only the double-action S&W N-frame guns in .41 Magnum and .44 Magnum can be relied on for good results, along with the Ruger single-action Blackhawk revolver chambered for the same cartridges. With either, the longest barrel available should be chosen (8⅜-inch S&W; 7½-inch Ruger) in order to realize the full potential of the cartridge and thus improve the percentage of 200-yard target knockdowns.

The choice between the two revolvers depends purely on economics and individual preference. The Ruger is by far the most economical,

Quite a few long-range competitors favor the S&W N-frame Magnums—either .44 or .41. The specimen shown has a 6½-inch barrel, which will do, but long-range pistoleros generally prefer the 8⅜-inch version.

Pictured with its interchangeable barrel and barrel extension detached from the frame, the massive Auto Mag is the only currently built autoloader suitable for long-range matches in which steel-plate game silhouettes must be knocked over.

The Thompson/Center single-shot Contender is offered with interchangeable barrels in a wide variety of calibers, several of which are ideal for a long-range game-silhouette shoot. (For this purpose, it cannot be scoped as in this photo.)

generally being available for only a bit over half the cost of the big N-frame Smith & Wesson. Either gun offers more than sufficient speed of fire for the Metallic Silhouette Matches.

Of all the autoloading pistols available in the world, only the big stainless-steel Auto Mag of limited availability is chambered for cartridges of sufficient power for the 200-yard stage of long-range matches. The Auto Mag does a superb job in calibers .41 AMP and .44 AMP, but it is temperamental and requires handloaded ammunition. In addition, even when the gun can be obtained, it is costly, ranging in price from about $400 up; and I mean way up.

Gun Selection: the Basic Battery

Oddly enough, this is the only kind of match shooting in this country that can be handled quite well by a single-shot pistol. However, the match does not require that one use the same gun for all stages, so if a single-shot is preferred for one reason or another, it might be used only at the longest ranges. The single-shot Thompson/Center Contender pistol in any caliber of power equal to or greater than the .41 Magnum will do a fine job. If this gun is used, it should be equipped with a 10-inch barrel in order to get maximum velocity from the cartridge. The Contender is fairly economical, costing roughly the same amount as the Ruger revolver, but its choice based on price alone would be false economy.

Balancing performance and economy, one is forced to conclude that the Ruger Super Blackhawk in .41 or .44 Magnum is the best choice for this type of shooting. That the 1975 champion used such a gun without any modification except custom grips is more than sufficient justification for this choice. During the 1975 matches, the .44 Magnum S&W M29 was the most-used gun, the Ruger ranked second, the Auto Mag third, with a sprinkling of single-shots and underpowered revolvers following. In 1976, the champion used a customized Remington XP-100 in .30 caliber. The XP-100, as most readers probably know, is a bolt-action single-shot designed much like a rifle.

An excellent revolver for long-range shooting is the Ruger Super Blackhawk, lowest-priced of all .44 Magnums. Like many single-actions, it has also been used by a few quick-draw competitors, but for such use its excellent sights become a hindrance rather than a help and therefore need alteration.

Remington's XP-100 single-shot bolt-action pistol is factory-chambered for the .221 Fireball, an inadequate cartridge for knocking over game silhouettes at long range. However, the gun is often customized to fire .30-caliber loads that perform well in such competition.

It cannot be over-emphasized that a metallic-silhouette handgun course, with targets shot at 50, 100, 150 and 200 meters, requires a very powerful cartridge. The gun simply must be chambered for a cartridge whose power at least equals that of the .41 Magnum out at 200 meters. An ultra-lightweight, high-velocity bullet, though it may produce greater energy at short range, is unlikely to be a good performer at 200 meters. Generally speaking, a relatively heavy bullet at the highest practical velocity is required. In .44 Magnum, 180-grain bullets represent the minimum, and in .41 caliber, 170- to 175-grain bullets, with a velocity of about 1700 fps, may represent the minimum. Exotic cartridges such as the various .357 and 9mm wildcats may look good on charts but when the bullet clangs into that heavy steel-plate target at 200 meters, they seldom possess sufficient striking energy to knock the target over. This is the one form of U. S. competition in which simply hitting the target is of no value; the target must be knocked off its feet if the shot is to score.

A decade or two back, the country was swept by the quick-draw craze. Very quickly, organized competition sprang up. It still exists but on a much, much smaller scale than at the time when an estimated 100,000 or more individuals participated. Today only a few thousand people continue in this type of shooting, whose gun requirements are unique.

As generally practiced, quick-draw, or fast-draw, matches prohibit the use of bulleted cartridges. The emphasis in this type of shooting has always been purely upon speed of draw and firing the first shot, with the time from the start signal to the sound of the shot measured precisely by sophisticated electronic equipment. The use of bulleted cartridges was banned in the interest of safety, and the only requirement for accuracy is that the gun be pointed at that portion of the timing system which is activated by the sound of the shot. Quick-draw also requires that the gun be of traditional single-action form, typified by the Colt SAA and such other guns as have copied it in general form.

Colt's Single Action Army six-gun is appropriate for only one brand of competition—quick-draw—but for that type of match it's the favorite, either in its factory form or extensively modified.

In this game, winning shooters generally use Colt SAA revolvers that have been heavily modified. However, such guns are not necessary for the tyro. It is especially important to note this inasmuch as a current-production Colt SAA and the modifications considered necessary by many experts may cost as much as $500.

The pure traditionalist will, of course, want to use the Colt SAA revolver. It should be chosen in .45 caliber, and as a first gun in 5½-inch barrel length unless you can find one with a 4⅝-inch barrel. While the experts with years of experience can get by quite well with longer barrels, the beginner has at least a psychological advantage with a short barrel that *appears* to come from the holster quicker and easier. The large caliber is chosen for two reasons: First, the large-diameter chambers lighten the cylinder, reducing the effort required in cocking or fanning to overcome inertia and thereby speeding up the process; second, this chambering allows the use of commercially available five-in-one blanks if one is not inclined to load his own.

Inasmuch as sights are never used in quick-draw competition, one should always choose a gun *without* target sights. This is not only an economy. Target sights invariably must be removed to prevent interference with rapid cocking, or to prevent ripping the hand when fanning if that method is used.

With the current-production Colt SAA priced in the $300 range, one might hope that there is an acceptable substitute at a lower price. There is. Several Colt SAA copies are being produced abroad and sold in this country for prices that often drop below $100. As this is written, the Dakota is available for around $90, but prices generally range somewhat above this. Several European manufacturers offer more or less similar models in this country under perhaps a dozen names. Almost any of them will do for quick-draw work. Some of the very cheapest might not be entirely satisfactory, as this type of shooting places severe stresses on the mechanism, and shoddy parts fail quickly. About the only advice that can be given is that you should examine several makes closely before making a purchase. By careful shopping, it is entirely possible to obtain a satisfactory first gun for quick-draw work for little over $100.

There is another alternative that should not be overlooked. The Ruger Blackhawk revolver is quite durable and reliable, and conforms to the rules regarding the proper type. Considering that it costs little more than the foreign models and hardly half the price of the Colt, it is really quite a good choice except for one factor. That is simply that the gun is not available without target sights—and as pointed out above, target sights are unsuitable. Probably the most practical approach is to obtain the Ruger in .44 or .45 caliber, then remove the rear sight and carefully file or grind the boss down to a smooth, flowing contour that approximates the shape of the Colt SAA in the same area. Even when that is done, a sharp-edged recess will remain. If this causes problems, it can easily be filled with a small block of steel soldered in place and then dressed down to match the surrounding contours.

After you've shot at least one full season of quick-draw, you'll know whether your talent and perseverence warrant an investment in more sophisticated equipment. You can either have your gun extensively modified or shop for a new SAA Colt and have it modified. The latter route, as mentioned, will cost you nearly $500.

There are other, less common types of competition in which a shooter can participate without too much trouble. Generally, they are oriented toward law-enforcement or personal defense, and require a powerful, heavy-caliber gun—generally an autoloader—though in some instances the use of a revolver is permitted. The oldest of these types of shooting is the Mexican Defense Course, quite popular south of the border and occasionally shot in this country along the northern half of the Rio Grande Valley. This course places a premium on fast movement, fast gun handling and just a modicum of accuracy.

It is shot with an autoloader, almost exclusively the Colt GM or a comparable model of other manufacture. In Mexico, the popular caliber is .38 Super, which is used mainly because of the prohibition of private ownership of .45-caliber autos. When the match is shot in this country, the .45 GM auto is generally used and is conceded by most to be the best choice. There is no doubt in my mind that our Mexican colleagues would use the .45 if governmental restrictions on handgun ownership allowed them to do so.

Great mechanical accuracy is not required for the Mexican Defense Course. All targets are shot at relatively close range, and are man-size. The emphasis is upon speed of movement and speed of gun handling, with scoring of hits only. Consequently, a standard Colt GM in .45 caliber will do the job nicely; there is no need for the match-type accuracy of the Gold Cup or the accurized jobs by custom pistolsmiths. Personally, I would lean toward the LW Commander or Combat Commander instead of the full-length GM, simply because it handles a bit better during the draw and in switching from target to target. However, when using the full-charge service ammunition many individuals find that the LW Commander has a bit too much recoil and jump. Therefore, the steel-frame Combat Commander is probably the best all-around choice. It has much more weight than the LW Commander; its recoil and jump characteristics are pretty much the same as those of the full-length gun, yet its shorter length makes it handier for this particular course.

Since the accuracy requirements are rather loose, almost any good-condition .45 auto with a perfect barrel and absolutely reliable functioning will perform quite satisfactorily. With new commercial .45 autos going at well over $200 these days, the $50 or so that can be saved by buying a used gun makes this solution most attractive.

Another match, just recently introduced in this country and becoming popular, is the Bowling-Pin Shoot organized by Second Chance in 1975. As this is being written, two National Championship matches have been held, and those who participated have been so enthusiastic about this type of shooting that we expect it to spread across the country within the next few years. The Bowling-Pin Shoot is unique in that it uses standard bowling pins for targets, five of them placed in a row upon a table top. Each pin must be knocked from the table for the shot to score. The range is quite short, and firing is undertaken under what amounts to a simulation of a combat situation. Scoring is based on the time required to knock over all five pins.

Obviously, the emphasis is on fast gun handling and rapidity of fire at multiple targets. Accuracy is certainly important, but the degree of accuracy required to hit a bowling pin fairly well centered at only a handful of yards is not great. A gun whose groups at a mere 15 yards compare to 50-yard X-ring groups in NRA competition will do well in the Bowling-Pin Shoot.

Ammunition is a significant factor in this match. It is important that the bullet transfer maximum energy to the heavy bowling pin if the target is to be knocked from the table. This rules out light loads and small calibers. Not even the traditional .38 or .45 wadcutter match loads will knock the pins far enough to produce winning scores, despite dead-center hits. Competitors to date have agreed that .44 or .45 caliber is required with the cartridge loaded to the maximum power allowed by the shooter's ability to absorb recoil and recover from jump. Generally speaking, standard .45 ACP ball cartridges do an excellent job; the smaller autoloading-pistol cartridges (.38 Super, 9mm P.) simply don't hit the pins hard enough except when perfectly centered. Bullet construction also is important. A good many shooters have found that a semi-wadcutter or expanding-type bullet seems to produce consistently high scores. This is an important distinction, and even more important when a bullet hits the outer part of a pin rather than the center. A bullet that tends to dig in rather than ricochet will produce higher scores. This accounts for the better performance of a medium-weight semi-wadcutter bullet over a round-nose FMJ type.

It is easy to see that a .45 auto is probably the best choice for the Bowling-Pin Shoot. Again, though, in the interest of speedy gun handling, the short Combat Commander or LW Commander will probably be better for most individuals than the full-length GM. The distinction between the two Commanders made in reference to the Mexican Defense Match also applies here. As long as the gun can be zeroed for the load to be used at the proper range for the bowling pins, there is no need for target-type sights, and it should be noted that fancy, curved and bulged target grips only get in the way of fast gun handling. It boils down to one basic choice—the standard .45 GM or the .45 Colt Combat Commander. A good, used, military GM is probably the best route for the beginner when economics are considered.

International competition is where it's all at. Anyone competing in such matches already has years of experience and hundreds of thousands of rounds fired in many types of events. All of the International matches require the absolute best in quality and accuracy that present-day technology can offer in a handgun and ammunition. There is no place for second-rate equipment or second-rate shooters. As a matter of fact, there is no such thing as a beginner in this kind of handgun competition. Anyone who demonstrates the level of skill necessary to obtain a berth, representing this or any other country, is among the top one percent of shooters. Consequently, there is little need here to recommend any particular make or model of International gun. I'll confine myself at this point to a brief enumeration of the types demanded, and will have more to say about them in Chapter 7, which describes the International matches.

There are four types of competition. First is the Free Pistol, or Slow-Fire, match in which 60 shots are fired over a long time at 50 meters into a target with a 10-ring diameter of only 25mm, about one inch. Second is the International Rapid-Fire wherein one fires strings of five shots at five different targets in time limits of eight, six and four seconds. Third is the Standard Pistol match, which comes closest to resembling NRA competition. And fourth is the European Centerfire, which originated as a combat-style match but has lost any resemblance to an armed encounter and now calls for firing single shots at a silhouette target within a relatively generous time limit. (As noted at the beginning of this chapter, I'll go into more precise detail regarding rules and procedures for such shooting events in my discussions of the major types of competition.) All except the centerfire match require a .22 rimfire pistol. The Standard Pistol and Rapid-Fire courses require an autoloader, and the latter demands as a practical matter that it must fire .22 Shorts. In the Slow-Fire match, a single-shot pistol is essential. This match is sometimes considered a contest of endurance, but it requires a gun delivering absolute maximum accuracy.

Highly-specialized .22 rimfire pistols are manufactured by several European firms especially for the 50-meter Slow-Fire competition. They are known as "free pistols" because, aside from caliber, almost no restrictions govern their construction or design. A typical specimen such as a Hammerli—probably the best-known make in this country—is a very finely made single-shot with a slender barrel about 10 inches long. It has an outlandish appearance by American standards, for the

This Hammerli M120 is probably the lowest-priced of the very sophisticated European .22 LR single-shots known as free pistols and designed specifically for ISU-type slow-fire courses.

This Hammerli M230, chambered for .22 Shorts, is an expensive, exquisitely built pistol intended specifically for International Rapid-Fire. The same basic design is also produced in .22 Long Rifle versions for Standard Pistol events, and in that form it also meets specifications for NRA competition.

rear sight is apt to be mounted on an extension and the grip is an over-sized affair with big rests for the thumb and heel of the palm. Often, such grips wrap partway around the hand.

Free pistols are all quite costly, with prices generally ranging from $400 upward. All are superb shooting machines, and though they may differ a great deal in detail of design, they are quite similar in overall form and style. Capable of superb accuracy, they incorporate various sophisticated refinements which usually include set triggers with multiple adjustments, superbly precise sights, dry-fire provisions, "orthopedic" grips, and so on. The International autoloaders, though somewhat more traditional in appearance, are also extremely sophisticated guns with comparable refinements. By the time a handgunner has done enough shooting to think about the Internationals, he is bound to find himself in the company of competitive marksmen who possess most of the available makes and models. He should try to shoot various makes and models extensively, then make a choice based upon results on target.

The centerfire match for the past decade has generally been one with the same type of gun that performs best in U. S. centerfire matches. The last time I attended International matches, by far the most common gun among centerfire competitors was the S&W M52 with factory-loaded .38 Special wadcutters. One cannot go wrong with this gun. There isn't much choice if a shooter wants a gun of American manufacture, but this is all right because the gun performs well in our domestic competition and is quite reasonably priced when compared to similar European products such as the Sig/Hammerli P240, which is also chambered for the .38 Special wadcutter but costs about $650 in the United States.

However, in recent years, various European makers have been developing highly refined versions of their .22 target autoloaders in .32 S&W caliber. To the best of my knowledge, the only such gun available in any quantity (as this is written) is the Walther GSP, which has its magazine forward of the trigger. This gun is a superb performer, and I feel that anyone who shoots well with the S&W M52 can probably—with a reasonable amount of practice—shoot a tiny bit better with the Walther. Unfortunately, the Walther costs nearly twice as much as the M52 and is available in this country only on a very limited basis. Consequently, the most practical and economical choice for an individual anticipating centerfire International competition is the S&W M52.

These represent the basic forms of competition throughout the world, along with reasonable suggestions for a starting battery. From time to time, other forms of competition crop up, one example of which is the LeClerc Military Matches conducted within NATO. One has no choice there, for only pure service pistols and ammunition are allowed. Another match, just introduced by an individual (at considerable personal expense), is the Money Shoot in Laramie, Wyoming. There, Dr. Robert Burgess has laid out his own range with a course of fire that is quite difficult. To date, gun requirements haven't really been refined by experience. The course (described in Chapter 9) places a premium upon both speedy marksmanship and athletic prowess, for the shooter *runs* over 200 yards while firing a total of 20 shots at 10 *small* targets.

Other forms of handgun competition will appear as time goes by; perhaps some of those outlined will die out, but the potential is there for the newer ones to grow and achieve national, even international acceptance. We can only wait and see. It's a certainty there will be plenty of guns from which to choose for whatever does develop.

3
Learning
to Shoot

"Just hold it and squeeze." That's the way handgun marksmanship has often been described—reduced to the barest essentials. It consists simply of holding the gun pointed directly at the target and squeezing the trigger without disturbing that alignment until the hammer falls and the shot fires. If the gun is pointed directly at the target at the instant the cartridge is fired, the bullet will strike the target. That is an oversimplification, of course, for there are many, many factors that affect one's ability to hold the gun directly on target and squeeze the trigger without disturbing the gun in the process.

If the human body could be made absolutely stable, and if a shooter could hold the handgun at arm's length without any movement whatever, and if the trigger could be manipulated without the slightest disturbance of the gun, then hitting the target would be easy.

Unfortunately, those conditions cannot be met. The human body is best at movement, worst at holding still. Even when completely at rest, asleep, we are a mass of movement. Respiration, pulse and various other involuntary movements disturb us even then. Awake and upright, movements multiply greatly, and it is impossible for us to hold any object completely immobile. This is especially true in the case of a two- or three-pound handgun held at arm's length, regardless of whether we use one or both hands. Many beginning shooters, thinking they *should* be able to hold the sights Gibraltar-solid on the target, become frustrated and take refuge in that old excuse, "I'm just not steady enough—too shaky, too nervous—to shoot a pistol."

When a handgunner realizes that a certain amount of movement will *always* be present, he is on the way to licking the problem. Knowing that the movement is controllable within limits and that it does not prevent precise shooting, he is prepared to learn how to keep his shots within the 10-ring.

Until quite recent times, so-called "bull's-eye shooting" was virtually the only type of pistol marksmanship practiced. Today, it is fashionable in many circles to denigrate this type of shooting for its lack of "practical value" to the use of a handgun for defense or hunting. This is a mistake. The ability to place a bullet on a precise point is the essential basis for developing other forms of marksmanship. Without this fundamental grounding, I do not believe anyone can become a truly effective pistolero, no matter how well he might ventilate silhouette targets at seven yards or how fast he might be able to draw and get off that first shot. Bull's-eye shooting formed the basic training of the winners in other forms of competition. The top men in IPSC, PPC, NSL and other forms of non-bull's-eye shooting all came up via the bull's-eye route. And I do not buy the notion that such shooting has no practical value. In the field, one seldom sees all of a live target, and the ability to shoot into a 1.695″ X-ring at 50 yards will also allow one to slip a bullet through a small opening in foliage to hit game. Or, for that matter, it's the same ability a soldier or law officer needs in a critical combat situation. Therefore, we will deal with bull's-eye shooting here in considerable detail.

No handgun is as suitable for learning the fundamentals and progressing rapidly as the .22 rimfire auto pistol. Obviously, of course, this beginning pistol must be capable of excellent accuracy and must be fitted with suitable target-type sights. A .22 autoloader possesses several advantages for learning. It is economical to buy and even more economical to operate. A great deal of shooting is necessary to develop basic skills, and centerfire ammunition costs from six to ten times as much as the .22 rimfire. Furthermore, the .22 auto produces negligible recoil, jump and blast. The beginning shooter has enough on his mind without being distracted by ear-splitting reports and hand-bruising recoil. Finally, the modern .22 autoloader is remarkably reliable; if merely kept reasonably clean and fed good ammunition, it will fire thousands of rounds without a malfunction. Again, the learning shooter needs no distractions in the way of assorted gun malfunctions.

Learning to Shoot

I do not believe the make and model of .22 autoloader is terribly important to a beginner. If he can afford it, certainly a top-grade target pistol is a good idea, but a good low-cost gun like the Ruger Mark I is adequate. It is not even necessary for that first gun to be new. A used gun in first-class condition can usually be purchased at a considerable saving and will serve the purpose just as well. Also, in the beginning, it is wasteful to spend extra money for match-quality ammunition, nor should one purchase the high-velocity or hollow-point cartridges most popular for hunting and plinking. The standard velocity .22 Long Rifle load, driving its 40 grain bullet at about 950 feet per second from a six-inch handgun barrel, is quite accurate and is economically priced. However, do not lean too hard on economy and attempt to use .22 Shorts. Only a very few (quite expensive) autos are made that will function reliably with the .22 Short cartridge. Second, the Short (even the expensive match-grade stuff) is less accurate at the longer ranges than the superb .22 Long Rifle. As you will note elsewhere in this book, the .22 Short is used only in the unique International Rapid-Fire match. In all else the .22 LR reigns supreme.

Let us now get into the meat of the matter. *Sight alignment* and *trigger squeeze* (the latter more properly termed *trigger control*) form the basis for marksmanship. Other factors are also important, but mainly as they affect these two areas. What was once known as the Patridge sight system is the almost universal favorite today. It consists of a flat vertical surface facing the shooter's eye, containing at its upper center a sharp-edged rectangular notch. The front element is a vertical, rectangular blade which presents flat surfaces to the shooter's eye. As shown in one of the illustrations, the proper alignment of these two elements presents to the eye a single image with the front element centered laterally in the rear notch with equal-width vertical strips of light visible between the edges of the two elements. Further, the flat top of the front element appears flush with the top of the rear element. This image should be crisp and sharply outlined. (This will present some problems, but we'll deal with them later.) The exact amount of light between the sides of the blade and the notch is not terribly important, except that it should be wide enough to be easily seen, yet not so wide that excessive effort is required to equalize the two strips. Most factory-installed sights are entirely adequate in this respect—though experienced shooters have decided preferences in this matter and sometimes switch to different dimensions. Until you have developed a significant level of skill, settle for what the factory sights offer in this respect.

Unless you are already familiar with Patridge sights, you may find it considerably more difficult than expected to achieve proper alignment.

Handgun Competition

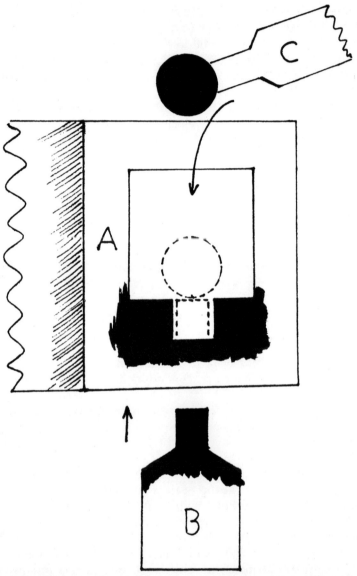

A simple, homemade sighting aid can be useful in accustoming yourself to getting the proper alignment of sights and target. Part A is a rectangular piece of cardboard, folded double so that the other parts can be slipped between the layers. Cut out the center of Part A to represent the rear sight notch and a generous amount of clearance above the notch. The shaded area along the left edge of this part is where the two layers of cardboard are taped or glued together. Part B is another piece of cardboard, cut to represent the front sight, and Part C is a third piece with a circular top to represent the target. Parts B and C are inserted between the layers of Part A from above and below, and are moved about to form a proper sight picture. The broken lines in the drawing show how the elements look, with relation to one another, when you have a "6 o'clock hold" and the sight picture is right.

Individual eyesight, plus the fact that two sighting elements are several inches apart, has a good deal to do with this. Such difficulty can be alleviated in the beginning by using a simple cardboard sighting device. While this device can occasionally be purchased, it can be made simply and quickly from scrap cardboard. The illustrations show how it is made and manipulated. The notch in the bottom of the front window forms a rear sight element, while the rectangular strip inserted from the bottom forms the front sight. All edges should be clean and sharp, and both elements should be colored a dull, flat black. While you're making this device, also make the bull's-eye element which is inserted from the top; we'll get to its use in a short while.

Take the sighting device, insert the front sight strip, then manipulate the two until equal space is visible between the vertical edges of the notch and the edges of the front sight, and the top of the front sight is flush with the top of the rear sight. If this sounds simple, rest assured that it is not. By performing this alignment with the sighting device, you can check sight alignment very carefully to *ensure* that everything is correct. If you were doing it on the gun, there would be no way you or anyone else could check. With the device, it is a very simple matter to check the width of the light gaps and the flushness of the two elements at the top. Once you've aligned the elements, displace the front sight completely. Then do it again. Repeat this until you can get it exactly right each time. Once you're satisfied with the alignment you're getting on the sighting device, then you can switch to the gun.

Immediately you'll notice that one or both of the sight elements will not be completely sharp. You'll also notice that it's more difficult to obtain alignment on the gun than on the sighting device. However, having practiced with the device, you'll be better able to judge when alignment on the gun is correct.

The slight fuzziness you'll notice in the sights is due to the inescapable fact that the human eye cannot focus precisely at more than one distance at any given instant. The eye does possess "accommodation"— the ability to shuffle rapidly back and forth, focusing alternately on two objects at different distances. If your vision is good and you look at both sights, the eye will do the rest automatically. However, some eyes can do this much better than others, so not everyone will see the sights with the same degree of sharpness. In my experience, it is better to concentrate on *one* of the sight elements, focusing it as sharply as possible while accepting a slight fuzziness of the other. I prefer to focus on the front sight, making it as sharp as possible and learning to live with a slight fuzziness of the rear element.

If your eyes are less than perfect, you may find the fuzziness more than you think you can handle. Corrective lenses, whether or not you already wear them, with the prescription ground specifically to pro-

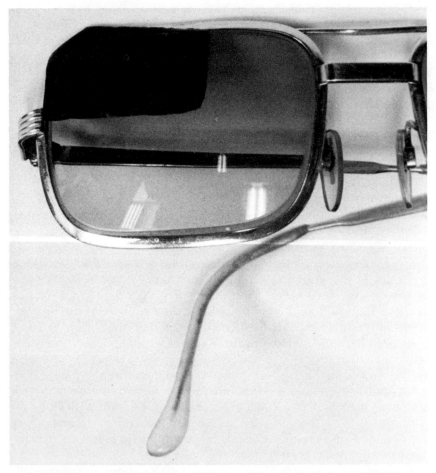

You can sharpen the composite image of rear sight, front sight and target by viewing that sight picture through a small hole. Do this by covering the upper right quadrant of the right lens of your shooting glasses (assuming you're right-handed) with flat-black paper and piercing a tiny hole in the paper. Commercial devices are marketed for the same purpose; they look neater—quite impressive, in fact— but the paper works about as well. You'll find that one of your eyes (normally the right one if you're right-handed) is the stronger one, the "master eye." Naturally, the lens over that eye is the one to equip with the little peep hole.

duce maximum sharpness of the sights when held at arm's length, will usually help a great deal. A good many elderly shooters find this essential.

Sharpness of the sight image (and also the target) can be substantially improved by positioning a small aperture in front of the aiming eye. Apertures are made specifically for this purpose, some of them with adjustable hole sizes, and they may be clamped onto spectacle frames.

Learning to Shoot

However, it seems to be equally effective if one simply tapes or glues a piece of dead-black paper over the spectacle lens with a tiny hole pierced in its center in the proper position for viewing the sights through it. Many shooters use a combination of corrective lenses and an aperture. The fairly expensive aperture device clamped on the spectacle frame is probably the best. Its hole is more sharply defined than one can usually produce in a piece of paper, and the more sophisticated types allow the size of the aperture to be varied. In addition, the aperture element may be rotated out of the field of view when not required. This is certainly more convenient than walking around between relays with one eye partially blocked or changing glasses to avoid that. After all, only a very small percentage of the time spent at a match is spent in shooting.

I feel that it is important to learn and practice proper sight alignment without the distraction of a bull's-eye in the beginning. Once you have become able to accurately position the front sight in the rear sight notch every time, it will be easier to add the bull's-eye to the picture. So, if you're satisfied with your ability to align the two sight elements, go back to the sighting device, align the sight elements, then insert the bull's-eye from the upper end of the device and position it so that its six-o'clock edge barely touches the center of the top of the front sight. This will place the center of the front sight directly under the center of the circular bull's-eye. This is known as the six-o'clock hold, and we'll go into it more later. It's absolutely essential that you learn at this point to center the bull laterally on the front sight, while maintaining proper front and rear sight alignment. Assuming correct sight alignment, if

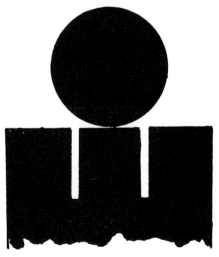

This is the correct sight picture. The front sight is centered laterally in the rear notch, and its top is flush with the top of the rear element. The top of the front sight is centered under the bull and barely touching its bottom edge at a point that would be 6 o'clock on a clock face. This "6 o'clock hold" is generally easiest and best to use on paper targets. A "center hold" requires the same alignment of front and rear sights, but with the top of the front sight against the center of the bull.

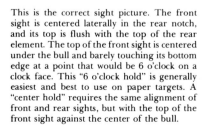

Handgun Competition

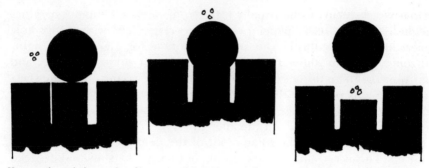

Here are the typical examples of improper sight-and-target alignment—and the results of each mistake. At left, both sights are correctly elevated, with the bull's bottom edge resting on top of the front sight, and the front sight's top level with the top of the rear notch—but the front sight is too far to the left in the notch, and the bullets will group to the left. In the example at center, the sights are correctly aligned with each other but too high on the bull; the shots will strike above the target. At right, both sights are too far below the bull and the front sight is too low in the notch, so the bullets will cluster well below the target.

the bull is displaced left, shots will theoretically strike to the right of the bull's center, and vice versa. If a significant gap appears between the top of the front sight and the bottom of the bull, the shot will strike low; and if the front sight intrudes up into the bull, then your shots will strike high.

But that isn't all there is to worry about. If the front sight is displaced left in the rear sight notch, shots will strike left, and vice versa. If the front sight is low in the rear sight, shots will strike low, and if the front sight rises above the rear element, shots will strike high. Obviously, quite a number of sighting errors can creep in if one is not exceedingly careful. A vast number of combinations of these errors is possible, and if they are allowed to occur even to only a very slight degree, shot groups on target will be greatly enlarged and you simply won't hit precisely where you want, except by accident.

Most inexperienced shooters fail to realize how great a degree of bullet displacement is produced by what appears to be a very small error in sight alignment. For the sake of simple computation, let's assume a six-inch sight radius (distance between the rear faces of both sight elements). At a range of 50 yards this sighting error will be multiplied 300 times. So, if the front sight is displaced $1/64$th of an inch, you can multiply that by 300 and discover that the bullet will be displaced approximately 4.7 inches. If, during the firing of a particular string, you allowed that much error to occur in all four directions, the smallest possible group you could obtain (all other factors being equal and perfect) would be nearly 9½ inches. With the 50-yard 10-ring measuring a mere fraction of that, the results of such slipshod sight alignment are readily apparent. Actually, when the variables of gun and ammunition are included, a group fired under those conditions would probably measure 12 inches or more in diameter. If you think a sighting error of $^{1}/_{64}$th-inch is more than you could possibly make, then consider that an error of only .010 inch will be equally multiplied, resulting in bullet displace-

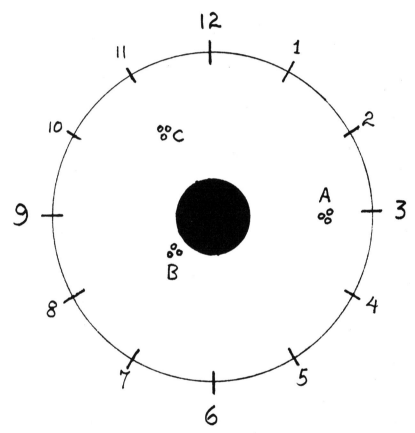

All shots should be called, with reference to their point of impact on an imaginary clock face. The bull's-eye (or whatever aiming point is used) is at the center of the clock face. In this illustration, the call for the shots in Group A would be "well out at 3 o'clock." Group B would be "close in at 7:30." Group C would be "out at 11 o'clock." When shooting at scored-ring targets, the value of the shots is also included in the call. A shot in Group A, for example, would be "a 7 at 3 o'clock." After a bit of practice, no effort is needed to visualize the clock instantly for each shot, and calling the shots in this way helps subtantially in making slight corrections for subsequent shots or for recognizing alignment errors immediately. One of the most common errors is canting the gun—tilting it a trifle to one side or the other. The bullets will strike the target away from center, in the direction toward which the top of the gun is tilted. Thus, the three shots in Group A—every one of them "a 7 at 3 o'clock"—could well have resulted from canting the gun to the right rather than from misalignment of the sights and bull.

ment of 3 inches at 50 yards, or 1½ inches at 25 yards. Even that miniscule error will make it impossible to shoot passable scores.

After you've worked with the sighting device and developed some skill in aligning both sights and bull's-eye, stick a small black bull's-eye on the wall of your den and practice aligning the sights of your gun on it. The proper method is to align the front and rear sight precisely, then by movement of the gun, without disturbing the sights, bring them into proper relationship with the target.

You'll notice two things that give you trouble. First, you'll find that it is impossible, no matter how hard you try, to keep the sights and the gun aligned rigidly with the bull's-eye. Most likely, the harder you try, the more the sights will deviate from the bull. After a few tries, if you observe closely, you'll probably notice that the sights appear to waver in a more or less horizontal figure-eight, with the intersection, or center, of the figure remaining fairly close to the bottom edge of the bull. This is the inevitable movement mentioned earlier, and even the world's finest shots can never eliminate it entirely; they merely control it, keep it within acceptable limits. The other thing you'll notice is that the bull's eye is not sharply defined; its perimeter will be fuzzy to some degree. Depending on your eyesight, the appearance of the bull may range from an almost-sharp black disk to nothing more than a grayish circular blob. It has long been established that it is preferable to have the sights appear as sharp as possible, and by the same token, to accept a somewhat indistinct bull.

The tendency among new shooters is to attempt to "sharpen" the bull by deliberately forcing the eye to focus on it. Unfortunately, this blurs the sights and makes accurate shooting virtually impossible. If the bull appears too fuzzy to work with, then the corrective lenses and/or aperture mentioned earlier should help a great deal. However, don't work too hard at sharpening up the bull. Surprisingly fine shooting can be done even when the bull is quite fuzzy.

Practice this form of sight-and-target alignment. Concentration is essential, but don't try too hard. There is a difference between the two. Bring the gun up, align the sights properly as quickly as possible, then bring them into correct alignment with the bull. If you haven't achieved proper alignment quickly, further attempts on that try will make things worse instead of better. If you can't get it in, say, three seconds, lower the gun and start over. If you do get it fairly close, and then continue to strain for 5 to 10 more seconds to get it better, it's almost certain to get worse as muscular tremors and eye strain interfere. Don't hesitate to admit that you muffed one attempt and start over. Most likely, your eyes won't be accustomed to this sort of exercise, so as few as 15 or 20 tries may be all you can handle at first.

Learning to Shoot

Continue to practice, and endeavor gradually to narrow the amount of visible movement. This takes a lot of practice, but when that practice is combined with the other points we'll bring, you should eventually be able to reduce the lateral limits of movement to the width of the bull's-eye. (This doesn't necessarily mean that everyone can reduce it that much, but most people can if they practice diligently for a short period every day or two.)

Even in your early practice, before the movement is whittled down, it's time to start *dry fire* and *calling the shot*. Dry fire is simply squeezing the trigger to drop the hammer on an empty chamber while maintaining proper sight-and-target alignment. Calling the shot is mentally and visually recording precisely the relationship of the bull's-eye and sights at the instant the hammer falls. In actual shooting, all other factors being correct, the bullet will strike precisely on the point where the sights are aligned at the instant of firing. If firing occurs at the center of the figure-eight of movement, then in theory that shot should be a pinwheel bull; if the hammer drops at the left limit of travel, the bullet will strike left, and so on.

Naturally, with no cartridges in the gun you won't be able to verify the accuracy of your calling. However, it will be good practice against the time when you do start shooting live ammunition. When actually shooting, every shot should be called, and each call should be verified by spotting the bullet strike. During slow fire this is easy if you have a spotting scope. It isn't really practical during rapid fire, but the competent pistol shot instinctively calls every shot fired, even when shooting is too rapid to verify individual shots. With practice, calling the shot does become instinctive, and you'll be doing it without any conscious effort. If it were to require effort, it might interfere with concentration on the other factors that are very important to getting the shot off properly.

Shots are called in reference to an imaginary clock face superimposed over the target. A shot at nine o'clock, for example, is centered vertically but off to the left.

If you've never tried dry fire before, you may question whether it serves any worthwhile purpose. It really does; it allows you to concentrate on sight alignment and trigger squeeze without being concerned about recoil or recovery. It also allows unlimited practice of those two techniques at no cost and without going to the range, for this practice may be conducted wherever you can stick a small bull's-eye up on the wall. Even if the bull is no more than 10 feet away, the practice can be very worthwhile. With this sort of practice, your trigger finger, your mind and your eyes slowly become integrated into a kind of control system that gets the shot off at the right time under the right conditions.

When mixed with live firing, dry fire can also expose flinching, which we'll discuss later.

Before dry fire can reach its optimum effectiveness, you must add a few more basics—breathing control, trigger control, grip and stance. And, of course, you must continue to improve your concentration. It is often said by top marksmen, "If you're concentrating fully on getting the shot off right, you won't hear the report or feel the recoil."

Breathing control requires you to oxygenate your system by taking several deep breaths and expelling them before raising the gun for the shot. The extra oxygen keys up your facilities and increases your ability to concentrate. After, say, three breaths, raise the gun, breathe deeply, align the sights as you do so—and as the gun settles on target, let out about half the breath. At this point, begin your trigger squeeze, finalize your alignment and concentrate on sights and trigger pull. If you're not in the best of physical condition, your ability to oxygenate your system before firing can be greatly improved by regularly performing any standard deep-breathing exercise. This will do most of us no harm, whether or not we intend to shoot, and it will eventually improve almost anyone's marksmanship.

Trigger control consists of carefully and evenly applying pressure to the trigger *directly rearward* with the first joint of the forefinger, while at the same time avoiding any movement or tensing of the rest of the hand. This pressure is applied (directly rearward, now) as the sights first come into proper alignment with the bull's-eye and is continued while you strive to keep movement to the minimum possible. If the sights do not move beyond the limits of the bull, the majority of shots will strike within the bull if all else is right. As practice progresses, you'll be able to get the shots off closer to the neutral center of sight movement, and thus increase the number of your shots that strike in the black.

You've undoubtedly heard that when squeezing the trigger one should never know exactly when the gun will fire, and that the fall of the hammer should come as a surprise. This may be an interesting theory, but after a few score shots—or at most a few hundred—from any particular gun, you cannot help but know almost exactly when the hammer will fall. And it is this *knowing* just when the hammer will fall that allows you to time the shot so that it occurs very close to the neutral center of sight movement. There is a terrible temptation to attempt to "snatch" the trigger quickly and thus fire the shot as the sights pass through that neutral center—but this is guaranteed to produce a lousy shot, probably a complete miss.

One of the major problems encountered in trigger control is the difficulty in applying pressure *directly* to the rear. When applying pres-

Learning to Shoot

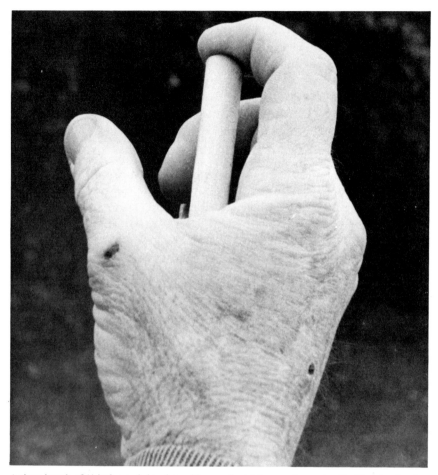

A short length of ½-inch wood dowel provides excellent trigger-pull exercise. Position the dowel as shown, between the ball of the trigger finger (just ahead of the finger's first joint) and the web of the hand. Keep it in line with the forearm while rearward pressure is exerted with the trigger finger. If the front end—the trigger-finger end—of the dowel moves to the right or left under pressure, the muzzle of the gun will move in that direction (and often downward as well) even though the sight picture looks fairly good. Initially, as a rule, the dowel tends to tip to the left. By carrying the dowel about and exercising frequently, this can be corrected, and direct rearward pressure becomes a natural movement, a kind of muscular habit.

sure, the finger tends to move in an arc, and thus (for a right-hander) the fingertip and trigger are forced to the left as well as rearward. This pulls or twitches the muzzle of the gun left and perhaps downward, destroying alignment at a critical time. Careful calling of the shot will disclose this if it is occurring, but it is simpler to train your trigger finger with an exercise requiring only a small length of dowel. The dowel should be cut to a length that can be comfortably fitted between the web of the hand and the pad of the first joint of your trigger finger, and it will probably help a bit if this length is the same as the trigger reach on your gun. The dowel is held between the web and finger, and the finger is moved rearward—as if pressing the trigger—while the dowel is observed and particular care is taken to ensure that it does not tip or move to either side. A few hundred repetitions of this exercise over a period of time will train your finger to apply pressure directly to the rear without any sideward pull and will thus avoid disturbing the muzzle of the gun. Personally, I feel the use of this dowel is more productive than practicing with the gun, mainly because any displacement is so easily seen and corrected; on the gun it is seen only as sight displacement.

A second troublesome tendency is that of tensing or moving the other fingers and the rest of the hand as pressure is placed on the trigger. Once the gun is gripped firmly, any change in that hold will result in some movement of the gun. If the hand tenses as the trigger finger moves rearward, alignment will be lost. To demonstrate this for yourself, align the sights on target, then clench and unclench your shooting hand deliberately. You'll see how much the sights move off the target. You must educate your trigger finger to move *entirely independently* of the rest of the hand—and also educate the rest of the hand to remain completely stable against the pressure applied by that finger. You'll find this easier to accomplish if your hand is relatively strong. This means hand exercises over and above the kind obtained by simply gripping and firing the gun. There are all manner of hand-exercising devices available; probably one of the best—and certainly the cheapest and simplest—is a stiff rubber ball as large as can be conveniently grasped. Many shooters carry such a ball with them and spend their idle moments squeezing and releasing it with the shooting hand. A couple of dozen squeezes three or four times a day on a regular basis will produce a remarkable increase in hand strength.

While on the subject of specific exercises, I must mention that building up the strength of the entire shooting arm and shoulder will certainly reduce fatigue during long strings of fire and will also facilitate control of that unavoidable gun movement. Over the years, a number of special weights and routines have been offered to strengthen the shooting arm, but I doubt that anything is much more efficient than a common five-pound dumbbell used in the regular one-arm routine with emphasis on extended-arm exercises. This gadget is in common daily use among the better shooters.

The hold on the gun must be firm and tight, but not so tight it will set up muscular tremors which cause the front sight to vibrate all over the target. Much has been made of the aid to be obtained from special

There's a common tendency, especially at first, to seat the gun in the hand improperly when simply picking it up with the shooting hand. Instead, grasp the pistol with the off-hand, pointing it upward, and seat the upper part of the back-strap solidly against the web of the shooting hand, between the bases of the thumb and trigger finger.

custom-fitted handgun grips, but in the beginning the standard factory grips on most target pistols are entirely adequate. In fact, so long as they possess a small thumb rest, they are to be preferred to the fancy jobs for initial training. Study the series of photographs showing the manner in which the gun should be seated in the hand, and also the manner in which the finger and thumb are folded around the grip and tightened to more or less "lock" the gun securely in place.

Some old-time shooters with whom I've spoken advise beginners to grasp the gun properly, align it on target, squeeze tightly until the muzzle of the gun begins to vibrate, then back off just enough for the muzzle to steady. With the .22 auto, a grip this tight probably isn't necessary—but it will be for the larger and harder-recoiling calibers, so it's just as well to learn it at this stage with the small gun. With a bit of

Keeping the gun pressed back against the web of the shooting hand, bring the muzzle down until the entire back-strap contacts the hand solidly and you can point your trigger finger forward along the trigger guard while you wrap the three bottom fingers tightly around the front-strap.

practice, you can educate your entire hand to grip the gun tightly, just short of tremor-producing tightness, and at the same time leave the trigger finger completely independent so that it may devote its full attention to trigger control.

Stance (body position) is quite important. In any form of handgun shooting, not just the NRA type under discussion, the shooter's body becomes in effect a *gun platform*. It must support the gun as solidly and uniformly as possible or accurate shooting simply cannot be done. In

When you're learning to achieve a good hold, there's no need to disturb that hold by cocking the hammer with the thumb of the shooting hand. Instead, cock it with the off-hand.

reality, the human body is a very unstable platform when upright and at rest. When we attempt to use our bodies as stable gun platforms, we're using them at their worst rather than their best. The upright human body is a loose-jointed bipod that trembles, pulsates, bends with the wind and is never entirely still. When upright, as it must be for this type of shooting, the body is probably at its most stable when the feet are 12 to 18 inches apart and slightly splayed, hips and shoulders level and arms hanging at the sides. This distributes its weight fairly evenly and symmetrically over the long bones of the legs and the feet. Even in this position it requires continuous effort by one's sense of balance, brain and various muscular movements to keep the body still.

In effect, what a target handgunner does is extend one arm more or less horizontally and attach a 2½- or three-pound weight at the end,

If you've seated the gun in your hand with the slide locked open, use the thumb of your off-hand to work the slide-stop, thus avoiding disturbance of the correct hold.

creating a condition of considerably poor balance. And the object is to keep that weight (the gun) as still as possible and accurately aligned upon a distant target. At the same time, the arm and head must be in such a position that one eye can view the sights correctly.

Try it like this. Face the target head-on, with the gun properly grasped in your shooting hand and hanging down at your side. Face left about 45 degrees (for a right-hander) placing the feet a foot or more apart and angled outward comfortably, then raise your shooting arm to point at the target and turn your head to the right to view the target. This will get most people into a position from which they can hit the target with some degree of success. However, minor adjustments must be made in the arm, head, and foot positions until the gun points precisely at the target while at the same time the shooting eye is aligned directly with the sights. This cannot be properly accomplished by twisting the gun appreciably in the hand.

The safety, too, can be worked with the off-hand to avoid disturbing the hold of the shooting hand.

Ideally—or theoretically—the barrel of the gun should form a direct prolongation of the long bones of the arm; but to accomplish this *and* have the eye in proper relationship to the sights would require relocation of the head by most shooters I have met. By twisting things around a bit, you'll be able to find a position, with chin tucked against shoulder and head cocked slightly toward the gun, where everything lines up well. But now you've thrown the bodily bipod out of balance. It wants to fall over in the direction of the gun, so some repositioning of weight is necessary. Thrusting the shoulders back a bit and arching the back slightly helps, but straightening the left leg and angling the right one a bit is more productive. Move the right foot more under the extended gun arm while straightening the left leg a bit, thus moving the center of gravity as near midway between the feet as possible.

A good, secure hold looks like this. The index finger is against the bottom of the trigger guard, with the ball of that finger on the trigger, ready to press directly rearward. The remaining fingers are wrapped tightly around the front-strap and pressed together. The heel of the thumb bulges around the back-strap, and the thumb itself is high, as shown, not bent downward. The hold must be very firm, but not quite so tight as to cause muscular tremors.

Of course, this results in tipping the hips off level, and the theorists tell us that's bad, but we don't care as long as the body's stability is improved.

It has been written many times that the position you eventually achieve, which gives maximum stability and control of the gun, should be comfortable and relaxed. Hogwash! I'll agree that there should be no great degree of stress or muscular tension developed by the stance, but your body is being forced into an unnatural position, and a certain amount of mental and physical effort is required to achieve and maintain that position. It can hardly be "comfortable and relaxed" in the normal sense of those words. Until you've practiced quite a good deal, the position may be decidedly uncomfortable, the degree depending to a large extent on your physique and physical condition. With practice, you'll be able to hold the proper stance without great conscious effort. Maybe that is what those people mean when they say "comfortable and relaxed."

The stance must be consistent from shot to shot, and equally so from string to string and match to match. Your body must be trained so that the position is assumed in exactly the same manner each time you prepare to shoot. Even minor variations will change the body's resistance

Learning to Shoot

Here's another view of the way it should look when you're ready to touch off the shot. The gun is wedded to the hand, and only the first joint of the index finger is on the trigger. Note that this finger cannot be held horizontally but must curve downward to meet the trigger; otherwise, too much of the finger—the part behind the first joint—will tend to wrap around the trigger and cause a sideward rather than straight rearward pull.

to recoil and this can affect the point of impact on target. Variations in foot positions and leg angles are especially likely to produce vertical stringing on target, and should be avoided. Variations in head and arm relationship can cause muscle or eye strain which increases fatigue and reduces accuracy. Consistency is the key.

During all this, nothing has been said about the position of the left hand and arm. If you've looked at photos of top shooters, you'll see a wide variation in this particular aspect of stance. Some stick the hand in their left pocket, some tuck it in their belt or place it on their hip, others allow it to hang straight down, limp and uncaring. An old Fifth-Army coach convinced me many years ago that the position of the off hand doesn't really matter, so long as it is absolutely consistent and does not detract from the stability of the gun-and-body combination. I do find that the off hand is less likely to cause problems if it is fixed by being thrust into the waistband or pocket. Somehow, it seems to me to require conscious effort to keep the hand and arm still if not anchored.

Even your clothing and footgear will have an effect. I consider footgear the more important of the two. Consider the difference if you are wearing a pair of thin, flimsy loafers or a pair of thick, heavy, stiff ski boots. This comparison may be extreme, but it makes the point. With the loafers, ground contact or "footprint" is very little greater than the soles of your feet; ankles and arch are virtually unsupported; and the foot can probably slip around a little bit on the slick insole of the loafer.

Further, the thin, flexible soles of the loafers can allow irregularities on the surface of the firing point to become a distracting influence. Now, look at those bulky, rigid ski boots; the footprint is substantially greater in area, the entire foot and ankle are well supported, the foot is not free to slip around inside, and irregularities at the firing point cannot be felt through the thick soles. The ski-boot soles grip the surface well, while the usual smooth loafer sole can slither about. It is also worth considering that the loafers weigh at most only a few ounces, while the ski boots are much heavier; consequently, wearing the latter tends to lower the center of gravity of the body slightly, thus making it more stable.

To achieve a good stance, start by facing the target squarely with your feet comfortably placed (usually about 12 to 18 inches apart and slightly splayed). You'll have to turn your feet and body before shooting, but this is a starting point—and a good time to remind yourself to keep your hips and shoulders level, your weight evenly distributed, balanced and relaxed.

While the example of the ski boots may seem extreme, International shooters have worn them in the past, and apparently with good effect. Far more practical and economical is the wearing of a snug-fitting pair of hiking boots whose tops are high enough to be laced snugly above the ankle. If you question the value of all this, some day when conditions are relatively good take low sneakers or loafers and a snug pair of hiking boots to the range. Alternate footgear between strings as you shoot once over the National Match Course, and note the difference in the feel and stability.

Clothing doesn't have much effect, but it has some and you might as well take advantage of it. In rapid-fire shooting, fired cases from your neighboring competitor's gun can be a distraction. Your shirt or jacket should not be cut or worn so as to funnel those cases—which are quite hot—onto tender portions of your anatomy. More than one old-time .45 shooter has scars on his chest or back where a hot case blistered his tender skin. Clothing should be loose enough to allow free breathing and movement, yet not so bulky or voluminous that it balloons in a breeze or otherwise distracts. It's not uncommon to shoot a match in a 15- to 20-knot breeze in some parts of the country, and a whipping,

When ready to take aim, turn at an angle so that your gun hand and the corresponding side of your body are toward the target, your off-hand and corresponding side away from it. Your shooting arm is extended straight toward the target, your head turned to line up your master eye with the sights and target, your chin tucked against your shoulder, and your head cocked slightly toward the gun to get your eye level with the sights. Position your feet comfortably, with the leg on your shooting side in line with the gun. Keep your shoulders back. If you're out of balance, bend the leg on your shooting side slightly and straighten the other one, to get your center of gravity about midway between your feet. The gun should now be parallel with your shooting arm, and you should be looking directly through the sights at the target.

fluttering jacket can pull the gun off target at a critical moment, not to mention the mental distraction it causes. Tight pants and a tight belt do not make deep breathing any easier, and might interfere with your concentration unless you are fully accustomed to them. A big-visored cap or broad-brimmed hat serves several purposes other than to prevent sunburn on your bald spot. Many ranges are not ideally oriented with the sun, and overhead protection from glare is needed. The visor or brim, combined with blinders on your glasses, will keep the eyes well shaded at all times. Actually, this overhead protection is more important in rain than in bright sun. Matches often continue in rain, and not all ranges have overhead cover. Just try shooting bare-headed in even a gentle rain and you'll be convinced; water on shooting glasses distorts the sight picture and can ruin your whole day. Choice of hat or cap doesn't make much difference until you shoot in a stiff breeze. Then, the large area of the hat brim can become a distinct disadvantage. Today, most people shoot with the typical "baseball cap," and in hot weather its lightweight, perforated, or otherwise ventilated crown is much cooler. If your neck sunburns easily, attach a light handkerchief to the cap at the rear.

Now let's get back to the actual shooting. You are familiar now with all of the elements of sight alignment, trigger control, grip and stance, and are on the range for some slow-fire practice. To save time and effort, you should have a good 20X spotting scope set up and focused on the target. Get into position, grasp the gun, breathe and settle down, raise the gun, align the sights, and *squeeze* off the shot—but remember to *call* the shot as it breaks. *Concentrate* on sight alignment and trigger control; blank out external influences and concern yourself only with directing that bullet into the center of the target.

It's a great temptation to look through the spotting scope immediately and locate the bullet hole. If you are more concerned with the accuracy of your call than with the placement of the shot, then go ahead and look. However, I prefer not to look until either three or five shots have been carefully fired. Looking through the scope after each shot tends to break down concentration, especially if a wild shot is noted. By firing at least three shots without spotting, one can concentrate more on the shooting and will produce a shot group which is far more indicative of the level of marksmanship than a single shot. After you're capable of producing small groups, then you can afford to take the time and break your concentration to spot individual holes.

It is common for the new shooter to concentrate too much on placing his individual shots in the center of the 10- or X-ring. He becomes overly concerned with his numerical score. This simply adds another factor of concern and can easily detract from one's progress. Instead, concentrate on *group size* rather than numerical score or placement of that group with respect to the target's scoring rings.

In fact, for this purpose I prefer to use blank targets containing only a black bull's-eye (of the same size as the 50-yard slow-fire target) and no scoring rings whatever. This eliminates the temptation to count score. Obviously, numerical score depends on two factors: first, the size of the group; second, the placement of that group with respect to the scoring rings. There is no reason at all for keeping score until such time as the shot group becomes relatively small and as near circular as possible in shape. When that has been achieved, the shooter can concern himself with the refinements that are usually needed to move the shot group until it is centered precisely in the bull's-eye.

There are two classic enemies of good shooting. First is the flinch and second is "heeling." The former occurs when one jerks or convulsively snatches the trigger and clenches the hand in getting off the shot. When this happens, the path of the bullet cannot be predicted accurately, but a right-handed shooter will put more of his bullets in the lower left quadrant of the target than in any other when flinching. Flinching is usually caused by an involuntary reaction to recoil, blast or report. "Heeling the shot" is the result of subconsciously anticipating recoil and actually thrusting forward with the hand to counteract the kick as the hammer falls. This action generally sends the shots into the upper right quadrant of the target.

Flinching is by far the greater of the two problems. Quite often a shooter is unaware of this involuntary reaction and will, in fact, emphatically deny that it is occurring. Usually, as soon as it can be graphically demonstrated that this is, in fact, what is spoiling his aim, the problem is half solved. The most common and effective method of eliminating flinching requires a coach or assistant. The coach loads the gun, out of sight of the shooter, and hands it to him for a shot. For the first two or three such shots, the coach actually chambers a round, and the student gets his shot off in normal fashion. Then, however, the coach will not chamber a round but will hand the gun to the student as if he had. If the student is flinching, it will become vividly apparent when he attempts to fire with an empty chamber. At the instant the hammer falls and he expects the gun to roar, the convulsive movement of the hand and arm and the gun will be visible. In some individuals the flinch is so strong that the entire body momentarily convulses. This isn't normally seen when a cartridge is actually fired, because recoil, report and blast mask the shooter's actions.

Once the shooter actually sees what he has done, continued use of the old "ball and dummy exercise" (as this is called in military circles) will usually clear up flinching in a short period of time. It should be

The shooting arm must be rigid, the elbow and wrist locked in positon to point straight at the target. Note the position of hand, arm, shoulder and head.

kept in mind that flinching is not restricted to neophyte shooters, nor is it something that disappears forever after correction. Even experienced shooters may occasionally lapse into flinching for no apparent reason.

To a lesser degree, heeling can also be corrected with ball and dummy exercises. However, it is usually a lot less trouble to convince oneself—or be convinced—that heeling is taking place by the consistent placement of shots in the upper right quadrant. Of course, this assumes that the gun is properly targeted in the beginning. This anticipation of recoil is far easier to deal with than the reaction of flinching. Once the shooter is convinced it's happening, a bit of extra concentration usually solves the problem with no great difficulty. Like flinching, heeling can sneak back on you, even after long experience in shooting. Firing a gun and cartridge of abnormally heavy recoil and blast will often precipitate flinching, whereas heeling usually develops when one's natural timed resistance to recoil gets a bit out of phase and occurs before the gun fires.

Once you've reached the point where reasonably small groups can be produced on target, it's time to look into a natural inclination (present in at least a modest percentage of shooters) toward "canting." Canting

Learning to Shoot

This photo illustrates a common mistake—canting the gun in an unconscious effort to attain a more comfortable stance. Because the top of the pistol is tilted to the shooter's right, the shot will strike to the right and low on the target.

is the deviation from perpendicular of the vertical center line of the gun and the sights. One will naturally take great care to keep the gun perfectly perpendicular during targeting; then, perhaps at some later date, a tendency may develop to lean, or "cant," the gun slightly to one side or the other. Canting may develop from muscular imbalance in the arm or wrist, from eye strain, or perhaps an unconscious attempt to reduce strain on neck and shoulder muscles. It may be to right or left, and the inevitable result is for the bullets to strike the target away from the center of the bull's-eye in the direction toward which the top of the gun is tilted. In other words, if the gun is canted to the left, even though the sight alignment remains otherwise perfect, shots will strike to the left and a bit low.

The greater the degree of cant, the greater distance will the bullets be displaced from the center of the target. If your shots start drifting to right or left and a bit low, canting is suspect. Inasmuch as one may drift into canting very gradually, it isn't always as easy to spot as you

This is the right way. The gun is vertical, and all the elements of the "shooting platform" are lined up solidly.

might think. A quick check is to go ahead and line up for a shot and then, without disturbing the vertical angle of the gun, swing it slowly over to the edge of the target or target frame and compare the angle of the front sight with the reference presented there. The front sight should be parallel to the edge of the frame; if not, canting exists. Another method is simply run a vertical stripe, consisting of target pasters or black tape, down the center of the target, then very carefully fire a three- or five-shot group while making certain that the front sight is parallel to the stripe. If, when this is done, the shots move back into their proper position, you may be reasonably certain that you have been canting the gun without knowing it.

Canting is not the only problem a shooter might drift into after having initially paid careful attention to sight alignment. Even after extensive shooting, it is possible to allow the front sight to ride high or low in relation to the rear, especially if you become a bit tired or aren't con-

In this photo, simulating recoil movement, another common mistake is illustrated. The shooter has allowed his wrist to "break" slightly under recoil. This permits the muzzle to rise higher than it needs to, thus slowing the process of aligning and locking all elements again for the next shot. Frequently, it also causes the shooting hand to shift its hold without the shooter's knowing that anything has slipped. Allowing the elbow to "break" during recoil will similarly slow down recovery for the next shot, and if both elbow and wrist are unlocked the undesirable results are all the more pronounced.

Here's another photo simulating recoil—this time with the shooter reacting properly. When the gun is fired, the wrist and elbow should be kept locked and straight. The gun's recoil and jump are absorbed by the hand and arm, moving up with the gun as a unit. Recovery of position and alignment for the next shot will then be rapid and easy, and the hold of the shooting hand is less likely to shift.

Handgun Competition

centrating on the shot as you should. If the top of the front sight rises above the top of the rear sight, and you still maintain the same relationship of target to front sight image, shots will go high; conversely, if the front sight is allowed to drop below the top of the rear, shots will go low. You may also find yourself letting the sights drift up deeper into the bull's-eye, or allowing a slight gap to develop between sights and bull. It is worth repeating that when the sights are aligned high on the bull, shots will go high, and vice versa. And even though you have drilled yourself religiously on keeping the lines of light on either side of the front sight equal in width, you may find that the gap becomes wider on one side. When this happens shots will be off the point of aim in the direction of the smallest line of light.

If you had to contend with only one of the above errors, perhaps correction wouldn't be much of a problem. Unfortunately, when you get careless or tired, or suffer from eye strain, sloppy sight alignment may incorporate any or all of those problems. When that happens, there's really no telling where the shot will land in relation to the intended point. So, if you start getting a series of wild shots and do not believe them attributable to flinching or heeling, correct each and every aspect of sight alignment and you'll probably get back into the black.

I've made several references here to fatigue, and it is surprising how small a number of shots will sometimes tire you to the point where it is difficult to do everything correctly. In the beginning, as few as 20 or so shots may frazzle your concentration to the point where nothing is to be gained by continuing. If you become sufficiently fatigued (mentally or physically) and you start doing wrong things and scattering

Here's another example of canting—a severe example—to show how the sights would look and where the bullets would group if the gun were tilted this much to the left. Canting is usually less severe (and therefore harder to detect) but its effect on target is so drastic that a shooter must take great care not to let himself slip into the canting habit.

your shots, it is often better to quit for the day—not even attempting to correct the problem—and start fresh another time. Continued efforts to correct the problems when you've become fuzzy are seldom very productive. In fact, the problems can become worse, and you may become convinced that the entire game isn't worth the effort.

I recommend that beginners limit themselves to short shooting sessions two or three times a week, rather than attempting to burn up several hundred rounds over the weekend. I have known some very experienced shooters who were capable of firing several hundred rounds each day, seven days a week. One acquaintance of mine shot an average of 30,000 rounds per year over a protracted period of time. Yet I have known other people of comparable shooting ability who simply could not handle more than 100 to 150 rounds at each session, two or three times a week. With respect to the amount of practice you can actually utilize, you'll simply have to seek your level and stay with it. Too much practice shooting can be worse than too little for some people.

4

National Rifle Association Competitive Program

Although the NRA—National Rifle Association—was originally formed for the purpose of promoting *rifle* marksmanship, the organization long ago became the governing body for national handgun competition as well. It acted as the official repository of records and data and did much to formalize and develop the so-called "American program," which differed from development in other parts of the world. International competition is covered elsewhere in this volume. This chapter will deal with NRA handgun competition as it exists today—and more specifically with that segment of competition generally known as NRA Matches. Other forms in which the NRA has become the principal influence, mainly police competition, are covered in detail in another chapter.

The current edition of the *NRA Pistol Rules* booklet, published by the National Rifle Association, may be purchased for a nominal fee and should be in the hands of anyone contemplating participation in organized NRA-type matches. It is probably best to start at the top, listing and describing briefly the various types of NRA competitions governed by these rules.

Handgun Competition

At the very highest level, International Matches are arranged by the NRA with national shooting organizations of various other countries. In such matches, the NRA operates as the authorized representative of the United States and coordinates all details (location, facilities, matches and courses of fire to be shot, etc.) with the officials of the other countries involved.

Directly beneath this we have the International Team Try-Outs which are U. S. matches (or tournaments) arranged by the NRA for shooters wishing to become members of a U. S. team (or individual U.S. competitors) participating in an International match. The shooters compete for the number of positions that exist. Such try-out matches, conducted by officials appointed or approved by the NRA, involve essentially the same courses of fire that will be utilized in the International matches. Depending on the nature of the matches for which the try-outs are conducted, they may be shot under the rules of the ISU (International Shooting Union) or NRA International rules, or a combination thereof. Anyone who has ambitions to shoot in International competition should obtain the appropriate rule book from the NRA. This book covers not only NRA rules for the conduct of International matches in this country, but the International Shooting Union rules which govern ranges, facilities, conduct of matches, guns, ammunition, etc., for *all* International competition.

The highlight of domestic pistol shooting is the National Championships, organized and conducted by the NRA and, in some cases, assisted by the National Board for the Promotion of Rifle Practice, Department of the Army. Participation by the National Board is generally limited to the conduct of the National Trophy matches, and the supply of such assistance to the matches is authorized by Congress. In recent years, this assistance has been greatly curtailed by Congress, by reduction in funding for the National Board, and by the activities of various anti-gun and anti-hunting legislators. In the past, much assistance was available from the National Board in the form of arms, ammunition, targets and target material, range construction and operation, and much more. In fact, in past years the National Pistol Matches (and rifle as well) were conducted almost exclusively with military personnel and equipment supplied by the several services under agreements arranged by the National Board. This situation no longer exists, due to the Congressional activities mentioned, and today the National Matches are conducted almost exclusively by member-volunteers of the NRA and with various costs paid by the NRA. Assistance by the National Board through the Office of the Director of Civilian Marksmanship (ODCM) is now limited to arms and ammunition for military and National Trophy matches.

Viewed from the ready line at Camp Perry, Ohio, these shooters are competing in the 50-yard slow-fire course.

From the beginning, the National Matches (composed of the NRA National Championships and the National Trophy matches) have been conducted at Camp Perry, Ohio, on the shores of Lake Erie. Camp Perry is a small military installation, used otherwise by the Ohio National Guard and owned by the state of Ohio. Though this is the historical location for the National Pistol Matches—and is the site of the 1977 matches—they may well move elsewhere in future years, due to various anti-gun pressures.

Any person, including Juniors (shooters under the age of 19), may enter the individual portions of the National Matches, provided they hold valid National Rifle Association memberships. However, it really isn't normal for one to simply decide he will join the NRA this year and shoot in the National Matches. After all, the very best pistol shooters of the nation congregate at the National Matches to seek the National Championship. An individual doesn't jump into that sort of competition without extensive preparation any more than he would trot over to the ball park with the intention of pitching for the Cincinnati Reds.

Most marksmen begin at the bottom and work their way up by joining NRA-affiliated rifle and pistol clubs, then gain experience in all of the lower-level matches. As a matter of fact, it is essential for an individual to begin this way if he is to participate in the National Championships as a member of a team. We'll get into that aspect later. Many different teams shoot at the National Matches, and invariably their members are selected on the basis of competitive performance at lower levels.

NRA-affiliated clubs may conduct informal matches for their members, and these generally serve mainly as training or practice and recreation and have no NRA standing. In fact, many clubs conduct few other matches simply because their main goal is fun, not serious competition. Above this, clubs may conduct either "Approved" or "Registered" (by the NRA) matches. Approved matches require a smaller registration fee; scores are not eligible as national records, competitors need not be NRA members, no minimum number of shots is required, there need not be a fixed award schedule, there will not be an official NRA referee assigned—and there are lesser differences. However, approved match scores do go toward NRA classification, and use of the NRA classification system is optional. Many clubs have their local matches approved but not registered simply because the administrative and logistic work is substantially less.

Whether approved or registered, club matches may be by invitation only or may be open to all comers. In addition, there may be Registered Leagues. Any group of clubs or organizations may form a league with a comprehensive schedule of matches for summer and/or winter seasons. In an active pistol-shooting area, approved or registered tournaments or registered league matches can be found two or three weekends each month throughout the season.

Above this level, we have State Championship Matches which are annual tournaments conducted by the State Rifle and/or Pistol Association affiliated with the NRA. Actually, the State Association may authorize an affiliated club to conduct those matches. The club is usually the one with the best range facilities available.

Beyond State Championships, we have Regional and Sectional Championships which are arranged between the NRA and a local sponsoring organization. This organization may be the State Association or a club with unusually good facilities. Setting up a Regional or Sectional Championship involves, of course, a great deal of liaison between the NRA and the sponsoring organization, and quite possibly other state and local organizations as well. A championship shoot at this level requires ranges and other facilities a good deal superior to those possessed by the average club or state association.

Thus, whether an individual is a tyro contemplating his first competition or an experienced shooter with a long series of matches under his belt, he may look forward to shooting in informal matches, approved and registered matches, registered leagues and state, regional, sectional and National Championships. The extent to which one may progress through NRA pistol competition is limited only by the time and marksmanship ability he can bring to bear on the project.

Matches are plentiful in the more thickly settled areas of the country, and they are surprisingly common even in the wide open spaces of the West. In the highly urbanized areas, range space is a problem, but even in places like New York City you'll find quite a few matches scheduled during the season. Some are on commercial ranges, some on police ranges, and in addition to the outdoor facilities there are quite a few indoor police and commercial ranges where certain types of matches can be conducted.

Basically, the NRA matches consist of only three types of fire, theoretically conducted with three different guns, but with sufficient overlap between two of the gun types so that they may be shot with a single gun and cartridge. All competition is shot over what is commonly called the National Match Course. There is the short course, consisting of 10 rounds rapid fire, 10 rounds timed fire and 10 rounds slow fire, for a total of 30 shots. Rapid and timed fire are shot at 25 yards. When slow fire is shot at 50 yards, it becomes the Standard National Match Course. Reducing slow fire to 25 yards makes it the NRA Short Course. The 30-shot course is fired with a .22 rimfire pistol (invariably an autoloader), a centerfire gun and a .45-caliber gun. A shooter may compete with one, two or all three guns, but it is customary to shoot all three, which means that over the standard course you'll fire 90 rounds. The maximum possible score with each gun is 300 points, and ties are broken by the highest number of shots striking the X-ring. (The diameter of the X-ring, 10-ring and other scoring rings on regulation targets will be listed later in this chapter.)

In addition, there is an aggregate score consisting of the total of the scores fired in each category, with a maximum possible of 900. There may also be 20-shot rapid-, timed- and slow-fire matches with each gun. Lastly, there may be a "grand aggregate," the total of the scores of all three guns. The end result is that in firing a total of 12 matches, four with each of the three guns, an individual winds up with 14 or more match scores. Championships are determined by the grand aggregate score, the maximum possible being 2700.

Rapid fire is shot in strings of five rounds, with 10 seconds allowed for the firing of the five shots in a string. Ideally this shooting will be at "turning targets," which are targets mounted on vertically pivoted

Here, the 50-yard slow-fire stage of the National Trophy Individual Match (service pistol) is in progress at Camp Perry. The photo shows a 50-target section of the much larger pistol ranges. To facilitate range management and scheduling, portable shooting stands are used even at national championships, and such stands are excellent for club use.

frames so that they can be rotated to face the shooter only for a specified period of time. However, many small clubs lack expensive facilities, so their shooting is done against targets that face the shooter at all times, with the beginning and end of the legal firing period indicated by whistle blasts. The higher levels of competition *must* be shot against turning targets, and the correctness of the time interval must be verified. The better ranges are equipped with the electrically or hydraulically operated targets controlled by electronic timers. Some less complex arrangements have the targets rotated by simple systems of cables, rods, and cranks that are operated manually.

In any event, then, the rapid-fire stage of each NMC will consist of two five-round strings, each fired in 10 seconds, beginning with the gun loaded and ready to fire. In an informal match, both strings (10 shots) may be fired on the same target. However, at registered and approved matches, each string will normally be fired on a single target in order to simplify scoring. It can become quite difficult to determine the value of some shots if a closely spaced group of 10 bullet holes exists on a single target. Both rapid-fire and timed-fire stages are shot at a range of 25 yards (that's yards, not meters).

Timed fire differs from rapid fire only in that twice as much time, 20 seconds, is allowed for each five-shot string. While it might seem that the allowance of twice as much time would cause scores to be appreciably higher, such is not generally the case. A thoroughly expert marksman will probably shoot perfect scores in both timed and rapid fire, or will drop no more than one or two points. Rather than developing two distinctly different rhythms for getting off five carefully aimed shots, a good many shooters concentrate only on the 10-second rhythm of rapid fire and use it for both the rapid and timed stages. However,

This is a section of the Camp Perry firing line during a timed-fire course. A close look (at top right) will reveal that one shooter is using a wire-screen barrier to prevent his neighbor's hot fired cases from striking and distracting him.

In NRA-type competition, when shooters and scorers go forward after a course of fire to record the scores, a shooter often carries his own replacement target and installs it in the frame as soon as scoring is completed.

the less experienced shooters often find that they can shoot higher scores with four seconds allowed per shot, as opposed to two seconds.

Slow fire is often said to be the stage that "separates the men from the boys." It is shot at twice the range of the others, 50 yards as opposed to 25 yards, and at a target with a larger black aiming area. A total of 10 minutes, one minute per shot, is allowed; however, this may be broken into two five-minute periods to allow separate targets to be used for each five-shot string. Scoring of 50-yard targets is not quite so critical, inasmuch as most groups will not be tight enough to produce scoring difficulties. Still, in the higher levels of competition, slow fire will usually be shot in two five-shot stages with scoring after each.

As already indicated, the above course will be shot in each of three categories. In .22 caliber, it is essential that one use a .22 rimfire pistol or revolver, with whatever standard .22 rimfire ammunition performs best in it. There are few restrictions on the ammunition, though generally speaking "Pistol Match" ammunition produces the best accuracy. Of the less costly varieties, .22 LR Standard Velocity generally shoots

In championship shooting, a single point can mean a lot, and scoring challenges are not uncommon. Here, NRA referees meticulously check challenged targets. Note the dollar bill lying on the far target—a payment that must accompany a challenge. Requiring payment (refunded if the challenge proves valid) helps eliminate frivolous challenges.

a bit better than the High Velocity version. At the higher levels of competition, carefully selected match ammunition is invariably used.

Paragraph 3.4 of the current *NRA Pistol Rules* booklet defines the gun to be used in .22-caliber matches as "any pistol (single shot or semi-automatic) or revolver using .22 caliber rimfire cartridge having an overall length of not more than 1.1 inches and with lead or alloy bullet not greater than .23 inch in diameter and weighing not more than 40 grains; barrel length, including cylinder, not more than 10 inches; sights may be adjustable but not over 10 inches apart; trigger pull not less than two pounds. All standard safety features of the gun must operate properly. Any sights including telescopic are permitted."

Within those limits, the shooter has a great deal of freedom, except that—obviously—a single-shot gun cannot be used in the rapid or timed stages. While either a revolver or autoloading pistol is allowed, very few revolvers are found in serious matches these days. The autoloader eliminates the time delay and disturbance of cocking the revolver, and thus is almost universally favored. There are those, also, who feel that the revolver cannot—because of its peculiarities of design —deliver accuracy quite as good as that of the autoloader.

For the centerfire stages of NRA matches, one is restricted by paragraph 3.2 of the current rules book to "Center-fire pistols (single-shot or semi-automatic) or revolvers of .32 caliber or larger (including 7.65mm and .45 caliber pistols and revolvers) . . . barrel length, including cylinder, not more than 10 inches; trigger pull not less than 2½ pounds except .45 caliber, semi-automatic pistols not less than 3½ pounds. Sights may be adjustable but not over 10 inches apart. All standard safety features of the gun must operate properly. Programs may specify particular calibers or types of center-fire guns which will be permitted or not permitted in the stated event. Any sights, including telescopic, are permitted."

This makes clear why a shooter need not necessarily fire three different guns in the three categories. The centerfire rules specifically allow the use of the .45-caliber semiautomatic pistol which is *required* in other matches. In years gone by, the Colt or Smith & Wesson target revolver in .38 Special (or occasionally in .32 caliber) was the chosen gun for this match with a special mid-range (low velocity) ammunition utilizing wadcutter bullets. However, over the past 15 or 20 years, fully reliable .38-caliber (and to a lesser extent .32-caliber) autoloading pistols have been developed. As described above regarding .22 matches, the advantage that the .38 autoloader offers over revolvers is obvious, so the auto has become the preferred gun.

Note that the centerfire rules do not define or limit ammunition as do the .22 caliber rules. The only ammunition limitations are those found in rule 3.17, which stipulates "ammunition of any description that may be fired without danger to competitors, range personnel, or equipment. Tracer, incendiary, armour piercing, and similar ammunition is prohibited." Generally speaking, a process of evolution has produced mid-range type, wadcutter-bullet loading of superb accuracy in .38 Special and .32 caliber. Similar loadings of .45-caliber ammunition have developed with semi-wadcutter bullets (required for feeding in all

SFC Hershel Anderson, a well-known Army marksman, has his gun box on the shooting stand at Camp Perry. Visible in the box are two .45 Colt autos; clamped behind them in the tray are others—including a .22—an entire complement of pistols for NRA matches.

.45 pistols) which are normally used when the chosen gun is .45 caliber. "Service" ammunition is specified for certain *.45-caliber* matches, but this does not apply to ordinary centerfire matches.

Guns for use in .45 Caliber Semi-Automatic Pistol Matches are defined in paragraph 3.3 as "any .45 caliber, semi-automatic, trigger pull not less than 3½ pounds. Sights may be adjustable but not more than 10 inches apart. All standard safety features of the gun must operate properly. Any sights including telescopic are permitted." Again there is no reference to ammunition, so any ammunition is permissible. However, it is important to note that .45 Caliber Semi-Automatic Pistol Matches are *not* the same as those designated "Service Pistol." Even though the caliber and type remain the same in the latter, the gun is considerably more limited by rule 3.1, which states: "U. S. pistol, caliber .45 M1911 or M1911A1 or the same type and caliber of commercially manufactured pistol. The pistol must be equipped with issue or similar factory standard stocks (i.e., without thumb rest). Trigger pull must be not less than four pounds. This pistol must be equipped with open sights. The front sight must be non-adjustable. The pistol may be equipped with adjustable rear sights with open U or rectangular notch, the distance between sights measuring not more than seven inches from the apex of the front sight to the rear face of the rear sight. The fore strap of the grip may be checkered. The mainspring housing may be either the flat or arched type. Trigger shoes may be used. Trigger stops, internal or external, are acceptable. Otherwise, external alterations or additions to the arm will not be allowed. The internal parts of the pistol may be specially fitted and include alterations which will improve the functioning and accuracy of the arm, provided such alterations in no way interfere with the proper functioning of the safety devices as manufactured. All standard safety features of the pistol must operate properly. It is the competitor's responsibility to have his pistol checked prior to firing of the match."

As can be seen, a gun meeting the qualifications for "Service Pistol" will meet the requirements of ".45 Caliber Semi-Automatic Pistol", but the reverse is not true. *Either* may meet the requirements for centerfire matches.

If a shooter wants to use the .45 Caliber Semi-Automatic Pistol in centerfire matches, he might even go further and substitute the Service Pistol, making no change in the gun but simply switching to mid-range ammunition. However, in Service Pistol matches, it is mandatory under rule 3.17 that the ammunition be "full-charge ball ammunition manufactured for or by the government and issued for use in service arms." Generally speaking, "Service Pistol" is specified only for the National Trophy Matches, and under those circumstances the use of ammunition supplied and issued at the range is mandatory. This eliminates any confusion or controversy that might arise.

Targets are clearly specified in paragraph 4 of the "NRA Pistol Rules" booklet. The basic target is the same for all three courses of fire —the X-ring being 1.695 inches in diameter, the 10-ring 3.39 inches, the 9-ring 5.54 inches, the 8-ring 8.00 inches, the 7-ring 11.00 inches, the 6-ring 14.80 inches and the 5-ring 19.68 inches. All shots outside

National Rifle Association Competitive Program

In 1969, U.S. Air Force PO 1 Donald Hamilton set the current NRA record at Camp Perry. His championship score, 2668 points out of a possible grand aggregate of 2700, beat the previous (1963) record by 14 points. This kind of handgunning is so demanding that only a small, elite group, called the "2600 Club," has ever topped 2600 points in registered competition. Here, Hamilton displays the 50-yard slow-fire target he shot at the 1969 matches; this target scored 100-8X.

the 5-ring score as misses even if they strike the paper. This target is used for 50-yard slow fire with the 8, 9, and 10 rings black; and for 25-yard rapid or timed fire with only the 9 and 10 rings black. The version for rapid and timed fire is known as target no. B-8, and the one for slow fire is B-6. Reduced versions are available for use at shorter distances where adequate range facilities are not available, and for use on the standard 50-foot indoor range. The reduction in scoring-ring diameter is not strictly arithmetical for the 50-foot target, which is used at one-third the normal slow-fire distance but has a 10-ring measuring only .90 inch. The reduction is by *more* than a factor of three, to account for other differences between indoor and outdoor shooting. On the other hand, when the 50-yard slow-fire target is reduced for outdoor use at 25 yards, the reduction is strictly arithmetical, by a factor of two; the 10-ring for the shorter range is exactly one-half its diameter for the longer range.

A great many more pages could be consumed in describing in detail other aspects of the NRA matches. The rule book contains 49 pages of data. It would be impractical to discuss all this in these pages. After digesting the fundamentals enumerated in this chapter, a shooter should obtain the rule book and should also read the various articles in *The American Rifleman* magazine about the competitive programs. With that under his belt, he will be able to understand the program and participate in it.

5

Police
Competition

Prior to the early 1960's, there was no *formalized* competition in police marksmanship. Of course, law-enforcement officers had competed from the very beginning, and some of the most outstanding pistol shots came from the ranks of police departments and federal law-enforcement agencies during the 1930's. However, these men were competing within the existing framework of NRA matches, shooting shoulder to shoulder with civilian and military shooters over the conventional courses of fire. Other than some oddball events such as "Hogan's Alley" at Camp Perry and perhaps similar local setups, there was no organized competition designed specifically for law-enforcement officers.

In the years following World War II, it became increasingly apparent that even a national champion of NRA-type paper-punching would be ill prepared for the kind of shooting that a policeman may be forced to do. Criminals don't stand up to present nice, easily recognized targets at 25 or 50 yards and wait for the range procedures found in typical competitive shooting. Years earlier, agencies such as the FBI and some very few urban departments had adopted suitable training methods and qualification courses, but there had been no competitive program employing such courses of fire to encourage better police marksmanship. During the late 1950's there was a good deal of independent

Handgun Competition

In recent years, police competition with the revolver has soared in popularity. The program culminates in an annual national championship match (which, incidentally, includes the use of shotguns as well as handguns). In this photo, competitors are loading preparatory to a course shot from behind simulated barriers.

Shooters move forward with their scorers to check the results on the targets.

This is a typical target after 30 rounds have been fired in police competition. The numerical score is not very impressive, but the shooter has kept his bullets grouped fairly close in the torso area of the target.

effort to develop such forms of competition. Among the pioneers of these matches were the University of Indiana, Colt Firearms and a number of individuals. The PPC—Practical Police Course—used by the FBI formed the basis for their work. Eventually, the NRA moved into the game and developed a nationwide program of police competition. It followed generally along the same organizational and administrative lines as the existing NRA bull's-eye-type shooting program.

The question of eligibility to shoot in police matches is a legitimate one. Only law-enforcement officers, including military police, are allowed. Civilians are out. NRA police competition culminates in the Na-

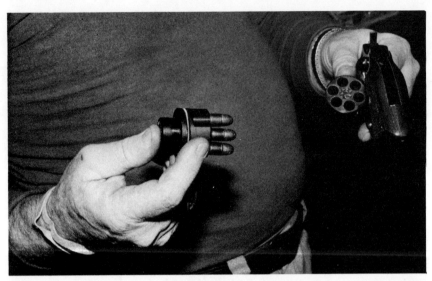

For PPC courses requiring a second string of well-aimed shots to be fired within a very brief time limit, speed-loading devices are favored by most marksmen. The cartridges are kept ready in the loader. After firing a string, when the cylinder has been swung out and the spent cases ejected, the loader is used to put the fresh ones in simultaneously. Using the model shown here, the shooter will press a release button with his thumb before pulling the loader clear of the cylinder, and the cartridges will be left in the chambers.

This is a perfectly acceptable two-handed hold in the kneeling position for police matches. The shooter is using a reworked Colt Python.

tional Championships, which have for several years been held in Jackson, Mississippi. Teams and individuals from local, state and federal departments and agencies all over the country meet there to determine just who is best in PPC shooting. The term "PPC" is widely (and less than correctly) used to describe this general type of shooting, mainly because the earliest FBI course of this kind was designated as the Practical Police Course.

The courses of fire for police competition have been developed, insofar as possible, to simulate the ranges, positions and types of firing that an officer might expect to employ in an actual shooting situation. The basic NRA National Police Course (Course No. 1) used in most matches is essentially the same as the older PPC. The NRA course eliminates the 60-yard firing of the FBI course and substitutes six-shot strings for the five-shot strings of the PPC. Admitting that no course of fire which can be conducted safely on a formal range in the presence of the public can really duplicate a combat situation, this course does possess sufficient similarity to combat shooting to be of practical use.

It consists of 12 rounds fired in 25 seconds at a range of seven yards, and of course this requires fully reloading the revolver within the specified time period. All 12 shots must be fired double-action from a crouched position, and the sights are not used. This constitutes Stage A. Stage B is shot at 25 yards with six rounds fired in 12 seconds from the standing position with no support; again, all shots are fired double-action, but the sights may be used. Stage C is fired at 50 yards, with six rounds fired single-action from the sitting and prone positions, followed by six rounds fired with the strong hand and six with the weak hand, from behind a simulated barricade. All Stage C shooting is normally single-action. The sights are used, and all 24 rounds are fired within 2 minutes and 45 seconds. Stage D is shot at 25 yards, with six rounds fired from the kneeling position double-action, then six rounds from each hand from the barricade position, double-action, all 18 rounds to be completed within 90 seconds.

In summary, all shooting is at 50 yards or less, and a total of 60 shots must be fired, 36 double-action, the balance in the single-action mode. With the exception of Stage A, fired from the crouch, the sights may and should be used, even when the shooting is double-action. Speed of reloading is stressed, as it would be in combat. Inasmuch as the National Police Course may be shot only with revolvers, reloading efficiency becomes extremely important. Few men have ever become speedy enough with loose cartridges to leave enough time for really first-class shooting. The development of speed-loaders, devices that allow an entire cylinder-load of six cartridges to be inserted simultaneously, has greatly facilitated reloading and produced improved scores.

Manufacturers are eager to make sure their guns perform well at police matches, and they send highly skilled gunsmiths to the national championships. These gunsmiths correct any mechanical trouble or malfunction as quickly as possible.

A wide variety of such loaders is available, and while some appear to possess mechanical superiority over others, practice in their use is probably a good deal more important than design.

While on the subject of reloading, I must say I fail to understand why autoloading pistols are not permitted in the NRA police matches. Even back in the 1930's when it was thought that the revolver was the universal police sidearm, a few departments and individuals preferred various autoloading pistols. The revolver is still the choice of most

Though reloading rapidly is essential, a few shooters—including the officer pictured here—still do it one cartridge at a time, without the aid of a speed-loader. It takes dexterity to avoid fumbling and dropping cartridges.

agencies, but more and more departments and agencies employ the autoloader. As it is the avowed intent of police matches to promote the development of service-sidearm marksmanship, it seems ridiculous to exclude the chosen standard of many departments. In speed of reloading, the auto possesses a distinct advantage over the revolver. It also has the advantage of a greater number of shots—which eliminates the necessity for reloading at all in many fire fights.

It is a paradox that the autoloader is banned from police competitive programs because of the very advantages it possesses over the revolver in genuine combat situations. The autoloader is apparently not allowed because it does possess these advantages over the revolver, and the original program was designed around the revolver. All other factors being equal, a typical 9- or 10-shot autoloader would permit shooting the entire course in less time—or, by reducing time and frequency of reloading, would allow the shooter more time for actual aiming and firing. These advantages could easily be evened out so that a true comparison of skill might be obtained, by simply reducing time limits and magazine capacities for autoloading pistols. Even if it could be said that no genuinely fair adjustment of time could be developed, any remaining inequities could be eliminated by simply having revolvers and autoloaders classified separately as were bolt-action and autoloading rifles for many years in military matches.

Of course, if we look at the revolver and autoloader closely, particularly in reference to the manner in which the former is employed in police competition, we find that the revolver is not entirely without advantages over the auto. Its principal advantage lies in the fact that it is generally used with ammunition loaded so lightly that recoil and blast are negligible. The autoloader cannot function reliably with loads anywhere near this light. Thus, recoil and muzzle jump with the sixgun are substantially less than with the autoloader.

While change has been steadfastly resisted and the revolver remains the standard arm for police competition, many of us anticipate that in the not-too-distant future the powers that be will be forced to allow the use of autoloaders in a separate category. This will make the conduct of matches more complex and time-consuming, but it is an essential step if the game is to continue to have practical value to law-enforcement officers.

There are few restrictions on the revolvers used in police matches. The course of fire requires a cylinder capacity of six rounds, and the gun must have double-action capability. On the other hand, even though the course of fire indicates single-action fire in some stages, double-action may be substituted (it generally being considered less accurate and more difficult) without penalty. The gun must be of no less than .38 caliber and may have a barrel length of no more than six inches. Adjustable sights are permitted. Telescopic sights are not permitted. Until now, there have been no limitations on the ammunition that may be used, and specially loaded cartridges of very low power are often employed because of their reduced recoil and jump.

The relatively few limitations on guns and ammunition have been, in my opinion, counter-productive. This is apparent when one sees the guns used on the firing line at many major police matches—guns so extensively modified with massive barrels and ribs, rebuilt actions, abnormally fast rifling twists, etc., that they bear virtually no relationship to a service revolver. A great many of the guns would not be satisfactory for duty use. The same may be said of the ammunition. The extremely low power level of the cartridges generally employed in matches would be totally unsuitable for service use.

With reloading completed, the officer resumes fire at the second-yard line. The shooter at his left is still reloading. Note that the stance and hold for this kind of shooting differs drastically from the stance and hold in bull's-eye matches.

If the intention is to promote more efficient use of the service revolver, only guns and ammunition suitable for service should be permitted in competition. It has been demonstrated many times that one may develop a very high level of marksmanship with specially modified guns and ammunition, and still not be able to demonstrate more than the most mediocre marksmanship with standard guns and full-charge ammunition. As a precedent, we need only to look at the rules set down for the National Trophy Match requiring the use of the service pistol. The permissible modifications on the standard .45 automatic are clearly set forth and defined; and, in addition, full-charge ammunition of the type issued by the military establishment is specified. Comparable rules in the NRA police matches would do much to increase their value to police training.

In addition to the basic course, there is the NRA 25 Yard Course (Course No. 2), which is exactly the same as the National Police Course except that Stage C is shot at 25 instead of 50 yards. The reason for this modified course is obvious in that it may be shot in its entirety on

Barrier shooting is important in police competition because it roughly duplicates a situation that might occur in the line of duty. It includes stages of fire from each side of the barricade, using both the "strong" hand (the hand normally used) to control the gun and the "weak hand." Here, a right-handed officer is going through the weak-handed stage, firing the gun with his left hand and using his right hand only for support.

a range which does not offer 50-yard firing points. A third modification of the course, for indoor ranges, is identified as the NRA Indoor PPC Course (Course No. 3). In it, Stage A is fired at seven yards, exactly as in Course No. 1, and is shot on the same target. All the remaining stages are shot in the same manner but at 50 feet on the NRA B-29 target or the reduced Colt target T-6. All outdoor courses are shot on the NRA B-27, or on the Prehel or Colt silhouette.

In police competition the FBI PPC Course (Course No. 4) is also sometimes encountered. Mentioned earlier as the basis for NRA Course No. 1, it consists of Stage A, 10 shots double-action in 25 seconds, fired at seven yards; then five shots single-action from the prone position at 60 yards for Stage B; Stage C at 50 yards, with 20 shots single-action, fired from sitting, prone and right and left side of the barricades; Stage D again double-action, with five shots kneeling, then five shots from each side of a barricade. Thus, the total number of shots in the FBI course is only 50 as opposed to 60 in the NRA course.

All stages of police competition are begun with the revolver fully loaded and holstered. Upon a signal, whether it be turning targets or a whistle blast, the officer draws his revolver and assumes the specified or appropriate position. If the particular stage requires reloading, then the officer fires his first six rounds and immediately reloads and resumes fire, without command, to complete the stage.

References are made to shooting with both the right and the left hand; a right-handed shooter's right hand is referred to as his strong hand while his left is referred to as his weak hand. The purpose of requiring both hands is to give the officer preparation for the time when his strong hand might be disabled. There are many otherwise impressive handgunners who have never fired a shot with the weak hand. I've had some experience in this, persuading individuals who shot quite well with their strong hand to try a few shots for record with the weak hand. Those who had never practiced this invariably scattered their shots all over the countryside.

If I've been critical regarding certain aspects of the current competitive police program, I must add that the situation is vastly better than it was 30 years ago. Then no such program existed at all. What we have now is far from perfect, but I think it's safe to assume that over the years it has saved a lot of lives. And we should be able to look forward to some desirable changes as the hidebound wheelgun enthusiasts realize their value to law enforcement.

6

Combat Matches

Terms like "combat shooting" and "combat matches" are frowned upon in polite society these days. Many people refuse to accept the unpleasant fact that armed encounters are part and parcel of the world we live in. Combat with handguns takes place daily, instigated by criminals against both police officers and private citizens. While one might expect that the majority of such encounters would take place with the police, media reports have convinced me that citizen-criminal armed encounters may well exceed those between criminals and police.

The prevalence of violent crime has created a tremendous upsurge among private citizens in learning to use a handgun for defense of self, family, home, and property. Unfortunately, thousands of these people fail to realize the importance of training before arming onself, but there are many, many others who do recognize the serious need for training. The latter group—essentially civilian but also including interested police officers—makes up the bulk of competitive combat shooters.

Civilian combat shooting is quite different from police competition, even though the latter is generally considered to be of the combat type. Civilians are barred from police competition, though police participate in civilian combat shooting. Police matches require the use of the re-

At the 1977 IPSC championships, a competitor goes through one of the draw-and-shoot two-handed courses of fire. The man standing behind him is a particularly interested observer—Jeff Cooper, director of the IPSC, head of the American Pistol Institute and the most prominent advocate of combat matches.

volver, whereas combat shooters generally elect to use the autoloader, though revolvers are permitted by the rules. Police matches allow the use of relatively small calibers and very weak loads, whereas combat matches require full-charge service-type ammunition. Police matches utilize formalized courses of fire, targets and range layouts; combat matches vary in all of these respects in order to avoid stereotyping and anticipation. Police matches place fairly strict limitations on the gun, while combat matches allow virtually any gun to be used, with penalties assessed only in regard to the power of the cartridge or loading if it is not sufficient for serious use.

Combat-shooting competition now has an international organization, formed in 1975. It is the International Practical Shooting Confederation. The word "practical" probably avoids some of the adverse comment that wide use of the word "combat" has generated in the past. The current director of the confederation is Jeff Cooper, whose name is probably most prominent of all in this type of shooting. The confederation is headquartered at Box 401, Paulden, Arizona 86334—the address of Cooper's pistol-shooting school, The American Pistol Institute. The IPSC conducted its 1977 National Championships in Golden, Colorado, followed in August of 1977 by the World Championship Matches in Salisbury, Rhodesia.

The confederation is loosely organized with affiliated clubs located in most major western nations, with the highest concentration in the U.S. The IPSC sets forth four principles of practical shooting:

1. DVC (Dilligentia-Vis-Celeritas), which translates "accuracy, power and speed." The motto is intended to convey the importance of an equal balance among these elements.

2. Diversity. The nature of the challenge must be continually varied to encourage a flexibility of response.

3. Relevance. Problems posed must relate directly to the realistic use of firearms.

4. Freedom of technique. No rule is a good rule. Regulations hold back innovation and, while necessary, must be kept to the absolute minimum consistent with the first three principles.

This broad statement of principles gives a good insight into the approach taken by members of the IPSC to handgun competition. The ultimate "practical" use of the handgun is interpreted to be defense against antagonists who are acting in violation of the law. This kind of competitive shooting is aimed at producing in the individual a combination of gun-handling speed, accuracy and rapidity of fire, and the conditioned reflexes needed to engage in armed combat if and when the necessity arises.

Toward that end, IPSC rules are somewhat in a state of flux as this is written. Generally speaking, the "Competition Rules for the Colorado Combat Pistol League" (a very active IPSC affiliate and the sponsoring organization for the 1977 National Championships) are representative of the type of rules employed. The league settled on 40 rules, which may seem like too many—until you read them. Those rules are reprinted herewith:

1. Pistols used in competition shall be serviceable and safe. If any pistol is observed to be unserviceable or unsafe, it shall be immediately withdrawn at the request of the contest director.

2. In any single contest, a contestant must use the same pistol, ammunition, and sight setting in all stages of the contest; except that a contes-

This shooter has just drawn his pistol and is bringing his hands up to assume a shoulder-high two-handed position to begin timed combat fire.

tant may use another pistol of the same type, action, and caliber as that with which he commenced the contest.

3. All types of pistols will compete together. No contest will be restricted to any one type of pistol, and the same condition of time, distance, and scoring shall apply to all pistols equally.

4. There shall be no restrictions on overall weight of pistols or weight of trigger pull.

5. There shall be no restrictions on sights, sight radius, length of barrel, or number of rounds loaded.

6. Detachable shoulder stocks are not permitted.

7. Extension magazines for auto pistols (containing a larger than normal number of rounds) are permitted only on reload, and may not be carried in the pistol in its ready condition.

8. No entrant shall wear or use two or more pistols.

9. The general lower limit of pistols used in competition is the 9mm (Luger) military hardball cartridge. Action type shall not be restricted.

10. In cases where metal targets are used which may be damaged by excessive penetration, the sponsoring body may prohibit cartridges that may damage the equipment. Metal-piercing and incendiary or tracer ammunition is prohibited.

11. Pistols shall be holstered and safe. Revolvers shall have hammers fully down. Auto pistols shall have hammer fully down or be cocked and locked by a manual safety.

12. A premature shot, in the holster or into the ground closer to the shooter than six feet, shall disqualify the contestant from further participation in any part of the contest for that day.

13. Optical sights shall not be banned, but must be used throughout the entire contest if the entrant desires to use them at all.

14. The minimum load (power) requirements shall be determined by the sponsoring body for each contest.

15. All contests shall require the shooter's pistol to be drawn from a holster.

16. No contest shall require the use of a particular type of holster nor shall any type of holster which is permitted in any contest be barred from any other contest; however, in contests requiring a draw from a concealed condition, the degree of concealment may be specified and ruled upon by the contest director or the sponsoring body.

17. The holster must hold the pistol against a withdrawal force of twice the weight of the loaded pistol, or be equipped with a latch which positively locks the pistol, or be equipped with a manually released latch for each draw.

18. The holster tie-down may be used if it is departmental issue or if it is concealed.

19. There shall be no restrictions upon the stance, position, or technique adopted by any contestant, except that no firing for score shall be conducted from an artificial rest. Simulation of a shooting situation on a course shall not be meant to imply a restriction on stance, position, or technique.

20. "Normal Ready" designates a position in which the pistol is holstered and safe, and neither hand touches the pistol, holster, belt, body, spare magazine, or spare ammunition. Spare ammunition must be carried in a manner suitable for continuous wear. The firing hand must

Here, the shooter has begun to get off his timed string. The gun is in recoil following the first shot. The light bulb is part of the timing system.

be sufficiently far from the pistol to permit a plane to be passed between gun and hand without touching either. Other "Ready" positions such as hands above shoulders or hands clasped may be used as designated in a particular match.

21. Once the ready position is assumed, it may not be changed before the signal to fire. "Creeping" (moving the hand towards the pistol in the ready position) is subject to penalty in score or forfeiture of a bout.

22. Pistols will not be loaded except as directed by contest officials.

23. During loading and unloading, and during remedial action in the event of a malfunction, the muzzle of the pistol must be directed safely downrange.

24. After a bout, no shooter may leave his position until his pistol has been unloaded and inspected by a safety officer.

25. In the event a pistol cannot be unloaded, due to a broken or failed mechanism, the shooter will notify the contest director who will take such action as he thinks best and safest. In no case will a shooter leave the firing line with a loaded pistol in his possession.

26. On courses requiring the contestant to run, pistols must be safe during movement. This means hammer fully down on all revolvers and double-action autos without condition one override; and condition one (cocked and locked) with single-action autos. Fingers must be outside the trigger guard.

27. During a contest, shooters not firing will refrain from handling their pistols except as absolutely necessary. Practice drawing, dry firing, or brandishing is prohibited. The normal condition of pistols not actually engaged is holstered and unloaded.

28. Aerial shooting is not permitted in connection with or in the vicinity of a contest.

29. The ready condition of pistols in competition shall be:

A. Single-action revolvers—hammer fully down on an empty chamber, or on the half-cock notch.
B. Double-action revolvers—hammer fully down. No half-cock.
C. Auto pistols—hammer fully down or fully cocked and with the thumb safety on safe, never on half-cock.

30. On paper targets, a shot the outside diameter of which touches any scoring ring counts for the value of that ring. Radial tears in the paper extending outside the actual bullet diameter do not count.

31. If a shooter fires after the signal to cease firing, he shall lose the maximum value of each shot so fired, to be subtracted from his total score.

32. If a shooter has more hits on his paper than allowed in a given string, the maximum value for each excess shot shall be subtracted from his score, except when it can be established to the satisfaction of the contest director that the hits in question are of a different caliber than that used by the competitor in question, or when it can be positively proved that another contestant was guilty of the excess shots. In the latter case, the contestant whose target was fired upon by another contestant will be allowed to fire the stage over.

33. When balloon targets are used, a balloon which is hit, but merely deflates rather than bursts, shall not count as a hit.

34. If a shooter fires before the firing signal, he shall forfeit the exchange in a man-against-man bout, or he shall lose the maximum value of one hit for each he fired before the firing signal, on a paper target.

35. In timed contests, differences of five one-hundredths of a second or less shall be considered a draw.

Handgun Competition

36. In man-against-man bouts, a draw [tie] shall count as if no action had taken place, and the bout shall be refired.

37. Ties shall be broken in a manner decided by the contest director. However, this shall always be done by shooting and not by chance and must be one or more stages of the contest being conducted.

38. It shall be the responsibility of each contestant to keep account of his score along with the scorekeeper. If there is an error in the scorekeeper's final tally, it shall be the responsibility of the contestant to protest the final results prior to the awarding of prizes. Failure to file a protest with the contest director prior to the awarding of prizes nullifies any claims made thereafter.

39. There will be two power categories in competition: "major" and "minor". The "minor caliber" power floor is the 9mm Parabellum cartridge in its service loading (military hardball). To qualify for competition in the minor caliber category, a load must move a ballistic pendulum as much or more than it is moved by the 9mm Parabellum round. To qualify as a "major" caliber, the load must move the ballistic pendulum as much or more than it is moved by the .45 ACP cartridge, in its standard service loading (military hardball). Thus it is possible that a full .357 loading, while of .36 caliber, may qualify as a major caliber cartridge, while a lightly loaded .45 ACP may not. It is also possible that a maximum loading for the .30 Luger cartridge could move the pendulum as much as the standard loading of the 9mm Parabellum. This would also apply to the .30 USC cartridge, if used in a pistol.

40. Refer to the target description that follows. [It is unnecessary to reprint that description here. In general—and for obvious reasons—the targets in such matches are silhouettes simulating a human antagonist in size and shape.]

Cases not covered in these rules will be decided by the contest director as sole authority in any dispute regarding any contest under his direction.

While the foregoing list of rules may seem lengthy, it actually leaves the contestant with almost complete freedom of choice concerning gun, ammunition and shooting techniques and positions. This is in keeping with the basic concept of developing maximum combat proficiency with a handgun.

Courses of fire are also quite flexible, and except for National and International championships, there are no rigid requirements other than that the spirit of the principles be supported. A match held in January of 1977 by the Colorado Pistol League is typical of what will be encountered. That particular match involved timed, "draw-and-fire" shooting

Combat Matches

Here is the target used in 1977 IPSC-sanctioned matches. It's a silhouette in camouflage colors and pattern, with alphabetically designated, rectangular scoring areas. The shooter has placed only one round out of the high-scoring vital area on the target shown.

at metal, man-size, silhouette targets at three different ranges, and then timed, rapid-fire shooting at a bank of three turning silhouette targets at three different ranges. Further curiosity about this type of shooting is best satisfied by the following reproduction of the match program.

One of the IPSC events requires the shooter to fire at a moving silhouette target from each side of a barricade. Here, the target has moved about halfway along its line of travel as the shooter gets off a two-handed string of shots.

MATCH I:

Target:	One metal League Silhouette
Distance:	15, 22, and 30 meters
Starting Position:	Weapon loaded and holstered; shooter facing the target with hands clasped in front of body.
Time:	Clock will run from starting signal to sound of hit on metal silhouette.
Procedure:	Standing at the 15 meter line, the competitor will, upon command, draw and fire until the silhouette is hit. When the silhouette is hit, the competitor will immediately holster his weapon and stand by for the signal to repeat. This will be done at the 22 and 30 meter lines also. The shooter will fire two sets at each firing line.

Number of Rounds: Minimum of six.

Penalties: Premature start, etc. will be assessed a 5 sec. penalty. Normal CPL penalty rules will apply.

Reloading: Reloading, if necessary, must be accomplished *while the clock is running.*

Score: The score for this match will be the total time used to make two hits from each distance, including reload, plus penalty times.

MATCH II:

Targets: Three IPSC Option targets spaced 18 inches apart on turning target apparatus.

Distance/Time: 7 meters—3 second exposure
15 meters—4 second exposure
25 meters—5 second exposure

Starting Position: The shooter will stand facing the center target with weapon drawn and held in front of him at waist level or lower. One- or two-handed grip is allowable. When targets are faced, the competitor will raise his weapon and fire six rounds, placing two hits on each target, before the targets turn away. This will be repeated at each of the three firing lines. A hit on the target that leaves a hole longer than twice the bullet diameter will be scored a miss. Misses will be scored as minus 5 points.

Score: The score for this match will be the total points earned after firing from each distance.

Number of Rounds: Total of eighteen.

The match winner will be determined by high score: match II score divided by match I time + points per second.

JACKPOT MATCH

Since there are several ranges available, we will be able to fire Match I and II concurrently. There will also be a fun match held which will not be scored in the aggregate of Match I and II, but will carry separate distinction. The details will be announced at the match. Bring 20 to 30 rounds for the jackpot match.

SUMMARY: Each match will be fired twice, requiring 48 rounds
Jackpot match will require 20 to 30 rounds
Total rounds needed: *68 to 78 rounds*

Handgunning enthusiasts of both sexes participate in IPSC matches. Here, a woman contestant is using a .45 auto to shoot the weak-handed stage of a "seat-at-table" course of fire.

This particular program shows clearly the emphasis placed upon a combination of speed and accuracy. Note that in Match II the first stage requires one to fire two shots at each of three turning targets in the exceedingly short time period of three seconds. This type of firing is quite similar to that found in International Rapid-Fire matches, with one terribly important difference. The International shooter is permitted to use a .22 Short autoloading pistol, which produces hardly any recoil and jump, but the IPSC shooter is required to use a big-bore, center-fire handgun and full-charge service ammunition or the equivalent. The recoil, jump and blast of such a combination make the firing of six shots in three seconds at three different targets a tremendous challenge.

These courses of fire place a premium on cartridge power. Cartridges equaling or surpassing the ballistic performance of the standard military service load in .45 ACP are awarded higher scores on the

Combat Matches

paper targets than are cartridges of lesser power. Cartridges producing less power than the standard military service load of the 9mm Parabellum (Luger) cartridge are penalized even further. Because of this, the shooter's gun-and-cartridge choice becomes a trade-off of power and controllability. A shooter might well be able to control a 9mm pistol better than one of .45 caliber, and thus reasonably expect to place his shots more closely and gain a higher score with it in spite of the penalty applied to the less powerful cartridge. It is interesting to note that U.S. shooters generally tend to use a .45-caliber gun because it scores the highest, while European shooters are more inclined to use the 9mm and attempt to overcome its scoring penalty by more accurate shooting. However, these choices may be due more to gun and ammunition availability than actual preference. Even less powerful calibers may well be used, but to do so would be unwise unless the contestant felt certain that a sufficient edge in accuracy could be obtained to offset a rather drastic scoring penalty.

The ammunition restrictions are not intended to force the individual to use only service ball ammunition in the calibers indicated. Commercial or handloaded ammunition of any safe type may be used, but when this is done the contestant must satisfy the match officials that the load produces the level of power indicated. This is currently done by having the ammunition fired into a standard IPSC ballistic pendulum immediately prior to the match. This pendulum is normally located at the range for this purpose. No esoteric formulas or calculations are involved in this ammunition qualification; the rules simply state that to qualify the load must move the ballistic pendulum the same or greater amount than it is moved by the reference service load.

These ammunition restrictions and qualifications have been established to prevent the game from being distorted and losing practical value by the use of underloaded ammunition (as described in the chapter on Police Competition). The foremost goal of IPSC competition is to develop competence with guns and ammunition that have the maximum *practical* combat value. In this respect IPSC competition is so far ahead of NRA police competition that there really is no basis for comparison between them.

Even though revolvers are employed by some contestants, the autoloading pistol offers several substantial advantages over it. For this reason, large-caliber autoloaders dominate the scene. In the U.S., the .45-caliber auto is by far the most popular. It offers all the advantages of the basic autoloader in rapidity of fire and speed of reloading, combined with the maximum scoring ability of the cartridge. A handgunner without previous experience in this type of shooting might well find himself in a quandary regarding gun-and-cartridge selection. If he

Handgun Competition

has demonstrated reasonably good rapid-fire capability with the .45 auto, I think it would be most logical that he use it from the very beginning. On the other hand, if no such capability has been demonstrated, I would be inclined to recommend the Colt Commander or similar design in 9mm caliber. Proficiency can probably be generated more rapidly with the lighter-recoil cartridge. Then, when reasonably good results are being obtained, it will be possible to switch to a nearly identical gun in .45 caliber and attempt to raise one's scores by use of the more powerful cartridge.

The IPSC and this particular type of extremely worthwhile competitive shooting probably would never have existed were it not for the untiring efforts and enthusiasm of Jeff Cooper. Nearly two decades ago, Cooper began promoting and developing this type of shooting. He eventually gathered around him a coterie of enthusiasts, mainly in California, who spread the word and the practice. For this reason, IPSC-type shooting has long been known as "West Coast style" combat shooting. Matches have been common on the West Coast for many years, but only recently have clubs been springing up elsewhere in the country. As this is written, there are about 30 IPSC-affiliated clubs scattered across the nation, with a healthy concentration on the East Coast and a relatively thin distribution from there to the Rockies. IPSC-type shooting has been gaining in popularity very rapidly, and it should not be difficult to locate a club within reasonable distance of almost any part of the country. The quickest way to do so is to write to the IPSC in Arizona and ask.

7
International Shooting

International shooting at any level is unique. The fluttering in the breeze of flags of many nations, the muted chatter of a half-dozen tongues behind the lines, the variegated costumes ranging from military uniform through ski suits to traditional native dress—all these combine to form a uniquely appealing picture. Whether the events be held in a great stadium amid the traditional elegance of the Olympic Games or in the austere but sweeping magnificence of the American desert at Black Canyon, Arizona, the sights, the sounds, the smells, and the feel are the same. In Munich, Montreal, Buenos Aires, wherever the contests are held, there is the feeling of the best, the sense of greatness that comes from knowing one is surrounded by the very finest of all the marksmen in the world.

At the International Shooting Games, one may encounter Russians and Spaniards rubbing shoulders at a refreshment counter; Filipinos discussing local shooting problems with Australians or South Africans; Chinese comparing guns, ammunition and equipment with Indians; a Bolivian lass in traditional dress chattering gaily with a haltered, shorted and sneakered American or a chic Parisienne. Gaucho boots may support one shooter on the line, flanked by Middle Eastern sandals and alligator-skin wingtips. In the vernacular, "International is where it's at."

International handgun competition may be as simple as a friendly match between two neighboring nations, or as complex and all-encompassing as the wide array of shooting events included in the Olympic Games where more than 50 nations compete not only to show the quality of their marksmen but to display the products of their political ideologies and to lay on a propaganda show.

Yet, stripped of the burden of political and ideological claptrap, shooters seem to be the same the world over. I've struggled through sign language and my few Russian words with a smiling, slender, ski-suited, Soviet feminine shooter as she showed me her .22 rapid-fire pistols; I've sat on the floor of a hotel room sharing a native lunch with Korean shooters whose enthusiasm for the game and eagerness to learn about our best American equipment knew no bounds. In my experience, it is not the individual shooters who make the political hay, but rather the commissars and ministers who use those shooters (as they use their athletes, race drivers, etc.) in the tired old political manner, boasting that their political and economic system produces the best shooters—and, by implication, the best of everything else. Even the clamoring propagandists themselves know this is so much hogwash, but the political propagandizing has a certain effect on the competitors. In brief, it places unnecessary pressures on the contestants, pressures that bear no relationship to the game being played.

But of course, our real interest in International shooting is the shooting itself. Over the years, the courses of fire and the arms and ammunition have developed along entirely different lines than in the United States. I think it may be truthfully said that the conditions, courses, and targets of International pistol shooting require a higher order of excellence (meaning mainly accuracy) of arms and ammunition as well as shooters. For example, an International Slow-Fire Match demands a far higher degree of shooting skill than a U. S., NRA-type Slow-Fire Match. The latter is shot at 50 yards, the former at 50 meters; the latter requires 20 shots, the former 60; the latter may be shot in 30 minutes, while the former might well require several hours. Add to that the fact that the 10-ring (and all other scoring rings) on the International target are smaller, and the differences become even more apparent. While near-perfect scores are common in the NRA course, they are seldom approached in International matches. The International Slow-Fire Match is physically much more demanding. A fellow can get through 20 shots in about 30 minutes without too much trouble, but 60 shots, fired over a much greater length of time, require a much higher standard of physical and mental conditioning. This holds true throughout the International pistol competitions; though the courses are relatively few, they require the firing of more rounds under more severe conditions than typical American shooting.

In the Free Pistol Match (International Slow-Fire Match) a total of 60 shots is fired at a target placed 50 meters from the firing line. Appropriately reduced targets are available for matches and practice at 50 yards and 50 feet (indoors) where range facilities will not permit the full 50 meters. Tryouts and informal matches and practice may be conducted on the reduced targets, but in matches sanctioned by the International Shooting Union (ISU), the 50-meter targets and range must be used.

The 60 shots are split into two series of 30 each, and may well be fired on different days, depending on range facilities and the number of competitors. Time is alloted on the basis of 2½ minutes for each shot, but obviously this cannot run continuously for a full series of 30 shots, and there are breaks for scoring. Free-pistol shooting is normally done from partially enclosed booths that not only protect the shooter from wind and extremes of temperature, but also provide him with a degree of isolation from adjacent competitors. In some permanent facilities, the booths are substantial structures, but more often they are light, simple frames covered with canvas or target cloth. Anyone doubting the usefulness of shooting booths will be quickly convinced after shooting a few strings on the Arizona desert (heat and brilliant sun) or the Kansas prairie (wind).

Free Pistol Matches must be shot with .22 rimfire ammunition, and invariably that which produces the very finest accuracy in a particular gun is chosen by the competitor. Selecting ammunition may be a rather lengthy process, requiring the careful testing of several different makes and lots; and, when the best is discovered, generally a substantial supply (preferably for an entire season of shooting) is laid in. Invariably, free pistols are chambered for the .22 Long Rifle cartridge, because the .22 Short is less accurate at 50 meters. However, low-velocity loadings are used because of their reduced recoil and report.

The "free pistol" is so named because it is almost free of restrictions. It has developed into a very finely made single-shot pistol with a slender barrel about 10 inches long, fitted with the most precisely adjustable target sights and a set trigger. The Martini-type action, with its tipping breech block and enclosed striker, has become the odds-on favorite because of the precision with which it can be fitted and the unusually fast lock time it permits when utilized with a top-quality set-trigger mechanism. This is not to say that other types of guns cannot be used, and many a free-pistol shooter entered the field with nothing more than a standard autoloader used in other types of matches. Such guns, though certainly useful for the tyro and as practice pistols, are distinctly outclassed by the traditional type of free pistol. Incidentally, free pistols that are truly competitive in accuracy and handling are mostly European and are by no means cheap. Adequate new ones generally cost $500 and up, up, up.

In addition to the aforementioned features, the set trigger of the free pistol is finely adjustable in pull weight and often in position, length of pull, angle of finger piece, etc. In fact, the portion of the trigger actually touched by the shooter's finger may be nothing more than a pin or screw head protruding from the side of the trigger proper. Set triggers must first be cocked, or set, before the gun can be fired. This may be done by a secondary trigger inside the guard or (a more popular system these days) a separate lever situated somewhere on the frame or receiver of the gun. The set trigger is a complex and very precise mechanism, almost as difficult and costly to build as a complete gun of some lesser type. It bears no relationship to the unsafe, so-called "hair trigger" of the gun-slinging desperado of the American Southwest.

The set trigger is actually a separate firing mechanism wherein, by a series of heavy springs and compound levers, a hammer is first cocked (by use of the trigger or cocking lever previously mentioned) and then released, or fired, by the secondary, or set, trigger actually contacted by the finger in firing. When this occurs, the "hammer" of the trigger mechanism strikes the sear of the main firing mechanism and thus releases the striker or firing pin to fire the cartridge. Only in this manner can the *firing* trigger be safely given an extremely light pull while retaining sufficient firing-pin energy for precise and consistent ignition. The system is by no means new; it actually predates firearms, having been first employed in rather crude form on crossbows.

Its purpose is to give the free pistol an unusually light trigger pull. Pull weights of one ounce down to as low as one-half ounce are not uncommonly preferred by the better shooters. A pistolero accustomed to the usual 2½-3½ pound pull of an NRA-type pistol will find a free pistol firing before he even realizes he has pressed the trigger. I've seen free-pistol triggers set with so low a pull that they could be fired by blowing upon them or by a slight shaking of the gun. Because of such unusually light trigger pulls, inadvertent firings on the range are not uncommon. A typical free-pistol shooting booth may well be marked by bullet holes in the earth ahead of the shooter's position. The rules recognize this problem, and such occasional inadvertent firings are not charged against the shooter if they occur during loading and/or if the pistol barrel is pointed downward at less than a 45-degree angle from the vertical. However, once the shooter is loaded and ready and raises

This marksman, representing the United States in competition, is shooting the International Slow-Fire Match. Note the massive stocks on his slim-barreled free pistol. As on many such highly specialized .22's, the stocks enclose his shooting hand almost like a glove. (Photo courtesy of National Rifle Association)

his pistol toward the firing position, an inadvertent firing above the 45-degree angle will be scored as a miss unless by chance it actually strikes the target inside the scoring rings. A ricochet hit on the target, incidentally, scores as a miss.

The grips of a free pistol are also quite different from those ordinarily encountered. Europeans sometimes call them "orthopedic" grips. They customarily enclose the shooting hand almost completely, and often the gun must be virtually "put on" like a glove. Considering all these aspects of the gun, its operation, safety, etc., it is easily seen why 2½ minutes is allowed for the firing of each shot.

Free-pistol shooters develop very specific routines and adhere to them rigidly to insure shot-to-shot consistency. The routine may include a certain period of rest, sitting on a stool or chair in the shooting booth after each shot, washing or wiping off the shooting hand, plus a stop-watch schedule for loading, seating, and grasping the gun, taking a sip of water, and so on. Though some of this may seem superfluous or even silly to a shooter schooled in NRA-type matches, it appears to be productive for the majority of free-pistol shooters. Those who adhere rigidly to set procedures, producing maximum relaxation between shots, maximum concentration on shots and maximum consistency of shots, seem to be the ones who win matches. It should also be pointed out that psychological makeup and conditioning appear to be more than a little important. The slow, phlegmatic person who is little affected by outside influences or the person who has the ability to simply "switch off" everything outside the shooting booth has the advantage. The more excitable types, those who can't tune out the rest of the world and those who are more than ordinarily elated by a superb shot or depressed by dropped points seldom do well with the free pistol.

Free-pistol shooting is probably the most demanding of all types of handgun marksmanship. I'm sure there are those who will say it is not quite so demanding as International Rapid-Fire work—but they are probably Rapid-Fire enthusiasts. In this respect, it should also be said that an individual must concentrate *full-time* on the free pistol if he is to achieve a high level of proficiency with it. Top free-pistol shooters seldom compete in any other matches. The gun, the shooting and the conditions are almost diametrically opposed to other types. Because of this, it is virtually impossible to switch, say, from rapid-fire one day to free-pistol the next in a tournament and remain competitive with the best marksmen.

Next in order of difficulty—at least in my view—we have the Rapid-Fire Course, which far, far exceeds in rapidity of fire any requirements placed upon the shooter by American-type competition. This match was originally intended to simulate or at least approach a combat situation in which multiple opponents had to be brought under fire, with each of them being fired at in a minimum period of time. The International Rapid-Fire Course is shot at a range of 25 meters at man-size silhouette targets with scoring rings. Shooting is done from the protective booth already described. Because of the very small time alloted per shot (though time is actually alloted per five-shot string), a basic requirement is a gun-cartridge-load combination producing absolutely minimum recoil and jump. This has evolved over the years into a very sophisticated (for which, read expensive) autoloading pistol chambered for the .22 Short cartridge. The typical .22 Short cartridge of years gone by was not noted for any high degree of accuracy, but ammunition manufacturers have developed .22 Short Match loadings. These loadings have been designed not only for maximum accuracy but relatively low (sub-sonic) velocity which produces minimum report and recoil. With recoil held to minimum levels, obviously, muzzle jump is also minimal, and this is essential to shooting high scores on the Rapid-Fire Course.

The quest for reduced recoil and jump did not end with the development of successful .22 Short autoloaders. In recent years, those autoloaders have been modified by venting or porting the barrel along its top centerline, usually in the form of a row of closely-spaced, threaded holes, about $3/32$-inch to $1/8$-inch in diameter. The holes go all the way into the bore, and in the past this has made it necessary either to finish the holes before reaming and rifling the bore or to re-rifle the bore after they are formed. Otherwise, slight burrs turned up at the inner edges of the holes would deform the bullets and reduce accuracy. However, with a modern method called Electrical Discharge Machining (EDM) it is now possible to form the ports in almost any shape, after rifling the bore, without any reduction in accuracy.

In any event, on such ported or vented barrels, the openings are closed or opened to control the amount of propellent gas that may escape and thus reduce bullet velocity, barrel pressure and recoil forces to levels that will produce a high degree of functional reliability in the gun. Due to manufacturing tolerances and practical, economic realities, individual guns will vary slightly in the amount of recoil force required for reliable functioning. Likewise, individual makes and lots of ammunition will vary substantially. Only by fine-tuning the gun-ammunition combination can reliability be obtained while at the same time holding recoil and jump to the absolute minimum.

Of course, the gun is designed and manufactured to function reliably with all makes and lots of ammunition that might be encountered. But this means that any given gun and any given lot or make of ammunition will most likely produce a substantial margin of recoil energy above what is actually required. To correct this, the shooter (or his gunsmith) can open or close the barrel ports at will, alternately test-firing the gun, until the desired results are obtained.

It is the nature and timing of the International Rapid-Fire Course that makes gun selection so critical. Five man-size silhouette targets are arrayed side-by-side, 25 meters in front of the firing point. The targets carry otherwise ordinary scoring rings that are elongated vertically. Except during firing, the targets are positioned with their edges toward the shooter, then for firing they are rotated very rapidly 90 degrees to face the shooter, remaining in that position for the specified period of time, then again rotated back to the edged position. Timing is critical, so the edging and facing operations are performed electrically, hydraulically or by compressed air, with the intervals controlled by electronic timers. Firing is conducted in five-shot stages, beginning with the shooter in the ready position and the targets edged.

The proper ready position is with the gun in hand and pointed down toward the ground at an angle of 45 degrees or less from vertical. Raising the gun above 45 degrees before the targets face is prohibited. Once the shooter has indicated his readiness, the targets are automatically faced for the prescribed period, during which the shooter must raise his pistol and fire one shot on each target, from left to right, before the targets are again edged. That may not sound so difficult until the time intervals are considered. Over the years, intervals of 10 seconds, eight seconds, six seconds and four seconds have been used. The course of fire consists of 60 shots, fired in two 30-shot increments—two five-shot strings at the longest time interval, which is usually eight seconds, two strings in a six-second interval and two strings in a four-second interval. Thus the entire course would consist of four five-shot strings at each of three time intervals, with a total maximum score of 600 points. Whereas near-perfect NRA-type rapid-fire scores are common, and perfect ones not terribly rare, no one yet has officially "maxed" the International Rapid-Fire Course.

While 10- and eight-second intervals are not particularly difficult to master, the problem gets decidedly tougher in the six-second stage, and at four seconds a neophyte might well decide that it's an impossible game. Until one has had considerable experience with the longer time intervals, getting off five *aimed* shots at five targets within four seconds seems an almost impossible task. Some shooters say that in the shorter time interval they simply move the gun smoothly across the row of targets, triggering off a shot as the sights come to bear on the 10-ring of each target; others say that they distinctly halt the gun, check sight alignment, then squeeze off the shot on each target. Either way, four seconds isn't much time. Yet, with practice, misses are surprisingly few.

International rules specify a target distance of 25 meters for the Rapid-Fire Course but, as with the other courses of fire, reduced targets are available for use at 25 yards and 50 feet on ranges that lack the space or are not set up for 50 meters.

The International Center-Fire Pistol Course is relatively new (since 1949). In it, one must use a center-fire pistol or revolver, and while the autoloading pistol predominates, some Soviet-Bloc nations still equip their shooters with highly-refined Nagant-type target revolvers. The

International Shooting

Since the International Standard Pistol Course is shot at 25 meters with a .22 rimfire autoloading pistol, an American shooter who is equipped for NRA rimfire courses does not have to buy a gun specifically for Standard Pistol competition. A fine-quality auto such as the High Standard Supermatic Trophy will perform well in either type of match, and it conforms to both NRA and ISU regulations.

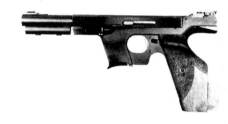

Second in difficulty only to International Slow-Fire, the International Rapid-Fire Course far surpasses NRA matches in rapidity of fire. Because recoil and muzzle jump must be minimized to achieve a respectable score in this rimfire competition, .22 Shorts are used in very accurate match loadings. A conventional pistol chambered for .22 Shorts will do for the average shooter who wants to learn this game, but the serious contenders prefer European pistols designed specifically for the purpose. One of the finest and most sophisticated is the Walther Model OSP pictured here.

In the relatively new International Center-Fire Pistol Course, revolvers may be used but autoloaders predominate. It is shot from 25 meters at turning silhouette targets with elongated scoring rings. Each shot must be very carefully aimed and fired without any waste of time. American shooters who have acquired fine pistols for use in NRA centerfire matches may be able to use the same guns successfully in the ISU matches. If such a gun is to be used without any modification beyond normal tuning, one of the best bets is the model shown here, the S&W .38 Special M52.

Unfortunately, no conventional American gun will fill the bill for the International Slow-Fire, or Free Pistol, Course. What's needed is a highly specialized single-shot chambered for the .22 Long Rifle cartridge and featuring such refinements as an adjustable, ultra-light set trigger, "orthopedic" stocks, fast lock time and the finest target sights. Such guns are made in Europe and are quite costly. A popular type is a Martini-action pistol like this Hammerli M104.

principal advantage of the autoloader is that it reduces reloading confusion and eliminates the need for manual cocking in preparation for each shot. At the last world championships I observed the most commonly used pistol appeared to be the standard Smith & Wesson M52 in .38 Special caliber.

All firing is done on a turning target at 25 meters and is, in fact, usually shot on the same range as Rapid-Fire, but with only one target in position instead of five. Thirty shots are made in what is called "precision fire," wherein five-shot strings are fired while the target is faced for six minutes. Sighting shots are allowed, and the 50-meter slow-fire target is used. The shooter must be in the ready position until his target begins to turn, pistol pointed downward at a 45-degree angle, as in Rapid-Fire. Six minutes for five shots allows ample time for cocking a revolver, so its use presents no significant disadvantage.

The second 30-shot stage is also fired in five-shot strings, but each shot is fired separately, after assuming the ready position, while the target is faced for three seconds. Intervals of seven seconds come between target exposures, allowing time to recock (if a revolver is used) and assume the ready position for the next shot. The target is that of the Rapid-Fire match.

The Center-Fire Course *looks* quite easy. This appearance of ease leads to overconfidence, and that can produce some surprisingly low scores. There is plenty of time for each shot to be very carefully aimed and fired, but there is really no time to waste. On the other hand, the time interval may seem short to some individuals, and they must resist the temptation to make a shot too quickly. Even if one uses up two-thirds of the time in sight alignment and getting ready for the shot, there's still plenty of time for a properly controlled letoff, which is essential if one is to do his best work. It is interesting to note that the International Center-Fire Course bears a great deal of resemblance to the turning-silhouette stage of the old U. S. Military Qualification Course for the .45-caliber autoloading pistol.

Finally, there is the Standard Pistol Course, also shot at 25 meters, but with a .22 rimfire autoloading pistol that is about identical to the pistol used in U. S. NRA-type .22 matches. This pistol is normally in .22 Long Rifle caliber, but considering that .22 Short ammunition of match type will deliver virtually equal accuracy at 25 meters, it is not inconceivable that it might be used.

The course differs only in detail from the U. S. .22 Caliber National Match Course. It is, however, substantially longer, requiring the firing of 60 rounds rather than the 30 of the NMC. The background of the Standard Pistol Course is interesting in that it began as an International Course intended to help bridge the gap between U. S. and ISU types

International Shooting

Melvin Makin, a member of a U.S. Army Reserve pistol team, is shown in position for International Rapid-Fire. Like many top shooters, he keeps both eyes wide open, and he puts his non-shooting hand in his pocket to keep it out of the way and help maintain a relaxed balance. Note the weights clamped over the muzzle of his pistol and the compensator ports cut behind the muzzle. (Photo courtesy of National Rifle Association)

of shooting, and also to permit the use of more common and less costly guns. Both Free Pistol and Rapid-Fire matches require highly specialized guns that are not even manufactured in the U.S., while the Standard Pistol rules allow almost any .22 rimfire autoloader that meets the requirements of NRA rules.

In the past, ranges with facilities for ISU courses of fire have been exceedingly scarce in this country. However, with increasing interest in recent years, more International-type ranges have become available. It would seem worthwhile to take a look at how one can most logically and easily make the transition from NRA-type shooting to the International Courses. I feel that the first step should be the Standard Pistol Course. This offers the advantage of a course similar to those with which an American handgunner is experienced, and it can be shot with a conventional pistol already in use. After that, I would consider the Center-Fire Course a fairly simple second step. Again, one would not need to purchase a new and very expensive gun. Generally speaking, an NRA-type centerfire pistol (or revolver) would be adequate in performance and acceptable by the rules of the International Center-Fire Course.

Beyond that, there is no simple, cheap or easy way to edge into Free Pistol or Rapid-Fire International Courses. To familiarize himself with those courses, a shooter can use any of the better .22 rimfire target autoloaders available in this country, but it is highly unlikely that competitive scores can be produced in that fashion. I think a shooter is more likely to progress reasonably well in the Rapid-Fire Course in this fashion than in the Free Pistol Course.

As I've indicated, ISU pistol shooting is the ultimate in handgun competition. The courses of fire are commonly shot abroad, and thus foreign teams generally have more experienced shooters to choose among and train when preparing for major competitions. In this country, where International ranges are available only to a very small percentage of shooters, it is not terribly uncommon to have people who have shot the courses only once or twice show up for team tryouts. Were it not for our military shooters, who do have access to fine International-type ranges, it would probably be most difficult for this country to field a first-class team. I would like very much to see more emphasis on the construction of International ranges and a distinct effort to introduce more people to this unusually difficult and rewarding type of shooting.

8

Long-Range Competition: Metallic Game-Silhouette Matches

Quite a number of years ago, a particular type of rifle competition became popular in Mexico and eventually moved north of the Rio
Grande. It is now a well-established sport, sanctioned and regulated by
the NRA. It consists essentially of shooting hunting-type rifles (and cartridges and loads) at steel-plate silhouettes of various game animals at
ranges out to 500 meters. There are no scoring rings on the target, and
a mere bullet strike on the target does not count as a hit unless the
heavy target is knocked completely from its stand.

A few years ago down in the neighborhood of Tucson, Arizona, two
handgunners named Dale Miller and Dutch Snow became interested in
adapting the game-silhouette matches to pistol shooting. After doing
some experimental shooting, they eventually arranged some informal

This photo was taken in 1975, when many shooters still preferred the prone position for the longer stages of the game-silhouette contests. Since then, this position has lost favor. The prone doesn't work with a handgun nearly as well as with a rifle, nor does it duplicate a method of shooting that's often practical in hunting with a pistol.

local matches. The matches generated considerable enthusiasm, and further club-sponsored matches were conducted although the originators had not yet finalized rules and/or targets.

At this time, along came Lee E. Jurras, then of Roswell, New Mexico. He was formerly the president of Super Vel Cartridge Corporation, which developed and marketed the first of a new "High Performance" type of police and defense handgun ammunition which is now offered in one form or another by major domestic manufacturers. An intuitive promoter of handgun shooting of all sorts, Jurras saw in the game-silhouette competitions an excellent vehicle for presenting handgunning to the public as a legitimate sport. Working with Snow and Miller, he arranged in 1975 for the first National Handgun Silhouette Championship Matches. I also participated to some extent in the preparation for those matches and attended them, so I am thoroughly familiar with what took place.

The competition consisted chiefly of four slow-fire stages fired at ranges of 50, 100, 150 and 200 meters. Strings of five shots were fired at each range, one shot to be fired at each of five targets, working from left to right, taking each target in sequence. The 50-meter targets were life-size silhouettes of large grouse, usually referred to as "chickens." The 100-meter targets were wild boar, the 150-meter targets were turkey and the 200-meter targets were mountain sheep. The targets, painted black and without scoring rings, were flame-cut and trimmed for neatness from steel plate about ¼-inch thick. They were provided with welded-on "feet" which allowed them to be placed upright on steel bases or rails; the feet also prevented the targets from being blown over

Lee Jurras, a pioneer in the development of high-performance handgun ammunition, has been very active in promoting the long-range metallic-silhouette matches, which come much closer than other forms of competition to duplicating the problems of handgun hunting. When he competes, he uses a long-barreled, specially sighted version of the Auto Mag pistol.

by the high winds often encountered in the Southwest. These targets were (and are) identical in size and design, including feet dimensions, to the NRA Rifle Silhouette targets.

In that first match, contestants were allowed to shoot any handgun chambered for virtually any cartridge, and they had complete freedom

Handgun Competition

The 200-meter target is a wild-sheep silhouette. Significantly fewer hits are visible on this target than on the 50-meter grouse, or "chicken."

of shooting position as long as no artificial support was used. Shots were scored only as hits or misses. A hit was scored when the target fell entirely from its stand. In that match, there were instances when a target was knocked *partially* from the stand, and those shots were scored as misses.

A fifth stage of fire was also included, requiring each contestant to run from a concealed position up to a shooting box, with gun holstered but loaded. Upon reaching the box, the shooter was to draw his pistol and fire at three different silhouette targets at three different ranges and angles. No limit was placed on the number of rounds that could be fired, but the total amount of time consumed by the shooter was utilized in calculation of this final score. Consequently, a premium was placed not only upon some athletic ability but upon speed of fire, economy of ammunition and, of course, accuracy under stress.

The rules for the first National Championship were quite loose and subject to some modifications as the three-day match progressed out-

These steel grouse silhouettes are the targets used at 50 meters. Note the deep craters (but no holes) punched in them by high-velocity Magnum bullets. Standing on heavy bases atop a steel rail, they're no cinch to knock over.

side Tucson, Arizona. There being no limitation on shooter position as long as no artificial support was used, many competitors relied heavily on the straight-on prone position at all ranges, but especially beyond 50 meters. I found this difficult to understand, as did some other observers, because it has long been established that the prone position, fine as it is for riflemen, is actually poor for use with a handgun. It places the sights in an improper relationship to the eyes; it places the head, neck and arms in an awkward, strained position; and muzzle blast is especially uncomfortable. Even though some relatively good shooting was done from that position in 1975, the current rules prohibit its use, mainly upon the basis that a prone position is very seldom practical in field shooting.

Many shooters, never having tried this kind of target before, tended to greatly overestimate the ability of some cartridges to knock over the targets. Though originally it was intended that no cartridges under .38 caliber be allowed in that first match, the organizers were willing to make exceptions for some wildcats known to develop high levels of energy and velocity. However, during practice and even more decidedly during the first day of the match, it became evident that cartridges with a power level below that of the .41 and .44 Magnums were severely handicapped beyond 100 meters; they simply did not retain the striking energy to knock a target from its stand.

The targets stood on feet approximately four inches wide (measured in line with the bullet's path), thus requiring considerable bullet energy to tip them over. Targets are most vulnerable to a bullet strike along a vertical line running halfway between the centerlines of the two feet —except in the case of the grouse and the turkey, which possess only one foot. On them, to be most effective, bullet strikes should be directly above the center of that foot. All other factors being equal, bullets striking either to the right or left of that vertical line will have some of their energy consumed in rotating the target about its vertical axis, thereby reducing the amount of energy available to tip the target over. The higher a bullet strikes along this vertical line, the less energy is required

Relatively large calibers and loads much more powerful than those used in traditional target shooting are needed to knock over heavy steel game silhouettes at the longer ranges. This photo shows a contestant's Ruger Super Blackhawk .44 Magnum in full recoil. Note the special sights.

to tip over the target. Unfortunately, even at the closest ranges, shooters cannot hope to invariably place their bullets on the vertical line, nor can they depend on placing them just barely below the upper limit of the target. Especially beyond 100 meters, it becomes a terrific chore (particularly if there is any wind) to place shots anywhere on the target, to say nothing of the ideal location.

It quickly became evident that many factory cartridges and wildcat loads, though normally considered quite powerful, did not have the punch to do the job at 150 and 200 meters, but merely clanged against the target without producing any score. Relatively slow, heavy-bullet loads such as the .45 Colt and .44-40 produced much the same results, though a perfectly-placed hit would sometimes topple the target.

It came about even without any rules limitations that only the most powerful, long-range loads could be considered competitive. I did not shoot in the matches but did do a bit of practice shooting and discovered that even the powerful .41 JMP cartridge (a 170-grain bullet with a muzzle velocity of 1900 fps and excellent long-range capabilities) would not topple the 200-meter target with a poorly placed shot. On at least three occasions, I clearly heard the clang of the bullet striking, and saw the target tremble, but it remained solidly on its perch. Similarly, I recall seeing a .44 Magnum shooter plant his big slug low in the neck of the 200-meter sheep, with the result that the front foot of the target came off the stand and dropped to the ground, but the rear of the target remained planted on the stand in a ludicrous rump-up position. That shot was scored as a miss.

As a result, definite ideas were developed with regard to guns, cartridges and loads to be used. In the beginning, this was somewhat complicated by the fact that in 1975 there was no rule requiring a participant to shoot the same gun or cartridge throughout the match. Since then, the rules have been amended to require the same gun (and therefore, necessarily, the same caliber) to be used for all stages. This does not preclude the use of different *loads* in that particular gun, but this would seem to be impractical, or at best inconvenient and likely to introduce error. There has also been discussion of a rules limitation on cartridges to allow the use only of standard handgun calibers. The word "standard" here means a cartridge that is now or has in the past been manufactured commercially in the U.S. for handguns, *and* for which standard-model handguns have been commercially manufactured and chambered. A rule change of this sort would prohibit the use of rifle cartridges such as the .45-70 in outsize SA revolvers, and the .30-30 or .308 cartridge in exotic single-shot pistols. I would welcome this rule. If this type of competition is to grow and gain in popularity, I believe it *must* be conducted only with conventional pistols and revolvers and only with cartridges in genuine handgun calibers. This may well be a minority opinion.

In any event, all of the top winners in 1975 shot the .44 Magnum cartridge, usually in the form of a hot handload with a relatively heavy bullet. They also shot either the double-action Smith & Wesson M29 revolver or the single-action Ruger Blackhawk revolver; the longest barrels regularly available in both models were the most widely used. The choice of barrel length is obvious, for a bullet launched from a 7½ inch or an 8⅜ inch barrel will possess somewhat greater energy at 150 or 200 meters than it would if it had been launched from a six-inch or four-inch barrel. Remember, striking energy at 200 meters is the major criterion here. The more energy is available, the greater the area over which the bullet can strike and still knock over the target. The increased sight radius provided by a long barrel is also of benefit to most shooters.

The consensus among shooters and observers alike was that a long-barreled .44 Magnum revolver or the Auto Mag .44 AMP pistol would be the ideal choice among commercially produced guns. Some indicated that they might get by just as well with a long-barreled gun in .41 caliber, inasmuch as it can be loaded to the same energy level as the .44 Magnum. In the final analysis, the choice for this type of shooting boils down to the gun and cartridge that will deliver the most energy to the target at 200 meters without exceeding the shooter's ability to withstand recoil and blast.

It's difficult to compare a handgun silhouette match with any other form of competition. Aside from accuracy, it does not place emphasis on many of the factors that are important in other matches. A descriptive name for it would be Hunting Handgun Competition. The targets, the courses of fire, the guns and ammunition in this match are reminiscent of a long-range or big-game hunting situation. A person who has shot in NRA competition for many years will have hardly any experience that might help him shoot a good score over the silhouette course. He will not be familiar with the type of guns and loads used, or with hit-or-miss scoring. In the various combat matches, again, the types of guns bear little relation to those of silhouette matches; the silhouette targets are quite different, too; and the ranges of combat matches, even the longest, are only a fraction of those at which one must be proficient in silhouette shooting. Thus, the long-range game silhouettes place special demands on the shooter and equipment, demands not found in any other shooting endeavor.

If one is attracted by handgun silhouette shooting, one of the first concerns involves the shooting facilities—a suitable range. Conventional pistol ranges are designed for distances of 50 meters, and very few can be adapted to silhouette shooting. Ideally, one needs range space at least 50 yards wide and 250 yards deep, just to accommodate shooters and the four banks of targets. And even this amount of space will not provide any degree of safety unless entirely barricaded. The cost of barricading being what it is, we need a much larger space, at least in length. Parallel side barriers of earth can provide lateral protection from stray bullets and ricochets, but the impact area needs to extend forward from the firing line more than 2,500 yards on level ground unless there is a natural terrain barrier.

A good site for a silhouette range would be in a level-floored valley or canyon with high sides and a high barrier downrange, beyond the 200-meter targets. Even this would present some problems of lighting, but they would not be insurmountable. A more ideal location would be a level field extending southward from a cliff or steep ridge that could serve as a backstop. Side barriers of earth could be bulldozed up, making the area safe while retaining the ideal condition of shooting to the north for best light. Firing would then be into a ridge that would stop all bullets.

The author (left) presents a silver trophy to the 1976 national champion, José Porras of Juárez, Mexico.

Actually, what I've just described is a typical 200-yard rifle range. With a reasonable amount of modification—not necessarily costly—the handgun silhouette course can be set up on almost any 200-yard or longer rifle range. The existing firing line can be used, and the stands for the four banks of targets can be constructed from metal or timber and made collapsible or removable so that they will not present a ricochet hazard when rifle shooting is in progress. With that accomplished, it's simply a matter of erecting the stands and positioning the targets to prepare for handgun silhouette shooting.

The 1976 National Matches were hosted by the Fort Bliss Rod & Gun Club, just outside El Paso, Texas, on the Fort Bliss Military Reservation. This time the billing was "National Hunting Handgun Silhouette Championships." The course of fire and the basic rules were revised somewhat. The surprise-target, rapid-fire stage was deleted. The course of fire thus became 10 rounds at each of the four ranges and targets, fired in separate, five-round stages. The prone position was

Unorthodox shooting positions and unorthodox guns are orthodox at the metallic-silhouette matches. This shooter's cross-legged sitting position evidently helps him steady his hold and keep the sights at the distance that works best for his eyes. He's using a heavily modified Contender pistol fitted with target-type rifle sights.

prohibited, all other positions allowed. Other minor rules changes were made, subject to formalization by a rules committee now established. Previously, rules were established by the match officials—a situation that can lead to argument.

While .44 Magnum revolvers remained the most common guns used by competitors, this second National Championship saw the introduction of single-shot pistols and cartridges devised specifically for the conditions of this match. The most common of these was the Thompson/Center Contender pistol modified with a longer barrel, rifle-type aperture sights and custom stocks. Most of the Contender pistols were chambered for the .30 Herrett wildcat cartridge. Unfortunately, they did not seem to hold up too well, with three out of four failing to finish the match. The problems were in the modifications, not the basic design or manufacture of the Contender. Even the one modified .30 Herrett Contender that finished did so with its sight-adjustment screws sheared off by recoil forces.

The most unusual guns developed for the 1976 matches were based on the Remington XP-100 bolt-action single-shot pistol. Two such guns were entered, both fitted with longer and heavier barrels than the stan-

Light, slim-bodied shooters have to accustom themselves to absorbing plenty of recoil when shooting guns powerful enough to knock down long-range game silhouettes. Look closely and you'll see that this young woman has both feet off the ground, having been rolled back by recoil. She's competing with a Remington XP-100 pistol, modified and rechambered for a hefty .30-caliber cartridge.

dard XP-100, as well as micrometer-type rear target sights intended for rifles. One was chambered for the .308/1.5-inch wildcat, a shortened version of the .308 Winchester, using 130- and 150-grain bullets at velocities up to 2600 fps. The other, shot by the winner of the championship, was chambered for the ".30 Dogie" wildcat, which is quite similar to the .308/1.5.

This trend toward smaller calibers and higher velocities has been brought about more by wind conditions than anything else. The high-velocity .30-caliber bullets are much less affected by crosswinds than even the most powerful of conventional pistol cartridges. To date, the matches have been shot in the Southwest where winds constitute a problem of major proportions.

The appearance of these costly, special guns has given rise to a recommendation that a rules change be made to separate "stock" and custom-built guns in distinct classifications. This is wise, because forcing owners of standard revolvers and autos to compete against such unconventional guns could stifle development of this especially appealing type of competition.

Another outgrowth of the 1976 Championship match was the forma-

Here's another unorthodox but evidently helpful shooting position used by a few shooters in long-range handgun competition. Like the woman competitor shown in another photo, this marksman is using a rifle-sighted XP-100 bolt-action pistol reworked to handle .30-caliber cartridges.

tion of a national organization to promote handgun silhouette shooting, and to regulate it in the best interest of the competitors. As this is written, committees are working on formal rules, classification programs and all the other details associated with any new sport. A network of affiliated clubs is being developed, with each club providing a suitable range.

In the absence of the formal rules now being established by the association, here are the regulations as they appeared in the 1976 match program.

COURSE OF FIRE:

Chicken	50 meters	10 shots
Pig	100 meters	10 shots
Turkey	150 meters	10 shots
Ram	200 meters	10 shots

Equipment: Any pistol of any caliber, weight not to exceed 4½ pounds, sight radius not to exceed 15 inches.

NOT ALLOWED: Optical sights, lanyards, slings, shoulder stock, or artificial rest.

PROCEDURES: Firing is in two five-round stages, 2½ minutes per stage. A two-hand hold will be allowed. Handicapped competitors may fire from a wheelchair. All other competitors will fire from a standing, sitting, or kneeling position. Each competitor has a bank of five silhouettes to fire against. One shot at each, left to right in order.

Hits out of sequence are misses, i.e., second shot hitting third silhouette is a miss and in this case a double miss. Only the two remaining silhouettes may be fired on. Shooter cannot fire his third shot at the untouched second silhouette. Only hits or misses are recorded and a silhouette must be knocked from its stand to be a hit. Turning a silhouette on the stand does not count. Ricochet hits on the correct silhouette count. There are no re-fires or alibis, except for pistol malfunction or defective cartridge. All re-fires will be conducted with a time limit of 30 seconds per shot.

Except when pistol failure occurs, the same pistol will be used at all ranges in a 40 shot match. Match director and committee will decide upon legitimate failures.

When called to the firing line, competitors place their pistols and 10 rounds of ammunition on the shooting stands and do not touch them until the command (Ready) is given. Then they may handle their pistols and load. 20 seconds are allowed before the command (Fire).

BICENTENNIAL PISTOL SILHOUETTE MATCH:

Each shooter may have one coach with him on the firing line who may have a scope or binoculars. The coach may tell the shooter where the shots are going, keep time, or otherwise advise. The coach may not touch the shooter during firing time.

SCORING: Competitors will score for the preceding relay. All shots are scored, a zero for a miss, an X for a hit, in the correct spaces on the score card. It is the scorer's responsibility to see that the shooter observes rules and time limits, fires no more than five rounds per series, and when strong winds exist, watch silhouettes so he can tell when a silhouette is blown over or knocked down by a bullet. When a silhouette is blown down before a shot, he will instruct the shooter to fire on remaining one in order, then go back to the left and fire unfired rounds at remaining silhouettes. All scoring differences must be resolved immediately on completion of the series before either shooter or scorer leaves the firing line.

TIES: All ties for awards will be broken by a shoot-off immediately following the match. The tied shooters will fire one shot each at the 200-meter distance first. If a tie still exists, the shooters will then fire one shot each at the 150-meter distance, the 100, then 50. If a tie still exists, the two shooters will repeat the tie-breaking sequence.

SAFETY: Pistols will not be carried in holsters. Pistols will not be fondled or handled behind the firing line. When a relay is called, the shooters will carry their unloaded pistols to the firing line with the muzzle pointed up and downrange. At the firing line, the pistols are to be placed on the stand with the cylinder or action open so that they may be readily determined unloaded. The shooters may not touch the pistols until the command (Ready). Firing will stop at the command (Cease Fire). All shots fired after cease fire will not count. Any shot fired before the command (Ready) will cause the shooter to be disqualified. Any shots fired after the command (Fire) will be scored.

Repeated violations of safety rules will cause violator to be disqualified. Match director and committee will be the final authority for all decisions.

CLASSIFICATION: Class AA based on 21-40 hits per 40-round match. Class A based on 11-20 hits per 40-round match. Class B based on 0-10 hits per 40-round match. Averages are derived from previous silhouette competition. Competitors not having a silhouette classification or those with an NRA pistol classification Expert must enter Class A. An NRA pistol classification of Master must enter Class AA. Any competitors may enter Class AA.

Here's part of the first National Shooters League range, developed by Dr. Robert Burgess at Laramie, Wyoming. The photo shows target positions 5 through 10. Only one firing point is close to one of these targets; the other four targets must be fired upon from longer range. Both speed and accuracy are essential in such competition. A shooter literally runs the course, and to score well he needs athletic prowess as well as shooting ability.

9

National Shooters League: Competing for Cash

More than once in recent years, a strongly motivated shooter has felt dissatisfied with the handgun-competition scene and has attempted to make changes. One such individual is Dr. Robert Burgess, a successful surgeon in Laramie, Wyoming, who cast about for a better way to obtain national recognition and favorable press coverage of the handgun as a sporting instrument.

Being an avid fan of several professional sports in which large cash awards command intense media attention and a tremendous public following, Dr. Burgess began seeking ways to apply the tenets of "big money" and "professionalism" to handgun shooting. By mid-1975, he had formulated his basic program—after much discussion with many others—and commenced promotion of the first professional handgun shoot in this country, *with a guaranteed purse of $10,000*. First place paid the unprecedented amount (among all shooting competitions) of $5,000.

That was to be but a single match, with only 40 competitors. While the purse was certainly impressive in the shooting world, it was a mere drop in the bucket when compared to the huge purses offered in bowl-

Handgun Competition

Dr. Robert Burgess sorts out the trophies and cash prizes at the 1976 NSL championship meet. He established the league and its unique matches because he is convinced that cash prizes and a dramatic athletic display, combined with great marksmanship, can gain press exposure and a public following for handgun competition. He has already demonstrated that target shooting can be a true spectator sport.

ing, golf, tennis, etc. This did not bother Dr. Burgess a bit. After all, he was plowing new ground out there in Wyoming, and had organized the very first *professional* pistol match in the world.

But neither the idea nor the large purse was enough. Dr. Burgess rightly felt that no existing competitive handgun course was well suited to a big-money match with spectator appeal. He also realized that police and combat matches certainly did not offer an ideal vehicle for wide public acceptance. The present social and legislative climate would have presented barriers, and even "hunting" matches would have been found objectionable by some segments of the populace. So he developed an entirely new course with no hunting, police or defensive overtones, and one that would place a certain value on athletic prowess.

After consultation with many associates, Dr. Burgess built a range on his ranch outside of Laramie. Shooting the course on this range requires the shooter to *run* over a 216-yard zigzag track, firing two shots

National Shooters League: Competing for Cash

Jimmy Clark, a pistolsmith most famous for his accurizing of Government Model autoloaders, is shown using a much-modified Ruger Security-Six revolver at the 1976 NSL match. Clark shot very well but couldn't run fast enough to place among the winners.

Shooting from behind a post that serves as a simulated barricade, one of the NSL contestants fires at target 5 from position 3.

The NSL pistol targets for the longer ranges aren't much larger than those used at short-range stations. The scoring area is easy to miss, especially when the shooter is shaky or breathing heavily after running from one firing position to the next.

at each of 10 different targets, all at different angles and at ranges varying from 16 to 60 yards. Furthermore, the running from target to target includes dodging around buildings and barricades, shooting from barricades or posts, and firing at three of those targets with the "weak" hand—that is, those three targets must be fired with the left hand by a right-handed shooter and vice versa. The course is laid out on uneven, rolling ground, requiring that most of the targets be fired at an angle upward or downward from the horizontal—providing an additional difficulty.

Dr. Burgess also designed unusual targets, with relatively small scoring areas and scoring values of 10 and 9 (with a tie-breaking X) *only*. The entire scoring area is black. Though the scoring rings appear unusually small, they are not much less in area than some standard targets. Two sizes, identical otherwise, are used, the smaller for the shorter ranges, the larger for the longer.

In order to place a value on time, a maximum of 3½ minutes was established as a cut-off or disqualification time for running the course and firing two shots at each of the 10 targets. If 3½ minutes sounds like a great deal of time to run a bit over 200 yards and fire 20 shots,

One of the 1976 NSL competitors used this modified S&W K-frame revolver. The gun has a slab-sided bull barrel, a Bo-Mar sight rib and big Pachmayr grips. Probably customized for PPC competition, it performed well in the rather different NSL match. Its owner checked his time with a stop watch on a leather wrist-cuff.

the tension, mental pressure, and physical stress generated by relatively short bursts of running between periods of shooting make the course quite difficult. In the words of retired U.S.A.F. Major Frank Green, a 30-year veteran of all other forms of handgun competition and 1964 Olympic medal winner, "This is absolutely the most challenging form of pistol competition I have encountered in my entire career, absolutely the best course I have ever known." The fact that Major Green made that remark while still out of breath after winning the $5,000 first-place prize in the 1976 competition—the National Shooters League Match—does not in the least detract from its validity.

Dr. Burgess saw no need—at least in the beginning—for placing any limitations upon guns or ammunition. The rules allow the use of any conventional revolver or autoloading pistol chambered for any center-fire cartridge of 9mm/.38 or larger size. No limitations are placed on modifications or accurizing procedures. Consequently, the first two matches saw most shooters equipped with either .38 Special revolvers heavily modified as for PPC competition or target versions of the Colt Government Model, principally in .45 caliber. Of course, not all shooters were so equipped. Both .357 and .44 Magnum revolvers were used, as were some S&W 9mm autoloaders, including the M52 Target Model in .38 Special.

This shooter placed second in the 1976 NSL match, though he had to contend with the recoil and jump produced by full-charge .44 Magnum loads in his long-barreled S&W M29. Bracketed to his belt are several speed-loaders, ready for fast use, plus a stop watch to help him keep track of time elapsed while running the course.

The rules specify that nothing smaller than 9mm or .38 Special may be used. It is the *intention* to eliminate cartridges of lesser power as well as of lesser bullet diameter. However, at the present, this is not clearly spelled out. Even though the spirit of the rules would prohibit the use of the .380 ACP and .38 S&W or similar cartridges, one might slip them in. Actually, no practical purpose would be served by doing so. No minimum velocity or energy is specified in National Pistol Institute's combat matches. Neither do the rules specify that the same ammunition must be used throughout the course, though it would be highly impractical for a contestant to use pipsqueak loads at the short ranges and switch to heavier loads for the longer-range targets.

Most revolver shooters to date have used the mid-range .38 Special wadcutter load originally developed for the more formal NRA-type

Retired Air Force Major Frank Green fires at target 2 from position 1 in the 1976 match. An Olympic medalist, Green won top honors and a $5,000 cash prize in this landmark match. He used a .45 auto and cross-draw holster.

competition. In autoloading pistols, the relatively light target-type loads in .45 ACP have predominated. However, there are exceptions—for example, the second-place winner in the 1976 match shot an S&W M29/.44 Magnum revolver with an 8⅜ inch barrel, using full-charge, jacketed-bullet handloads developing a velocity of nearly 1900 fps. His justification for the use of full-charge loads was not based on flatness of trajectory or long-range performance (for the 60-yard target) but on the fact that in a machine rest his M29 delivered better accuracy with that load than with any other.

The 1976 winner, Frank Green, stated that he felt the .45-caliber autoloader offered the best combination of speed and accuracy to produce high scores. In view of the small target involved, Green believes that the gun and ammunition should produce machine-rest groups measuring no more than one inch at 50 yards. Not many pistols or revolvers are capable of such accuracy, and certainly none have that capability as they come direct from the factory. This, of course, means a shooter must use a first-quality customized target gun and ammunition carefully matched to it. This is not to say that one cannot qualify for a match and even win one of the smaller cash prizes with a factory gun, but certainly a highly-refined gun and ammunition will be necessary to place in the top five.

With regard to selection of caliber, another factor can be decisive—albeit a factor that has long been controversial in standard NRA competition. All other factors being equal (mechanical accuracy and shooter ability), the larger the diameter of the bullet, the higher one's score will be. A .38-caliber bullet striking in the 9-ring, with its center .175-inch from the edge of the 10-ring, will score as a 9; a .45 bullet striking exactly the same place will score as a 10. The larger diameter of the .45 bullet will cause it to touch the 10-ring and thus score a point higher. This factor assumes greater importance in the National Shooters League Match than in any other because only two scoring rings are used. A bullet striking outside the 9-ring of the NSL target scores as a miss, while the same strike on an NRA target would score as an 8. Thus, on the NRA target such a shot costs only one point, but on the NSL target, it costs nine points and scores as a complete miss. A .38 or 9mm bullet barely missing the nine can knock a handgunner completely out of the running, while a .45 bullet at the same point can keep him in there.

In most other forms of handgun competition, anyone wishing to compete simply fills out a registration form and mails it in, accompanied by whatever the registration fee might be. If there happens to be a limit on the number of competitors that can be handled by the facilities available, entry acceptance is on a first-come, first-served basis. This is not true with the NSL. As it now exists, the National Championship Match may be shot only by those individuals who have qualified previously and been selected on the basis of their qualification-shoot scores for participation in the biggest match.

In preparation for the 1976 Championship, hopeful shooters were invited to schedule their qualification shooting well in advance of the match, the range being open for qualification at several periods. Each shooter was then allowed to go over the course five times, being timed and scored just as he would be later in the Championship, with the

National Shooters League: Competing for Cash

On the official NSL targets, any bullet striking outside the 9 zone is scored as a miss, and the targets for the shorter ranges have a scoring area about the size of a man's fist. The station shown here is target 1 on the Laramie range, and it's 16 yards from the shooter.

highest of his five scores posted for qualification. This qualification shooting went on throughout the summer. It had been determined in advance that a total of 40 shooters could be processed during the one day allotted to the match. Therefore, on the eve of the match, the 40 top-scoring shooters were selected in descending order of their qualification scores, and all others were eliminated.

This presents problems, but Dr. Burgess is well aware of them and progress is being made to iron them out for future matches. First of all, a qualifying shooter would not know until the evening before the match whether he is to compete. Unless he lives within a few miles, it will be necessary for him to travel to the match site and wait around, prepared to shoot on the appointed day.

Such problems can and probably will be eliminated by a series of regional matches conducted throughout the country in the future. At least three or four regionals will be held in preparation for the next Championship. As of this writing, one NSL range has been constructed and is ready for operation in New Jersey, while ranges are under construction or well into the planning stage in five other states.

There has been a substantial amount of controversial discussion revolving around the range—that is, its physical and mechanical layout. The facilities for all other forms of handgun competition have been built according to rigid specifications, with the result that every range is virtually a duplicate of all others intended for the same type of matches. This is not true of the NSL home range at Laramie, with its rolling ground that requires running uphill and downhill, shooting both uphill and downhill, and shooting at various angles in relation to light and wind. It is not possible in other parts of the country to create an exact duplicate of this range except, perhaps, at the tremendous cost of building a precise topographical model.

The answer to this controversy is simple. Dr. Burgess makes the comparison between NSL ranges and golf courses or field-archery courses. Golf courses where professional tournaments take place are never identical. They differ substantially in topography. They are only approximately equal in yardage and hazards, and are precisely identical only in the number of holes—which he compares to the number of targets and shots in the NSL course.

Most of the people involved in the NSL endeavor feel that a loose similarity of topography is entirely adequate so long as the total distance to be run is approximately the same as that of the home range, and so long as the distances and number of targets and shots are identical. Drawings and complete specifications of the NSL home range at Laramie are available. It is only necessary for a sponsoring club or individual to approximate this range within the framework described.

Only one thing more needs to be said about the National Shooters League and this initial effort to develop professional pistol shooting for money. Ambitious plans are in the making, and I expect that within the next few years a great deal of progress will be made. For the first time, handgun shooting will be elevated to the position of a legitimate sport and will receive far greater public attention than ever before.

10
Sights and Sight Installation

Proper sights are so crucial that even guns intended for instinctive or point shooting are generally provided with sights to make them suitable for other purposes. Some guns are made with sights so vestigial as to be unworthy of the name, but a "sightless" sidearm is obviously useless for the varieties of shooting discussed in this book.

Flintlock and early percussion pistols occasionally lacked sights, and those that had them usually had poor ones. But then, most of those guns were so inaccurate by modern standards that it hardly mattered. At the short ranges for which they were intended, pointing rather than aiming was adequate. Among the first revolvers, notably the early Colts, sights became standard. The Colt design established a pattern wherein the front element was a simple brass cone (later a blade) let into the barrel near the muzzle, and the rear element was a very small V-notch cut into the hammer nose. Since the hammer was pivoted and moved through a considerable arc in normal functioning, the rear sight was in a position to be used only when the hammer was at the full-cock. This presented no problem, for only at that time could the gun be fired. However, the combination of an upright V-notch in the rear and an inverted V in the front, combined with the very small size of the two components, produced relatively poor results. These sights continue to be made today in reproductions of Colt percussion revolvers, and they aren't any better now than they were 140 years ago.

With the coming of solid-frame revolvers such as the Remington of 1858, the V-shaped rear notch was transferred to the upper rear of the frame. This resulted in no improvement of sight shapes, but eliminated the wobble of the rear notch, inevitably produced by any looseness of the hammer.

Relatively soon, even before cartridge guns displaced the percussion revolver, the front sight changed from a brass cone to a brass or silver blade resembling either a half-disk or half a tear drop, with the larger vertical dimension to the rear. This produced some improvement in accuracy of aim, but the bright surface and rounded edges of these sights made aiming rather haphazard, especially in bright light. As is well-known among competitive shooters, a bright front sight will cause a gun to "shoot away from the sun." This means that reflected light on the side of the front sight toward the sun gives the illusion (to the shooter) of a thicker blade, resulting in lateral displacement which causes the bullet to strike away from the point of aim in a direction opposite the sun. This occurs even with the most modern sights except when the front element is fully shaded.

During the late 19th century, two notable exhibition handgunners developed their own particular types of sights which produced for each vastly better accuracy than they had been able to obtain earlier. One of these devices, the Patridge sight developed by E. E. Patridge in the 1880's, consisted of a rectangular notch at the rear and a front blade that represented a perfect vertical rectangle to the shooter's eye. The dimensions of the two elements were such that when the front sight was centered in the rear notch, a thin strip of light could be seen between the two sides of the notch and the edges of the blade.

These strips of light were to be made equal by sight alignment, and were generally about one-sixth the width of the front sight. The top of the blade was to be aligned flush with the top of the rear sight. The bullet would then strike the point indicated by the exact center of the top surface of the front sight.

The second exhibition shooter, Ira Paine, devised sights of almost opposite form. His front sight consisted of a horizontal rod-like element on top of a very slender stem so that it appeared to the shooter as a disk or dot on top of a thin post. This was doubtless adapted from the "pin-head" front sights that had been popularized on muzzle-loading match rifles. Paine's rear sight consisted of a semi-circular notch. The sights were aligned by centering the bottom edge of the front bead on the bottom of the notch at six o'clock. The Paine system was then

Introduced by Smith & Wesson in the 1930's, this type of target sight is now employed on all S&W revolvers that feature adjustable sights, and is widely used by pistolsmiths who install it on autoloaders as well as revolvers. The sight leaf shown here has a white-outlined notch, also originated by Smith & Wesson; it's quite popular, and is available not only on production-line sights but from suppliers of replacement leaves.

targeted so that the bullet struck the point indicated at the twelve o'clock edge of the front element.

For quite a few years, both types were very popular. However, as shooters of less expertise than Patridge and Paine utilized both sights, it became apparent that proper sight alignment was more easily obtained with the Patridge type. By the early 20th century, the Paine sight had faded from the scene. Most handgun sights today, even the most sophisticated and precisely adjustable types, are of the Patridge design. Numerous minor variations exist, such as placing the rear element at an angle rather than vertical, cutting the rear of the front element at an angle, and using colored inlays or outlines to emphasize the sighting elements under varying light conditions. Dimensional relationships also have varied a good deal.

Variations notwithstanding, modern sights on the majority of handguns differ from the original Patridge type only in dimensions, details and complexity. Even the latest Bo-Mar target sight, with very small adjustment increments in both windage and elevation, differs only in having those precise adjustments and in overall size. The matching front sight differs even less, though it may be tapered on the top and sides to produce a sharper image, and its rear surface may be at an angle other than perpendicular.

Almost all major handgun manufacturers gradually changed from the V-notch rear element machined in the frame to a neat rectangular notch in Patridge fashion. This was certainly an improvement; however, it was not accompanied at the time by a necessary change in front sights. The Patridge notch alone could improve sighting accuracy, but it could not achieve its full potential with the several different shapes of rounded front sights then in use. The typical S&W front sight of the period was integral with the barrel, consisting of a broad base surmounted by a half-disk about $^{1}/_{16}$-inch thick. All the edges of the disk were neatly radiused and polished, and those rounded edges prevented sharp front-sight definition to match the sharpness given by the rear sight. At the same time, Colt used a roughly triangular front element brazed to the barrel. It, too, radiused and rounded, and somewhat tapered toward its top. It presented most of the same problems as the Smith & Wesson, and its tapered shape made accurate alignment more difficult. It was not until well after World War II that all of our major handgun makers finally revised their front sights on service guns (fixed-sight, large-caliber models) to provide a front sight that would perform properly with the rear sight. Today, though the precision and quality of many front sights leave a good bit to be desired, the Patridge design dominates American handguns in both fixed and target-type models, with a very few exceptions.

Some older Colt target revolvers contained only windage adjustment in the rear sight; elevation was provided in the base of the front sight. This was done by pivoting the front blade at its rear in a slot in the sight base and spring-loading it downward. A screw was threaded horizontally into the base from the front, contacting the underside of the blade with its coned point. Turning the screw in forced the front of the blade upward; backing the screw out allowed the sight spring to force the blade lower. Corrections required the sight to be moved opposite the direction it was desired to move the bullet.

Some modern slow-fire pistols are fitted with a front sight in which aiming elements of different size and shape may be interchanged to suit the shooter or match conditions. This type is essentially the same mechanically as the interchangeable-insert front sights regularly used on target rifles. Inserts include a plain post, post and bead, pointed post, aperture, or whatever type the shooter prefers under the most exacting conditions of International Slow-Fire. Naturally, the rear element must be compatible with the front, so it is also interchangeable.

Still, the basic Patridge target design overshadows all other target sights. I'm talking here about sights intended primarily for competitive shooting, or general-purpose sights that are suitable for competition of one form or another. Most people think of target sights as being large and containing very fine click-adjustments. It would be difficult to find a gun in competition today which did not have that type of sight. However, it should be pointed out that under many conditions, properly made and targeted fixed sights would be fully as suitable. For example, in competition where a single gun and load is used at a single range, those precise adjustments are of no avail once the gun is properly targeted. They are certainly a great convenience in initial targeting, but after that they can become a liability in that they make the sight more prone to failure, damage or accuracy-reducing looseness. Even in American-type competition, where shooting takes place at both 25 and 50 yards with the same gun, relatively few shooters utilize the rear sight adjustments to make changes between ranges. Instead, they either shift aiming points or use different loads for the two ranges. In fact, in most competition—including the long-range handgun hunting championships shot out to 200 meters—one could probably get along nicely with properly targeted fixed sights of the good design and configuration.

The targeting is the thing. Precise rear-sight adjustments in both windage and elevation make it possible to target almost any gun for any load or range in a few minutes. On the other hand, targeting with fixed sights requires a great deal more time and ammunition and very often includes minor gunsmithing to make the necessary changes. A fixed rear sight dove-tailed laterally into the slide or frame of the gun may be moved to accomplish windage changes by a "pusher" or simply by tapping it with a hammer and drift. This doesn't present any great problem, except that the shooter cannot predict with any great accuracy the exact amount that any movement will shift point of impact. Elevation changes require the shooter to begin with a front sight that is too high, then file it down until the proper point of impact is obtained. It isn't really all that much trouble, except that once the sights have been set for a given load, the front sight may too high or low for some other load.

As a consequence, target shooters demand rear sights with a wide latitude of adjustment in both windage and elevation—and with those adjustments available in uniform, precise increments. So long as the sights are of good quality and made to precise tolerances, this is great. However, some of the cheaper replacement sights on the market and some of the sights supplied on factory guns lack the necessary precision. It is becoming fairly common to pick up a brand-new handgun fitted with a target sight and discover that the sight will not repeat adjustments or that there is too much slop in the adjustments and in the assembly. Assuming a revolver has a four-inch barrel and a sight radius of approximately six inches, a mere .005-inch slop in the rear sight or any component thereof can cause shots to spread through an inch at 50 feet, 1½ inches at 25 yards, three inches at 50 yards. A slight amount of play in a rear sight leaf can cause you to drop several points with a single shot on ring targets, or produce a complete miss on the small targets involved in some of the specialized matches.

Probably the most common problem with target rear sights is backlash, which prevents accurate repetition of adjustments. This can generally be overcome by always approaching the adjustment you wish from the same direction; that is, always turning the sight adjustment screw in the same direction, even if this means backing it up first and then making the necessary adjustment. This applies equally to windage and elevation. The other problem I've encountered most often is a looseness of the rear sight leaf, the piece of metal carrying the sighting notch, when it is a separate piece seated in the sight proper. If this part is loose, it simply bounces around from shot to shot. Obviously, this will enlarge group size.

In the sights we have today, both windage and elevation adjustments are found within the rear sight, but it was not always so. When Colt first began producing target-sighted revolvers, the windage adjustment was in the rear sight, but the elevation adjustment was in the front sight. This was accomplished by pivoting and spring-loading the front blade into a slotted base or ramp; a screw was utilized to apply pressure to the blade, rotating it about its pivot and thus raising or lowering the rear face. This system was relatively fragile and required very careful hand-fitting of the components in order to obtain the desired degree of accuracy.

Today, when the average pistolero thinks of a revolver target sight, he almost invariably thinks of the basic design found on Smith & Wesson revolvers. This design dates back to the early 1930's and achieved its present more or less definitive form as installed on the .357 Magnum revolver in 1935. It is an excellent sight, as it must be in order to have achieved over 40 years of shooter popularity. During that same period of time, the sights of competitive makers have been changed many times. The S&W sight possesses the virtues of compactness, light weight, good design and a high degree of accuracy. It is also better adapted to the top-strap mounting of almost all revolvers than any other design. Even though the installation operation is complex and costly, many thousands of these sights have been fitted to other revolvers, including Colts, and a large number of autoloading pistols as well. We'll touch on this, and the procedures involved farther along.

Sights and Sight Installation

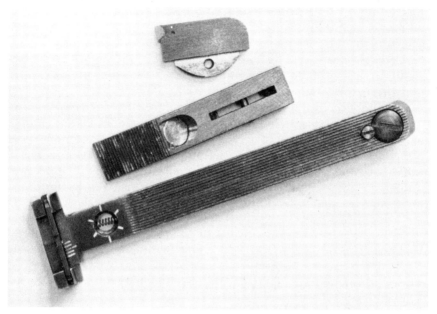

Before World War II, the King rib-and-sight unit shown here earned acclaim as one of the best. Note its similarity to the current target sights found on S&W revolvers. At the center of the photo, between the rear rib and the front sight, is the "mirror" front-sight base, containing a chromed button angled to reflect light against the front sight, which has a colored plastic insert.

From time to time over the years, various independent designers and manufacturers have produced target-type sights for all makes of handguns. They have been prompted to do so mainly because the gun manufacturers did not meet the standards of the more difficult-to-please shooters. Also, the gun manufacturers produced sights only for specific models of their own, and thus they offered no sights that were easily adaptable to guns that did not originally carry target sights.

One of the earliest such manufacturers was King Gunsight Company. In the 1930's, King target sights were reckoned to be the best available; in fact, at one time Colt installed them on some of its own target guns. More recently, the well-known Micro Sight Company has specialized in finely adjustable sights. The basic Micro rear sight may be had for either revolvers or autos, though in these days I suspect only a few are sold for revolvers. The Micro model that is probably the most popular today is the so-called "High Micro," designed so that the shooter may fit it directly into the original rear sight dovetail of the Colt Government Model pistol without any particular difficulty. Naturally, Micro produces matching front sights for a wide variety of autos and revolvers. My experience with Micro sights goes back nearly a quarter of a century, when I shot competitively on a regular basis. My custom-built guns of those days were almost invariably fitted with Micro Sights.

A newer entry into the target-sight field is Bo-Mar. Bo-Mar rear sights are unusually massive and heavy, and they are thus quite sturdy and precise. Bo-Mar does not limit its production to rear and front sights. It specializes also in a sight-rib combination that may be fitted as a unit to almost any gun. Essentially this consists of a fairly massive rib contoured to fit the gun and carrying properly fitted rear and front sights. The rib itself serves two useful purposes, in addition to greatly simplifying the installation of the sights upon the gun. First, it provides a smooth sighting plane, which reduces glare by virtue of its finish; second, it adds weight to the gun to improve its balance and/or controllability.

Only a very few years ago, an outfit called MMC (Miniature Machine Company) introduced a so-called Combat Sight containing adjustments for both windage and elevation. This sight is designated "combat" because it is intended for guns used in combat competition and in active combat service. Its greatest features are that it is extremely low, light and compact. When properly installed, it is comparable in height with the original front sight of a number of big-bore autoloading pistols. Further, it is designed so that the average owner of a big Colt or Browning pistol can install it himself in minutes with nothing more than hand tools. This obviously presents a great advantage. For serious target use, the adjustments and the size of the rear element of the MMC sights are not as suitable as those of true target sights. Nevertheless, the MMC sight has become quite popular in combat matches. MMC has also produced a very good install-it-yourself replacement rear sight for the S&W M39 and M59 pistols. This unit contains both windage and elevation adjustments and may simply be snapped into place on the slide to replace the original S&W sight. A sad lack in that S&W sight is in the absence of any elevation adjustment; windage adjustment is provided, but the even more important elevation adjustment is not.

In 1976, Austin Behlert, proprietor of the Custom Gun Shop in Union, New Jersey, introduced a new replacement sight for S&W target revolvers. This sight is designed for quick and easy home installation into the recesses occupied by the original rear sight. Though the S&W target sight is a good one, Behlert's new design provides a much larger rear element, more precise construction, and very fine windage and elevation adjustments. It also costs a good bit more than the original. Other companies produce various sights and accessories but, to the best of my knowledge, those just listed are the major suppliers of sights proper.

Sights and Sight Installation

This target sight, made by the Micro Sight Company, has been fitted by the author to his replica Remington .36 Navy percussion revolver. Such installation is very simple. A flat is filed into the back-strap, and the sight is secured by two small screws.

One of today's highly regarded sighting systems is the Bo-Mar combination. The front and rear sights are available separately or in combination with a solid full-length rib. Installation is much simpler with the rib than when the sights are attached individually. See the text for tips on preparing the gun and installing sights.

The Bo-Mar sight rib is available for autoloading pistols as well as revolvers, and it's particularly easy to install on an auto.

Intended for use on service pistols and on guns used in combat matches, the adjustable MMC Combat Sight is easily installed in the existing dovetail on a big-bore autoloader. It can also be attached without much difficulty on a revolver whose top-strap is thick enough to permit the filing of a shallow dovetail.

These drawings show how to accommodate a Low Micro Sight. At left is the rear portion of the slide with its original sight dovetail. The shaded area represents the metal that must be removed to provide a low seat for this sight model. Saw cuts are made within scribed lines, as indicated in the drawing at right, to remove the bulk of the metal before filing the dovetail and seat to final shape.

As I mentioned in passing, installation of some target sights is very simple. For example, the High Micro can be installed in a few minutes with a hammer, soft drift and files. Installation of the MMC sight for the S&W autos is even simpler and quicker. On the other hand, many sight installations (often depending more on the particular model of gun than on the sights) can require a great deal of work. The individual accustomed to doing a reasonable amount of his own pistolsmithing, and equipped with basic hand tools, can probably install most sights properly and accurately if he exercises reasonable care. Some jobs, though, are beyond the average home workshop and depend on accurate machining by a professional pistolsmith. A classic example of this is fitting the S&W rear sight to an autoloader.

Ignoring the very simple installations, for which the brief instructions supplied with the sight are more than sufficient, let's take a look at several typical jobs you can do yourself, and also the more difficult ones which you must farm out.

The low Micro sight for the Colt Government Model, popular on pure target guns, may also be used on other autoloaders of similar design and construction. This sight achieves its low position by being seated in a cutout at the upper rear of the pistol's slide. The original sight dovetail is cut away and a second one is formed lower in the slide. Because a new dovetail must be formed and a large piece of the slide cut away, most people consider this installation strictly a machine-shop job, but anyone handy with tools and able to accurately control a hacksaw and files can do the job in a few hours of careful and patient work.

The job begins with stripping the slide of all internal parts, then accurately scribing the outline of the section of metal to be removed. The bulk of this metal can be removed by just two accurate hacksaw cuts; one vertical from the top of the slide, and another horizontal from the rear to meet the first. If one uses a fresh, new, high-speed steel hacksaw blade of about 32 teeth to the inch and lubricates the blade and cut with any good cutting oil, both cuts can be made in a few minutes. The cuts should be very carefully kept just inside the scribed outline of the notch, leaving sufficient metal to true up the surfaces with files. Filing

Here's the completed installation of a Low Micro on a Colt GM pistol. The necessary amount of metal removal is clearly visible.

should progress slowly and carefully, and the surfaces should be checked frequently with a small square to make certain they remain at right angles to the sides of the slide; checks should also be made frequently to keep the bottom of the recess parallel to the bottom of the slide. As the filed surface approaches very near the scribed marks, it will be useful to use layout blue or candle soot on the surfaces to ensure that you aren't rocking the file and that you know exactly where it is removing metal.

Once the surfaces of the sight recess have been filed smooth and flat, the lateral dovetail to accept the sight base must be very carefully scribed on the front of the floor of the recess and on both sides of the slide. Again with a new hacksaw blade, very carefully make a series of parallel, vertical saw cuts at right angles to the sides of the slide within the outline of the dovetail. These cuts should not quite reach the scribed outline of the bottom of the dovetail. A good deal of care is required in making the cuts and it is especially important that the saw blade not be rocked. A small cold chisel may be used to remove the metal between cuts. Alternatively, the metal can be removed with files, but it takes a lot longer.

With the surplus removed, take a medium-cut, narrow pillar file and true up the bottom of the notch, right down to the scribed outline of the dovetail bottom. This will leave a rectangular notch, rather than a female dovetail. Check the floor of the notch with the square to make certain it is perpendicular to the sides of the slide. Then with a dovetail file (available along with many other choice tools from Brownell's in Montezuma, Iowa) begin to cut the front and rear portions of the dovetail. This is done by laying the smooth side of the file flat on the floor of the notch, with the toothed side facing upward and in the direction you wish to remove metal. Hold the file flat and use it in short even strokes, undercutting the edge of the notch to form the dovetail. File both front and rear until you reach the scribed outline, but try the sight's male dovetail in it before you get too close to the outline, just in case your scribed marks might be a bit off. It will be helpful if you develop a slight taper to the dovetail as you approach the scribed outline. Make the wider part on the right, and frequently try the sight dovetail until it will just begin to enter. Then you can begin reducing the taper so that the sight can be drifted home. Go slow and easy in this operation, to avoid making the dovetail too big. If somehow you do remove too much metal, the completed dovetail may be peened to close it up slightly and give it a good grip on the sight.

It remains only to deburr all the filed edges and use touch-up blue to cover the bright metal. The sight is then drifted into place, centered as accurately as possible, and secured by the binding screws in its base. The security provided by these screws against any lateral shift can be improved by drilling shallow holes in the slide into which they may seat. Seat the sight properly with the screws removed, then carefully punch-mark the bottom of the dovetail through these holes. Added security can also be obtained by peening or staking the edges of the slide dovetail and/or very carefully applying a drop or two of cyanoacrylate adhesive at the edges of the dovetail. It will flow inside and fill the joint to form a very tight bond. If this adhesive is used, be especially careful that you do not allow it to get on any of the working parts. It sets in seconds and will freeze the parts.

The basic Bo-Mar rear sight (and a few others of earlier vintage that might still be encountered) can generally be installed in approximately the same manner as the Micro. If the differences in shape and size between the two sights are noted, the differences in installation will be readily seen. One might also encounter the Bo-Mar sight (and even the Micro) without any male dovetail. These models are primarily for revolvers, but may be used just as easily on autoloaders. Lack of the dovetail means simply that a flat seat must be sawed and filed for the sight, after which holes for the installation screws must be carefully aligned and then drilled and tapped. The sight is simply screwed into place.

However, I am reluctant to trust the security provided by only a couple of small-diameter screws. In earlier years, such sights were often installed by first completely stripping the base, then tinning the base and seat, after which the sight was screwed and clamped tightly into place and sufficient heat was applied to melt the solder on both surfaces and thus sweat the two together. I have never known a sight installed in this manner to shoot loose. But when this was not done, I have known such sights to shear the screws. Today, though, with modern epoxy compounds and cyanoacrylate adhesives, one need not resort to soldering. Simply use one of those adhesives, drawing up the screws very tightly and clamping the sight until the adhesive is thoroughly cured.

This is a typical front-sight replacement on a big-bore auto. The blade has been silver-soldered into the original sight seat. It's low one, and light enough so this method should keep it securely in place. However, a greater joint-contact area must be fashioned for a larger, heavier sight or it may shoot loose.

Though front sights may look simple, their installation can be much more of a chore. This is particularly true of a sight installed on the slide of an autoloading pistol. The major problem is that the contact area between the slide and new sight is very small in most instances. Very careful fitting is required if the inertial forces are to be resisted during recoil so the sight stays securely in place. The original means of installing a front sight on the Colt Government Model (the model most often encountered) consisted of a small stud on the underside of a plain sight blade; this stud entered a hole through the slide and was riveted on the inside. Silver solder was then flowed into the joint. This worked well with a small, light military front sight, but with target sights—which are several times larger and heavier—the installation is not adequately secure unless very, very carefully performed.

It is for this reason that I am not particularly fond of installing a plain, straight blade on any big-bore autoloader of significant recoil. A ramp-type sight offers several times more joint area and can be made thoroughly secure with silver solder and one or more screws or pins. I prefer to make my own front sights form ⅜-inch-wide bar stock, cutting and filing a flat on top of the slide into which the flat base of the ramp fits. It is important to keep the front and rear edges of the flat sharp and square and tight against both ends of the ramp. These ends then form shoulders which resist the forces of recoil and counter-recoil to further stabilize the sight. The sight may be then secured simply by two screws, but I prefer silver solder in addition to the screws. If by chance you are not set up to drill, tap and counterbore holes for the screws, then simply clamp the sight in place and drill vertical holes for a couple of tight-fitting drill-rod pins. Tin all the surfaces, including the holes, seat the sight, seat the pins and clamp the entire assembly tightly together while sufficient heat is applied to melt the solder. After this is done, remove excess solder and scale, trim the pins flush, and you have a very neat installation that will not shoot loose, no matter how many high-performance loads you fire.

Handgun Competition

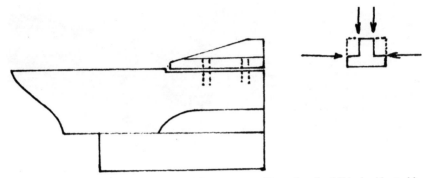

Here's how to cut and attach a good front sight on an auto. First, a length of ⅜-inch-wide steel bar stock is sawed to the profile shown, and saw cuts are made as indicated by the arrows to produce approximately correct blade width while leaving the base a full ⅜-inch wide. The sight is then filed true and smooth, and a flat just large enough to accept the underside of the base is filed at the front of the gun's slide. With this much joint area, low-temperature silver solder will hold the sight securely, but the joint can be strengthened by a pair of pins or screws passing vertically through the base and the roof of the slide.

Installation of a new front sight on a revolver is even more difficult. Screws should be used, but in many instances the barrel walls are so thin that drilling and tapping to provide even a couple of threads for engagement is a critical operation. Then, even after the holes are drilled and tapped, it is easy to spoil the threads or pull them out by over-tightening the screws. With a ribbed barrel, a great deal more metal is available for threaded holes, and it is much easier to file a flat and fit the sight base closely to it. Then both screws and solder will make an entirely satisfactory installation. If the original barrel length is to be retained, the old front sight may be utilized to secure the new sight. Sights are available from Micro (and perhaps others) with a recess in the base which slips down over the original front sight (usually after shortening it). Then the two are pinned together. This is an entirely satisfactory installation, and if the pins are hardened there is no need for solder in the joints.

Installation of both front and rear sights is greatly simplified if one uses a rib-sight unit such as that currently available from Bo-Mar. This unit, made for both autoloading pistols and revolvers, consists of a full-length rib with both sights already properly installed. As this is written, the unit is available for Colt, S&W and Browning autos and for a limited number of S&W revolvers with ribbed barrels. The underside of the rib is contoured to match the surface of the slide (or a revolver's rib and top-strap) and holes for attaching screws are already drilled and counterbored in the unit. Installation is simply a matter of carefully locating the proper holes, drilling and tapping them, then turning in the attaching screws.

Rib installation on an autoloading pistol is the easiest. The attaching screw holes forward of the ejection port can be simply drilled through the slide roof, then tapped, after which the holes must be deburred carefully. If one of the holes is in the locking-lug area of the slide, careful deburring is especially important or burrs and protrusions might interfere with proper locking.

The one or two screw holes that fall back on the breech portion of the slide may be drilled roughly ¼-inch deep, though special care must be taken to ensure that they do not run into the firing-pin hole or other working-part recesses. Before drilling and tapping, the rib should be very carefully aligned and clamped solidly in place on the slide. Then a hole-fitting center punch is dropped into each of the attaching holes and rapped smartly to indicate the hole location on the slide. The rest of the operation is obvious, usually with four large-diameter, hardened screws doing the job. Security of the installation is adequate without any solder or epoxy.

Installation naturally requires that the original front and rear sight be removed. The rear sight may normally be drifted out of its dovetail without difficulty. The rigidly attached front sight is best filed or ground away, flush with the surface of the slide. However, the empty rear-sight dovetail may offend one's sensibilities since it will be visible from the side beneath the new rib. A dovetail blank may be drifted into place, peened for security and then filed flush with the surface of the slide. Lacking a blank and the inclination to make one, the rear sight itself may be cut down to serve the same purpose if you anticipate no further need of it.

Installation of this type of rib on a revolver (that is, on those few models for which it is made) is essentially the same, though removing the original sights might be a bit more complex. In any event, careful examination of the sights will show how it must be done. Once the sights are removed, again carefully align and clamp the rib to the gun and then mark the holes. Those holes which fall in the top-strap may be drilled completely through, after which the inner edges of the hole should be carefully deburred. Those holes falling on the rib require a bit more care. Determine the total thickness of metal between the surface of the rib and the bore, then drill and tap holes to a depth that will not approach closer than $1/16$-inch to the bore surface. It might appear safe to approach the bore more closely than that, but to do so makes it likely that the point of the drill and the pressure of drilling will produce a slight irregularity on the bore surface—and this will not help accuracy. Keep in mind that the bore surface can be distorted even though the drill does not break through.

For maximum security of installation, use a bottoming tap to finish the threads in the holes, so that full threads reach all the way to the bottom. The more threads the screw can engage, the more secure the installation will be. Where the screws enter blind holes, make certain you trim the screws short enough to draw up tightly without running into the bottom of the hole.

Installation of Micro, Bo-Mar or similar rear sights on revolvers originally fitted with fixed sights does not present any great problem. The sights for this type of installation have flat bases, without a dovetail, and contain holes for securing screws. Locate the sight in the proper fore-and-aft position, then carefully file a flat on that portion of the top-strap. This flat must be parallel to the bore's center line (as near as you can determine), perfectly flat and perpendicular to the sides of the frame. Once the flat is formed, clamp the stripped sight base in place and mark the location of the securing screw holes as already outlined. Drill and tap the holes and check everything for fit.

Now, this installation is especially weak; only the two thin screws hold the sight in place, and they are not adequate to withstand heavy recoil forces. Of course, if you will be shooting nothing but .38 mid-range wadcutters, they will *probably* do the job satisfactorily. Nevertheless, the sight needs to be affixed more securely. Sweating the two together, keeping the solder molten while drawing up the screws very tightly, produces the best installation possible under these conditions. Epoxy or cyanoacrylate adhesive may also be used, but such a bond is not as permanent as solder. Some sights contain sufficient metal in the base so that the original screw holes can be enlarged for stronger screws, or in some instances there may be room to install one or two additional screws. However, even when that is done, I still feel strongly that the joint should be reinforced throughout its entire surface with carefully applied solder. Soft solder is sufficient in this instance, though a low-temperature silver solder will certainly produce a stronger joint.

11

Production-Line Guns for Competition

In the second chapter of this book, I made recommendations (and offered my reasons for those recommendations) regarding a basic battery of guns to be used in the principal types of competition. On the basis of those suggestions, a handgunner who has had little or no experience in target matches should be able to choose a gun (or guns) suited to the kinds of competition that most appeal to him. For that matter, even an experienced competitor may well find information in that chapter to help him make a selection when he is in some doubt as to which of two or more models to choose when he wants to try his hand at various courses of fire in which he hasn't yet competed. But of course, a great many more sidearms are available than were described in Chapter 2, and many of them are suitable for serious target shooting.

Catalogs, dealers' and manufacturers' listings, magazine articles and books on guns can sometimes be confusing—or less than complete—in their enumeration of specifications, features and advantages (or disadvantages) of guns commonly used for various kinds of target shooting. Over the years, specialized target-shooting events have proliferated, and guns suitable for them have more or less kept pace. In several previous chapters, I've described the major types of matches and have made some observations about the guns used in those matches. But the more experienced competitors among my readers would undoubtedly like to have a handy reference to the guns—a reasonably detailed listing. And many tyros, as well, are probably curious as to what's available, even if they aren't ready yet to enlarge their basic batteries.

The present chapter will therefore provide a descriptive list of the production-line guns that are currently available and particularly suitable for one or more forms of competition. The list will be limited to standard-production models, just as they are shipped from the factories. Home-accurizing, sight replacement and various other kinds of modification are discussed elsewhere in the book, and custom-built target guns will be discussed in the next chapter. I will make some personal observations in describing the production-line models, but any favorable comments should not be taken as specific recommendations unless I actually say so. I'm not promoting any makes or models, and to avoid any appearance of favoritism I will list the guns alphabetically by the manufacturers' names. The prices quoted were applicable when I compiled the list, in mid-1976. They are included only as a rough reference, because many if not most prices will have risen slightly. In almost all cases, a photo will accompany the specifications for the gun being described. Only three of the costly, highly specialized foreign pistols will lack illustrations; these guns, designed for specific ISU courses of fire, are imported only in very limited quantities, and at press time no photos of the latest versions were available, nor could I locate samples of the pistols—the Domino and two Hammerlis—to borrow and photograph.

CENTERFIRE AUTOLOADERS

Auto Mag: This is a highly unusual and massive gun introduced in the 1960's. It first appeared in small numbers, much to the displeasure of many potential owners who had placed orders and made advance payments, then received neither their guns nor a refund when the original company was bankrupted. Only a few deliveries were made. Since that time, several thousand Auto Mag pistols have been manufactured by a new company, TDE Inc., and though production remains small the guns are available at prices ranging upward from approximately $500.

The Auto Mag is not even remotely suitable for any form of competition other than the long-range Metallic Silhouette matches, which require the firing of 10 shots at different steel-plate game-silhouette targets at ranges of 50, 100, 150 and 200 meters. The Auto Mag possesses the weight, stability, long sight radius, power and flatness of trajectory,

Production-Line Guns for Competition

Auto Mag

not to mention superb accuracy, which are essential for this type of shooting.

The pistol had the distinction of being probably the only self-loading handgun designed in conjunction with special cartridges since the development of the .45 Colt autoloader. Both gun and cartridges were designed specifically to function at working chamber pressures in the 50,000 C.U.P. (copper units of pressure) range. The cartridges were adapted from the shortened 7.62mm NATO case, necked down to accommodate bullets of .44, .357 and, to a much lesser extent, .41 caliber. Other bullet diameters have been used experimentally, but no production guns exist for them. The Auto Mag was further designed for complete manufacture from stainless steel, and for maximum use of the latest in investment-casting technology.

Of greater size and weight than any other currently produced autoloading pistol, the Auto Mag utilizes a front-locking, rotating bolt whose multiple locking lugs engage abutments in the barrel extension. The barrel and extension are mounted slideably on the basic frame, or receiver, and the short-recoil system is utilized, whereby barrel and extension recoil a very short distance upon the frame, during which a cam slot and pin rotate the bolt to unlock and allow it to travel rearward under its own momentum. Because of the substantial weight of the recoiling parts, this design is fitted with an accelerator, which is not, to the best of my knowledge, found on any other currently produced autoloader. The bolt is powered by twin, small-diameter recoil springs housed in long tunnels on either side of the frame and connected to the bolt by thin rods attached to the rear of the bolt. Firing is by a conventional firing pin driven forward by an exposed hammer at the upper rear of the frame. A conventional manual safety, slide-stop and takedown lever are employed. The magazine is large and housed within the butt, held there by a push-button catch behind the trigger, quite similar to that on Colt and Browning designs. The barrel carries a welded-on, ventilated rib and fully-adjustable, target-type sights.

The design is not only sophisticated but complex and more than a little temperamental. The gun requires very careful attention to cleanliness and the use of special lubricants to ensure reliability. Many brand-new guns have required careful tuning before proper functioning could be assured. It is a gun nut's gun which requires a degree of care and attention not generally needed for any other domestically produced big-bore, autoloading pistol. When it receives that care and attention, and when the shooter thoroughly understands the gun, it will perform feats of long-range accuracy that cannot be duplicated by any other autoloader.

AUTO MAG PISTOL

Caliber & magazine capacity:	.44 Auto Mag or .357 Auto Mag, 7-shot
Barrel:	6½", 8½", 10½"
Length (overall):	11½"
Weight:	57 oz. (.44), 54 oz. (.357)
Stocks:	Checkered polyurethane
Sights:	Target-type ramp front, fully adj. rear
Features:	Short recoil, rotary bolt system. Made of stainless steel. Conversion unit available to change caliber using same frame. Comes in plastic carrying case with extra magazine, wrenches, lubricant and manual. Custom variations available on special order. From Lee E. Jurras & Associates.
Price:	.44 AMP, .357 AMP .... $500.00.
	Conversion unit (6½") .... $185.00.
	Conversion unit (8½ or 10½") .... $195.00.

Browning Hi-Power: Designed by John M. Browning before his death, this gun became a production reality in 1935 and has been manufactured ever since by the famous Fabrique Nationale in Belgium.

Production-Line Guns for Competition

Browning Hi-Power

During World War II, excellent copies were produced in Canada, and other copies have been produced elsewhere in small quantities.

The Browning HP was designed purely for military and police purposes, and it is or has been the official military sidearm of dozens of nations. Chambered only for the 9mm Parabellum cartridge, it is, of course, suitable for the various forms of military pistol competition as practiced in the armed forces of many nations. The only other form of competition for which I deem it suitable is the combat-type matches promoted and governed by the International Practical Shooting Confederation, headquartered in Paulden, Arizona, and currently directed by the well-known Jeff Cooper. Though not used extensively in such matches by U.S. shooters, it is the favorite in some other countries. Its acceptance for this type of shooting is low in this country because of our shooters' devotion to the .45 ACP cartridge. This gun is also known as "P.35" or "GP" (Grande Puissance).

The design utilizes the basic rising/falling, breech-locking barrel actuated by a cam slot on the barrel and cross pin in the frame, rather than the swinging link of earlier big-bore Brownings. All parts are steel, and the design incorporates an unusual trigger-sear linkage which contains a pivoted bar inside the slide that also functions as a disconnector. This linkage has been damned by many pistolsmiths because of the difficulty encountered in producing a first-class trigger pull. The trigger proper incorporates a magazine safety, which many shooters do not like. An exposed hammer, conventional slide-stop and manual safety are employed. The basic production gun has conventional fixed sights; however, some military models were fitted with a tangent rear sight adjustable only for elevation, and commercial production since the early 1960's includes a modest percentage carrying a so-so target-type, adjustable rear sight and matching front element. The single feature of the Browning that is considered most outstanding by many shooters is the 13-shot double-column magazine. This is of no particular value in combat-type competition, though it alone has been responsible for wide law-enforcement use of the Browning HP.

This pistol has a well-deserved reputation for high-quality manufacture and functional reliability. The only exceptions to this might be some portion of the quarter-million or more guns manufactured by Fabrique Nationale for the German military establishment during the occupation of Belgium in World War II.

BROWNING HI-POWER

Caliber & magazine capacity:	9mm Parabellum (Luger), 13-shot
Barrel:	$4^{21}/_{32}''$
Length (overall):	$7^{3}/_{4}''$
Weight:	32 oz.
Stocks:	Walnut, hand-checkered
Sights:	Fixed
Features:	External hammer, thumb and magazine safeties. A blow on the hammer cannot discharge a cartridge; cannot be fired with magazine removed.
Price:	With standard fixed sight .... $272.95.
	9mm with fully adj. rear sight .... $288.95.

Colt Government Model & Commander: The Colt GM .45 is second in fame only to the Colt Single Action Army revolver. As developed in the early 1900's from John M. Browning's basic design, it's one of the most durable and reliable big-bore autoloaders in the world. Several million have been manufactured by Colt, other contractors, the U.S. military establishment, various Spanish and Argentine arms companies —and copies in small quantities have been turned out by assorted small establishments in other parts of the world.

In its as-issued form, as well as the light-weight and all-steel shortened Commander versions, the GM is the best suited for matches of the International Practical Shooting Confederation, and to a lesser degree for the matches of the National Shooters League. It also performs quite well in the so-called "Bowling-Pin" Shoot which has gained some

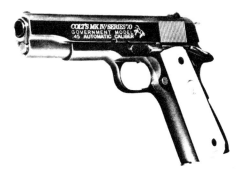

Colt GM .45

prominence in the past few years. As manufactured—without accuriz-ing or modification—the GM is no longer considered competitive in conventional NRA matches. At one time it was used extensively in such matches, but it has long been surpassed in accuracy by the Gold Cup and by itself when customized by the top pistolsmiths of the country.

In one form or another the GM/M1911A1 has served this and other nations through all the major wars since 1914 and through countless revolutions, police actions and other military or quasi-military opera-tions. It has achieved a most enviable record for durability and reliabi-lity under the most severe conditions, ranging from arctic cold to rain-forest humidity and from steaming Asian swamp to North African desert.

Mechanically, the GM is probably the simplest of all big-bore auto-loaders in the world. Design and functioning are discussed elsewhere in this volume.

COLT COMMANDER

Caliber & magazine capacity:	.45 ACP, 7-shot; .38 Super Auto, 9-shot; 9mm Luger, 9-shot
Barrel:	4½″
Length (overall):	8″
Weight:	27 oz.
Stocks:	Sandblasted walnut
Sights:	Fixed, glare-proofed blade front, square-notch rear

Features: Grooved trigger and hammer spur; arched housing; grip and thumb safeties.

Price: Blued .... $213.50.

COLT COMBAT COMMANDER

Same as Commander except steel frame, weight 36½ oz., 9mm and 38 Super

Price: Blued .... $213.50.

Satin nickel .... $217.50.

COLT GOVERNMENT MODEL MK IV/SERIES 70

Caliber &
magazine capacity: 9mm, .38 Super, .45 ACP, 7-shot

Barrel: 5″

Length (overall):   8⅜″

Weight: 40 oz.

Stocks: Sandblasted walnut

Sights: Ramp front, fixed square-notch rear

Features: Grip and thumb safeties, grooved trigger. Accurizor barrel and bushing.

Price: Blued .... $213.50.

Nickeled (.45 only) .... $225.95.

Colt Gold Cup: Back in the 1950's, Colt introduced a new target version of its Government Model .45 pistol. It was intended to be a pro-

Production-Line Guns for Competition

Colt Commander

Colt Gold Cup

duction gun that would compete successfully (at a lower price) with the rapidly growing family of custom-built target pistols based on the GM. Essentially, it was the GM pistol with refinements and additional hand-fitting to ensure better accuracy. It was fitted with fully adjustable target sights, a skeletonized wide trigger with a trigger-stop built into it, and a number of other refinements (which were added as the model continued in production). Eventually it sported a ribbed and somewhat heavier slide, and after 1970 a special collet-type barrel bushing that improved accuracy without the necessity of careful handfitting. In .45 caliber this gun retained the typical Browning locking system—but eventually a .38 Special model was introduced and it dispensed with the locking system, thereby converting the design to straight blowback. The earlier .38 models contained annular grooves in the chamber to delay unlocking slightly, in effect making it a "delayed-blowback" system.

In the beginning, the Gold Cup sold fairly well in .45 caliber, though it never really displaced the custom-built guns. In fact, many shooters wishing the best .45 pistol available purchased the Gold Cup instead of the standard GM and then had the custom pistolsmith do his work on it. The production-line Gold Cup shot considerably better than the average GM, but it was never quite the production-gun answer to the serious target shooter's prayer. The .38 model achieved far less acceptance and was eventually dropped from the line for lack of interest and sales.

The .45 Gold Cup in its latest form (MK IV/Series '70 Gold Cup National Match) is still available. At the moment, it is the only .45-caliber target autoloader in production. As such, it is considered suitable for virtually all types of competition conducted in this country in caliber .45, and is often considered suitable for the other centerfire stages of NRA-type matches.

COLT MK IV/SERIES '70 GOLD CUP NATIONAL MATCH

Caliber & magazine capacity:	.45 ACP, 7-shot
Barrel:	5″
Length:	8⅜″
Weight:	38½ oz.
Stocks:	Checkered walnut with gold-plated medallion
Sights:	Ramp-style front, Colt-Elliason fully adj. rear, sight radius 6¾″
Features:	Arched or flat housing; wide, grooved trigger with adj. stop; ribbed-top slide, handfitted, with improved ejection port; new barrel-bushing design.
Price:	Blued . . . . $284.95.

Heckler & Koch P9S: Though bulky and, in the opinion of some shooters, ugly, the double-action P9S is probably the most sophisticated autoloading pistol of its kind to come out of Europe. Designed well after World War II, it first became available in limited quantities in this country in the late 1960's. It is still not widely available, but supply and delivery are improving.

The P9S, even though offered in a special "competition model," does not appear to be suitable for any of our competitions except the combat matches of the International Practical Shooting Confederation.

Mechanically, it is most interesting. Both the slide and the frame are fabricated from sheet-metal stampings to which have been welded the necessary spacers and functional parts. The frame is particularly skeletonized, with the trigger guard and front-strap formed by a screw-attached plastic molding, and the back-strap formed by the molded-plastic wrap-around grip. In a departure from most other big-bore autos, the recoil spring encircles the barrel, a position made possible by the fixed barrel of the roller-lock Vorgrimmler locking system also utilized by the West German G3 service rifle. The extractor functions as a loaded-chamber indicator, and the enclosed hammer activates a cock-

Hechler & Koch P9S

ing-indicator plunger whenever the hammer is at full-cock. A slide stop is present but not visible, and it can be manually operated by working the cocking and uncocking lever that protrudes from beneath the left grip behind the trigger. A manual safety resembling that of the Walther is installed at the rear of the slide, but engaging it does not drop the hammer. Engagement simply disconnects the trigger from the sear and at the same time makes it impossible for the hammer to contact the head of the firing pin, even if it were to fall.

The P9S barrel is unusual in that it utilizes polygonal rifling which contains no sharp corners. It is claimed by the maker that this form of rifling produces a 10 percent increase in velocity and a substantial increase in accuracy. Factory tests which prove the claim are quoted by Heckler & Koch, but field experience has not yet borne this out among U.S. shooters.

In the past, the Heckler & Koch P9S has been available only in 9mm Parabellum. I have seen sample guns in .45 ACP, and shipments of some are reported in this country at this time, but I haven't yet encountered any in the hands of shooters. Availability in .45 caliber, combined with the double-action first-shot capability should make the P9S a very popular gun here.

HECKLER & KOCH P9S

Caliber & magazine capacity:	9mm Para., 9-shot
Barrel:	4″
Length (overall):	5½″
Weight:	33½ oz.
Stocks:	Checkered black plastic, wrap-around

Sights: Open combat type

Features: Double-action; polygonal rifling, roller-lock action with stationary barrel. Loaded-chamber and cocking indicators; uncocking lever relaxes springs. Imported from Germany by Security Arms.

Price: Standard P9S . . . . $285.00.

Target Model (5½" bbl., target sights, bbl. weight) . . . . $315.00.

Competition Model (similar to Target except with wrap-around match grips, bbl. weight, 4" or 5½" bbl.) . . . . $478.00.

Llama (Gabilondo) MVIII & MIXA: Since the late 1920's, the Spanish firm of Gabilondo, in Eibar, has produced copies of the Colt GM in several calibers. There are minor differences, mainly externally and in barrel length, but internally all parts and their appearance and functions are identical to those of the Colt except for dimensional differences.

Though target models of the Llama pistols have been offered, they have never been popular in this country. The basic, fixed-sight version in .38 Super or .45 caliber (Models VIII and IXA respectively) are generally quite suitable for combat-type matches, though the quality of fit and workmanship is often not quite equal to that of the Colt.

LLAMA MVIII & MIXA

Caliber &
magazine capacity: .38 Super (MVIII), 9-shot; .45 ACP (MIXA), 7-shot

Barrel: 5"

Length (overall): 8½"

Weight: 40 oz.

Stocks: Checkered walnut

Llama

Sights: Fixed

Features: Grip and manual safeties; ventilated rib. Engraved, chrome-engraved, or gold-damascened finish available at extra cost. Imported from Spain by Stoeger Industries.

Price: ....$184.95.

SIG/Hammerli P240: The P240 is the latest centerfire target pistol from SIG, the well-known Swiss company, chambered for the factory-loaded, flush-seated, .38 Special mid-range wadcutter load. This gun exhibits the superb manufacturing quality for which SIG has long been known. It is the ultimate refinement of the basic SIG P210 design that appeared at the end of World War II as a service pistol. There is no interchangeability of parts between the P240 and the P210, however. The locking system is a variation of the old Browning system, but only a single locking lug is used, and it fits into a segment of the ejection port rather than into internal grooves in the slide. Vertical movement for locking and unlocking is produced by a cam slot on the underside of the barrel breech and a cross pin passing through the frame.

The trigger is fully adjustable and features an unusual double-stage pull with a long, soft take-up leading to the final let-off; the transition from take-up to let-off is quite distinct and occurs at a point where only very slight sear engagement remains. Thus, there is no danger of accidental discharge or doubling, as often occurs with guns having more conventional searing systems. When the hammer is at full cock, there is an abnormally large amount of sear engagement to prevent any such occurrence. Engagement is reduced and transferred to a different area of the sear only when initial take-up is completed.

SIG / Hammerli P240

The SIG/Hammerli P240 is ideally suited to International centerfire matches and also to the centerfire stage of NRA matches. It is not suited to combat-type or long-range matches.

SIG/HAMMERLI P240 TARGET PISTOL

Caliber & magazine capacity:	.38 Special wadcutter, 5-shot
Barrel:	6″
Length (overall):	10″
Weight:	44½ oz.
Stocks:	Walnut, target style, unfinished
Sights:	Match sights; ⅛″ undercut front, ⅛″ notch Micro rear click, fully adj.
Features:	Recoil operated; meets ISU and NRA specs for centerfire competition; double-pull trigger adj. from 2 lbs., 15 oz. to 3 lbs., 9 oz; trigger-stop. Comes with extra magazine, special screwdriver, carrying case. Imported from Switzerland by Gil Hebard.
Price:	. . . . $650.00.
	.22 conversion unit . . . . $300.00.

SIG/Sauer P220: This double-action auto is the most recent Swiss development in a military and police arm. It has been many years in the

SIG / Sauer P220

making. Its suitability for any form of competition is yet to be proved, but it appears to have all of the basic characteristics—including future availability in .45 caliber—to adapt it very well to the matches of the International Practical Shooting Confederation and, perhaps, the matches of the National Shooters League. It does not appear that it would be suitable for NRA-type competition or for long-range work.

The P220 was designed from scratch as an economical replacement for the famed SIG P210 series which has been so highly regarded since its introduction at the end of World War II. The P220 was designed to take maximum advantage of the latest technology in investment casting and sheet-metal stamping. It utilizes a slide made up of a stamped shell with spacers and internal components welded or pinned in place. The frame is a finished-machined casting. The gun departs radically from tradition in that it has no conventional manual safety. Instead, it is fitted with a cocking and uncocking lever on the left side and an automatic firing-pin safety which prevents discharge except at the instant when the trigger is deliberately pulled fully rearward. It also possesses double-action capability for the first shot, and thereafter the hammer remains cocked for deliberate SA fire of subsequent shots.

It utilizes a variation of the basic Browning M1911 locking system, wherein the breech of the barrel rises and falls for locking and unlocking. In this instance, barrel movement is guided by cams, while the traditional multiple locking lugs seating in the top of the slide are replaced by a single lug seating in the top of the ejection port. The details differ greatly, but the principle is the same. This is also the first production-line gun with the front of the trigger guard roughly squared and hooked to provide a secure seat for the forefinger of the hand in todays popular two-handed combat and field-shooting grip. It carries a conventional slide-stop and a fixed sight.

At present, the P220 is available only in 9mm Parabellum. It will later be offered in 7.65mm Parabellum, .38 Colt Super Auto, .45 ACP and .22 LR. Further, SIG/Sauer brochures state that the gun can be converted to any of the other calibers by simply installing the correct combination of slide, barrel, recoil spring and magazine. This degree of caliber conversion has never before been offered in a big-bore autoloader and should greatly enhance the desirability and versatility of this gun. Of course, such conversion kits are unlikely to be available until initial demand for one-caliber guns has been substantially met.

SIG/SAUER P220

Caliber & magazine capacity:	9mm, 9-shot; .45 ACP, 7-shot
Barrel:	4⅜"
Length (overall):	7¾"
Weight:	28¼ oz. (9mm)
Stocks:	Checkered walnut
Sights:	Blade front, rear drift-adj. for w.
Features:	Double-action; uncocking lever permits lowering hammer onto locked firing pin; squared combat-type trigger guard; slide stays open after last shot. Imported by Hawes Firearms.
Price:	Not determined at press time.

Smith & Wesson M52 .38 Master: This is a very sophisticated and highly developed variation of the basic S&W M39 service autoloader. Introduced in the early 1960's, it features the basic firing mechanism of the M39, and the locking system is also identical. Early-production guns were so similar to the M39 internally that by backing out an adjusting screw one could put into play the first-shot double-action capability of the M39. Later production, however, dispensed with this feature inasmuch as the serious target shooter has no use for double-action. The M52 utilizes a massive steel frame similar to but not quite identical to that of the M39. The slide and barrel are both longer and heavier, proportioned to a barrel length of five inches.

Production-Line Guns for Competition

Smith & Wesson M52

The M52 introduced an unusual barrel-muzzle and barrel-bushing setup wherein a semi-circular-section bulge surrounds the muzzle and is closely fitted to the bore of the barrel bushing so that it provides line contact completely around the muzzle when the gun is in battery. This constitutes a significant improvement over the older system employed by custom pistolsmiths in accurizing Browning designs, wherein maximum surface contact was sought between barrel and bushing. The M52 system allows a much closer fit of barrel to bushing in battery, yet does not interfere with angular displacement of the barrel necessary for locking and unlocking.

In addition, the M52 is fitted with very precise and accurately adjustable target sights of excellent design. As shipped from the factory, it is quite snugly fitted and generally capable of delivering better accuracy than any other domestic production-line autoloading pistol.

This gun is chambered only for the .38 Special wadcutter cartridge in its factory-loaded form with the bullet seated flush with the case mouth. It will not accept or feed cartridges loaded with the bullet protruding significantly from the case.

Since its introduction, the M52 has been widely accepted by target shooters of all sorts. It can be found in use throughout the Western world wherever a reliable centerfire autoloader of top accuracy is required. It was developed for the NRA-type bull's-eye matches that predominate in this country, and its immediate success in that area led to its use elsewhere. It is often seen in International matches, the Pan-American games, Olympics, etc.

It will serve admirably for any type of match in which centerfire shooting is done at ranges not much exceeding 50 meters and in which a magazine capacity of five rounds is adequate. It has performed well in National Shooters League matches, and is also seen occasionally in combat-type matches—though with the new rules placing a floor on cartridge energy, it is not likely to see much use in matches conducted under the auspices of the International Practical Shooting Confederation.

SMITH & WESSON M52 .38 MASTER

Caliber & magazine capacity:	.38 Special mid-range wadcutter, 5-shot
Barrel:	5″
Length (overall):	8⅝″
Weight:	41 oz.
Stocks:	Checkered walnut
Sights:	⅛″ Patridge front, S&W Micro-click rear, fully adj.
Features:	Top sighting surfaces matte-finished. Locked-breech, moving-barrel system; coin-adj. sight screws. Dry firing permissible if manual safety is on.
Price:	...................................$267.50.

Smith & Wesson M59 & M39: The basic model is the M39, first made in the early 1950's and later revised to accept a double-column 14-shot magazine to become the M59. In design the two guns are identical except for the magazine, and the complete slide-and-barrel unit is interchangeable between the two. These guns possess double-action first-shot capability and utilize a hammer-dropping, hammer-blocking manual safety installed in the left rear of the slide. Thus, they may either be fired double-action for the first shot or cocked manually; naturally, the hammer remains at full cock after each shot. This design cannot be carried in the "cocked and locked" mode. Though the double-action mechanism is often compared to that of the Walther P-38, the S&W system is far simpler. A yoke (drawbar) connected to the trigger straddles the magazine well. Hooks on its rear engage corresponding surfaces on the foot of the hammer; pulling the trigger moves the drawbar forward and rotates the hammer about its pin, with the drawbar camming off the hammer at the proper point (at the same time moving the conventional sear out of the hammer's path) and allowing the hammer to fall and strike the firing pin.

Smith & Wesson M59   Smith & Wesson M39

The locking system is based on the early Colt/Browning system of 1911, but utilizes camming surfaces rather than the pivoted link or cam-and-pin system of other Browning-type designs. These two S&W models are built on high-strength aluminum-alloy frames which have proven quite satisfactory and durable over roughly 20 years of field service. A few M39 pistols were made with steel frames in the beginning, but today these are encountered only as collector's items.

The M39 and M59 are the only domestic big-bore autos fitted with adjustable rear sights in standard form. Unfortunately, the sight contains only windage adjustments, and the system of sight installation does not permit fitting of a better rear sight without extensive (costly) gunsmithing.

In their basic form, the M39 and M59 are suitable only for combat-type competition. Available only in 9mm Parabellum, they have the capability of performing well in such matches, though to date they have not become popular for this purpose.

SMITH & WESSON M59

Caliber &
magazine capacity: 9mm Luger, 14-shot

Barrel: 4″

Length (overall): 7⁷/₁₆″

Weight: 27½ oz.

Stocks: Checkered high-impact nylon

Sights: ⅛" serrated-ramp front, square-notch rear adj. for w.

Features: Double-action; furnished with two magazines.

Price: Blued ....$178.50.

Nickel................................$194.50.

SMITH & WESSON M39

Caliber &
magazine capacity: 9mm Luger, 8-shot

Barrel: 4"

Length (overall): 7⁷/₁₆"

Weight: 26½ oz.

Stocks: Checkered walnut

Sights: ⅛" serrated-ramp front, square-notch rear adj. for w.

Features: Magazine disconnector; positive firing-pin lock and hammer-release safety; alloy frame with lanyard loop; locked-breech, short-recoil double-action; slide locks open on last shot.

Price: Blued ....$148.50.

Nickeled ....$164.00.

Star: The big-framed Star pistol is offered in .45 ACP caliber as the Model P, in .38 Super Auto as the Model AS, and in 9mm as the Model BS. A smaller, lighter model in 9mm is designated BKM, but with its aluminum-alloy frame and small size, it is not generally considered suitable for competitive purposes. The most recent Star is the .45-caliber Model PD, which is very much shortened and lightened; though in-

Star

tended primarily as a concealed defense gun, it does have a capability of performing well in combat-type matches.

All of the foregoing Star pistols (manufactured by Star Bonifaccio Echeverria in Eibar, Spain) share the same basic design. The slide, barrel and locking system are those of the 1911 Colt Browning. However, the lockwork and the inner details of the slide are much modified. The Browning grip safety and separate mainspring housing are dispensed with, the frame being solid in these areas, and the mainspring rides in a simple vertical hole. The Star's manual safety is the most positive of its type. It acts upon a protrusion at the tail of the hammer to lift the sear notch off the sear nose and positively block the hammer in this position. This system is so secure that it is necessary for an impact to break the hammer or the sturdy safety shaft before firing can result from impact. The fire-control mechanism is also quite different from the Browning, consisting of a pivoted trigger and a single rearward-reaching trigger bar which engages the sear directly. Disconnector function is provided by a small plunger riding vertically between the trigger bar and the underside of the slide.

Though there appears to have been very little use of Star pistols in competition in this country, the design is capable of doing anything that can be done by the Colt GM. The gun could be accurized and therefore be suitable for NRA-style competition, or it could be used more or less as issued for combat-type matches. Given the same tuning and attention that is often lavished on the GM, it should perform just as well as the latter.

STAR MODEL AS

Caliber &
magazine capacity: .38 Super, 9-shot

Barrel: 5″

Length (overall): 8½"

Weight: 37½ oz.

Stocks: Checkered walnut

Sights: Fixed

Features: Magazine and manual safeties; wide-spur hammer. Imported from Spain by Garcia.

Price: Blued ....$195.00.

Chromed ....$209.00.

Walther GSP-C: This pistol is identical to the Walther GSP and OSP (listed with rimfire pistols) except that it is modified to function with the .32 S&W rimmed revolver cartridge as factory-loaded with flush-seated wadcutter bullets. In fact, it is possible to convert the .32 to .22, or vice versa, by the installation of a conversion kit consisting of barrel, bolt, barrel extension and magazine.

The GSP-C is ideally suited to any centerfire match that allows the use of a cartridge of .32 caliber. The principle advantage is in the very light recoil of this cartridge. The small caliber generally restricts its use to International centerfire matches or to the centerfire stage of NRA-type matches. The gun is superbly accurate, and with reasonable attention to maintenance and load selection, it is quite reliable.

WALTHER GSP-C MATCH PISTOL

Caliber &
magazine capacity: .32 S&W wadcutter, 5-shot

Barrel: 5¾"

Length (overall): 11⁴/₅"

Weight: 49²/₅ oz.

Stocks: Walnut, special hand-fitting design

Sights: Fixed front, rear fully adj.

Walther GSP-C

Features: Available with either 2.2 lb. (1000 gm) or 3 lb. (1360 gm) trigger. Spare mag., bbl. weight, tools supplied in Match Pistol Kit. Imported from Germany by Interarms.

Price: . . . .$569.00.

      .22 cal. conversion unit . . . .$309.00.

Walther P38:   Introduced in the late 1930's and adopted by the German military establishment in 1938, this model was the first successful big-bore autoloader to feature double-action first-shot capability. Today it has been well proven by nearly 40 years of arduous military service throughout most of the world, and many millions have been manufactured.

The design is unusual in the use of a hinged locking block that rides in a recess in the underside of the barrel breech and is cammed upward and downward to lock and unlock the barrel and slide. This permits a short and open slide design—which does not enclose the barrel. It is driven by twin recoil springs fitted in tunnels in either side of the frame. The firing mechanism of the P38 is unusual and—by today's standards—unnecessarily complex. It was copied more or less directly from the Walther PP pistol of the 1920's. This basic design is not found in any other make or model except for copies of the various Walther models. Its chief problem is that the double-action function is gained through the use of additional members connecting the trigger bar to the hammer. These members not only add friction to the system but generally produce a rather heavy double-action trigger pull and greatly increase the cost of manufacture.

To the best of my knowledge, the Walther P38 has seen only military competitive use. It does not lend itself well to the usual methods of accurizing, so it has never been seriously considered for NRA-type competition. It has never made any inroads in combat-type competition

Walther P-38

because of its unusually muzzle-light feeling and rather clumsy grip and appearance. Though made primarily in 9mm Parabellum, it is also available to a lesser extent in 7.65mm Parabellum and .22 LR.

WALTHER P38 AUTO PISTOL

Caliber & magazine capacity:	.22 LR, .30 Luger, 9mm Luger, 8-shot
Barrel:	$4^{15}/_{16}''$ (9mm and .30), $5^1/_{16}''$ (.22 LR)
Length (overall):	8½"
Weight:	28 oz.
Stocks:	Checkered plastic
Sights:	Fixed
Features:	Double-action; safety blocks firing pin and drops hammer; chamber-loaded indicator. Matte finish standard; polished blue, engraving and/or plating available at extra cost. Imported from Germany by Interarms.
Price:	.22 LR .... $375.00.
	9mm or .30 Luger .... $340.00.

CENTERFIRE REVOLVERS

Colt Python: This is the premier double-action revolver of the entire Colt line and, as such, is the most costly of the lot. It's built on the old

Colt Python

Official Police frame and action, fitted with a heavy figure-eight-section barrel that carries an integral ventilated sighting rib and is cut away on the underside to shroud the ejector rod. The lockwork is the old-style DA Colt system, which has been manufactured in essentially the same form for nearly three-quarters of a century. (It is not the more recent Mark III design.) The differences between the Python and standard service revolvers based on the same design are simply in quality of workmanship, both internally and externally, and the improved cosmetics. The Python possesses the smoothest double-action pull of any production-line revolver available today. It is chambered only for the .357 Magnum cartridge but, as everyone knows, this chambering handles .38 Special loads with equal facility.

While the Python could be considered suitable for NRA-type centerfire matches, revolvers have been superceded in such competition by .38-caliber autoloaders. The Python has become quite popular in police or PPC matches. These are the only shoots in which medium-caliber revolvers play a significant part today.

COLT PYTHON

Caliber & cylinder capacity:	.357 Magnum, 6 shot
Barrel:	2½", 4", 6", with ventilated rib
Length (overall):	9¼" (4" bbl.)
Weight:	38 oz. (4" bbl.)
Stocks:	Checkered walnut, target type, square butt
Sights:	⅛" ramp front, fully adj. notch rear

Features: Ventilated rib; grooved, crisp trigger; target hammer.

Price: Blued . . . .$318.95.

Nickeled . . . .$329.95.

Colt Single Action Army: Colt's "SAA" is the traditional "frontier six-shooter" spread across all the T.V. tubes and movie screens of the world and virtually unchanged since its introduction in 1873. For that matter, the 1873 SAA differed hardly at all internally from Colt percussion-revolver designs of the 1850's.

Great though its appeal may be for other reasons, the Colt SAA has probably the most limited competitive application of any handgun. Its use in matches is limited almost exclusively to the quick-draw shooters who draw and fire blanks against time. Though there are several fairly good copies and slightly modified copies of the Colt SAA which also see this sort of use, the favorite is the original item. Actually, in .45 Colt or .44 Special, with properly handloaded ammunition, this old favorite may also be considered marginally suited for long-range handgun silhouette-target shooting.

COLT SINGLE ACTION ARMY

Caliber &
cylinder capacity: .357 Magnum or .45 Colt, 6 shot

Barrel: 4¾", 5½", 7½"

Length (overall): 10⅞" (5½" bbl.)

Weight: 37 oz. (5½" bbl.)

Stocks: Black composite rubber with eagle-and-shield crest

Sights: Fixed. Grooved top strap, blade front

Price: Blued and case-hardened 4¾" or
5½" bbl. . . . . $288.50.

Production-Line Guns for Competition

Colt SA Army

7½″ bbl. . . . .$293.95.

Nickeled, with walnut stocks . . . .$338.95.

Ruger Security-Six: Though intended primarily as a police service revolver, the .357 Magnum Security-Six (M117) is suitable for PPC and police or other combat matches that allow medium-caliber revolvers. This, of course, applies only to the target-sighted version which carries a substantial integral sighting rib on the barrel and is fitted with excellent, adjustable target-type sights. As an indication of the design suitability for this use, consider that at least one or two custom pistolsmiths are currently using the Ruger Security-Six as a basis for heavy-barreled PPC competition revolvers.

The Security-Six is one of the very few *new* revolver designs to appear in over three-quarters of a century. Developed in the late 1960's, the lockwork combines features of both Smith & Wesson and Colt into a relatively original design that contains very few parts and may be disassembled without tools. This latter characteristic is not shared by any other modern revolver. Of special interest, the frame of the Security-Six is solid on both sides and symmetrical; it does not have one side cut away for the traditional side plate found on almost all other DA designs. This makes the frame much more rigid and should contribute to longer durability.

RUGER SECURITY-SIX (M117)

Caliber & cylinder capacity:	.357 Magnum, 6-shot
Barrel:	2¾″, 4″, 6″

Ruger Security-Six

Length (overall): 9¼″ (4″ bbl.)

Weight: 35 oz. (4″ bbl.)

Stocks: Hand-checkered American walnut, semi-target style

Sights: Patridge front on ramp, rear fully adj.

Features: Music-wire coil springs throughout; hardened steel construction; integral ejector-rod shroud and sighting rib. Can be disassembled using only a coin.

Price: ....$152.50.

Ruger Super Blackhawk: Bill Ruger, the designer of this gun, is the party responsible for the comeback of the single-action revolver in the 1950's. His first design in .22 rimfire was shortly developed into a large-frame gun capable of handling the .44 Magnum and all lesser revolver cartridges. The ultimate development was the New Model Super Blackhawk, introduced in the early 1970's. The principle difference between the New Model and the previous version is the inclusion of a transfer bar between hammer and firing pin, activated by the trigger in such fashion as to eliminate the possibility of an inadvertent firing—or any firing except when the trigger is held deliberately to the rear. Inadvertent firing has been a recognized hazard with single-action revolvers. Several attempts have been made to eliminate the hazard by the means of various safeties, both manual and automatic, but the Ruger transfer bar is by far the simplest, most effective and most convenient.

The chief competitive use of the Ruger Super Blackhawk is in long-range silhouette shooting. In fact, the first National Championship was

Ruger Super Blackhawk

won in 1975 at Tucson, Arizona, with a *stock* .44 Magnum Super Black-hawk.

This Ruger has also seen some use by the quick-draw crowd, but it requires more modification than the Colt, particularly because the large adjustable sights must be removed to protect the shooter's hand. Consequently, it is very popular for this type of match.

RUGER NEW MODEL SUPER BLACKHAWK

Caliber & cylinder capacity:	.44 Magnum, 6-shot
Barrel:	7½″ (6-groove, 20″ twist)
Length (overall):	13⅜″
Weight:	48 oz.
Stocks:	American walnut
Sights:	⅛″ ramp front; Micro-click rear, fully adj.
Features:	New Ruger interlocked mechanism; non-fluted cylinder; steel grip and cylinder frame; square-back trigger guard; wide serrated trigger and wide-spur hammer.
Price:	.....................................$170.00.

Smith & Wesson K-Frame: Several target models fall in this category —target-type and target-sighted .38 or .357 revolvers built on the standard M10 or Military & Police frame and lockwork. As has been

Smith & Wesson K-Frame

pointed out, revolvers play a significant part only in PPC or police competition today. They have been superceded by autoloaders in all other forms, even though they dominated the field prior to about 1950. The basic Smith & Wesson design reached its definitive form during the first decade of this century and has been manufactured with virtually no significant change since. The mechanism is well proven in durability, reliability and accuracy. Generally speaking, the S&W lockwork is preferred over others for double-action shooting. This isn't to say that it is mechanically superior, but that the average competitive shooter finds that it *feels* better. The various K-frame S&W revolvers will normally outnumber other makes and models in most PPC or police matches. The K-frame series is also by far the most popular basis for custom-built guns which many shooters prefer for this type of competition.

The S&W models falling under this heading are the M14 (K-38 masterpiece); the M19 (Combat Magnum), which is essentially the M14 with a heavier barrel and chambered for the .357 Magnum cartridge; and the M66, which is the M19 fabricated entirely from stainless steel. All three are fitted with a relatively heavy barrel carrying an integral sighting rib and micrometer-adjustable sights of the same type S&W has offered since the 1930's. In fact, these are the sights introduced on the original .357 Magnum in 1935.

SMITH & WESSON .357 COMBAT MAGNUM (M19)

Caliber &
cylinder capacity: .357 Magnum, 6-shot

Barrel: 2½", 4", 6"

Length (overall):   9½" (4" bbl.)

Weight: 35 oz.

Stocks: Checkered Goncala Alves, target style

Sights: Front, ⅛″ Baughman Quick Draw on 2½″ or 4″ bbl.; Patridge on 6″ bbl.; Micro-click rear, fully adj.

Price: Blued or nickeled .... $167.50.

Smith & Wesson N-Frame Guns in this category are mechanically identical to those of the K-frame series but are built on the .44-size frame introduced in 1908. These are the basic so-called "Magnum" revolvers, and some individuals with large hands prefer them to the K series for the same forms of competition.

However, in the larger Magnum calibers (.41 and .44) these N-frame revolvers are also suitable for long-range competition such as that conducted with metallic game silhouette targets out to 200 meters. Because of their size, they accommodate the very powerful cartridges needed for this type of competition, and their greater weight makes it possible for the shooter to handle the high recoil of these cartridges without difficulty.

Smith & Wesson M29

SMITH & WESSON .44 MAGNUM MODEL 29 REVOLVER

Caliber &
cylinder capacity: .44 Magnum, .44 Sp., .44 Russian, 6-shot

Barrel: 4″, 6½″, 8⅜″

Length (overall): 11⅞″ (6¼″ bbl.)

Weight: 47 oz. (6½″ bbl.) 43 oz. (4″ bbl.)

Stocks: Oversize target type, checkered Goncala Alves

Sights: ⅛" red ramp-front, Micro-click rear, fully adj.

Features: Includes presentation case.

Price: Blued or nickeled 4", 6½" bbl. . . . . $235.00.

8⅜" bbl. . . . .$241.50.

Dan Wesson: This is another new design. It was developed during the late '60's and manufactured by the Dan Wesson Arms Company, founded and operated by the great-grandson of Daniel B. Wesson, one of the original founders of the famed Smith & Wesson company. The Wesson design is quite modern and uses the very minimum number of parts for full SA/DA functioning. It was designed for the latest methods of metal fabrication, including sintering and investment casting. The action was also designed to focus all tolerances into a single point (the hand, or pawl) in order to eliminate most of the handfitting that is required in the assembly of traditional designs. While the Wesson frame encorporates a slideplate in the traditional fashion, it dispenses entirely with a grip frame, substituting a squared tenon over which a one-piece wood grip fits and is secured by a socket-head screw.

The most outstanding feature of the Wesson design is its quick-change barrel system, not found in any other make. Rather than a one-piece barrel, threaded and pinned securely to the frame, the Wesson uses a thin-wall, tubular barrel threaded loosely into the frame, after which a heavy cast or extruded shroud is slipped over the barrel and secured by a jam nut at the muzzle. This locks the barrel proper in place (the shroud is aligned by a stud on the frame) and the tightening of the nut places the barrel in tension. To change to a lighter or heavier, shorter or longer barrel, the nut is simply unscrewed, the shroud slipped off, the barrel turned out by hand, and the appropriate replacement parts installed in the reverse order. Barrel-to-cylinder gap is properly established by use of a feeler gauge furnished with the gun. This interchangeable-barrel setup also allows for regulation of the barrel-to-cylinder gap at any point during the gun's life. Conventional revolvers with rigidly installed barrels often develop excessive gap which can be corrected only by installing a new barrel and by costly gunsmithing; such a condition can be corrected in moments on the Wesson at no cost whatever.

Dan Wesson M9-2

With a barrel of proper weight and length installed, the target-sighted Wesson is quite suitable for PPC or police matches, or any other form of competition for which a medium-caliber revolver is considered acceptable.

Note also that the design of the Wesson lockwork produces very short trigger and hammer travel and has the development capability of an extremely light double-action pull without introducing ignition problems.

DAN WESSON M9-2 & M15-2

Caliber & cylinder capacity:	.38 Sp. (M9-2); .357 Magnum (M15-2); 6-shot
Barrel:	2½", 4", 8"; Quickshift interchangeable barrels
Length (overall):	9¼" (4" bbl.)
Weight:	36 oz. (4" bbl.)
Stocks:	Quickshift Powerwood Target, checkered walnut grain; interchangeable with three other styles
Sights:	⅛" serrated blade front, rear fully adj.
Features:	Interchangeable barrels; four interchangeable grips; few moving parts, easy disassembly.
Price:	Bull barrel shroud, 2½", 4", 6" . . . . $187.35.
	As above 8" bbl. . . . . $206.10.

Vent-rib barrel shroud, 2½", 4", 6" .....: $190.60.

As above, 8" bbl. .... $207.65.

Models 9-2VH, 15-2VH (vent-rib, bull barrel shroud, 2½", 4", 6" .... $207.65.

As above, 8" bbl. .... $226.35.

RIMFIRE AUTOLOADERS

Colt Woodsman Match Target: At one time, the Match Target Woodsman was *the* .22 rimfire target pistol in this country. It is an excellent gun by the standards of a quarter-century ago, but it has not been updated since. It possesses the inherent accuracy and proven durability and reliability to make it suitable for NRA-type .22 matches, but it lacks the additional features and sophistication of more recent designs and revisions by other manufacturers. It is a sound, basic gun, and certainly no neophyte or medium-class shooter will be able to fault its accuracy.

The Colt Match Target is the basic Browning-developed straight-blowback action, utilizing a short slide and fully exposed fixed barrel which set the standard in 1915 for future development of superb .22 rimfire autoloading pistols. Almost every successful .22 rimfire autoloader in existence today owes much to the pioneering done in the development of the basic Woodsman from which the Match version grew.

COLT WOODSMAN MATCH TARGET AUTO PISTOL

Caliber & magazine capacity:	.22 LR, 10-shot
Barrel:	4½", 6"
Length (overall):	10½" (4½" bbl.)
Weight:	39 oz. (6" bbl.), 34½ oz. (4½" bbl.)
Stocks:	Checkered walnut with thumbrest

Production-Line Guns for Competition

Colt Woodsman Match Target

> Sights: Ramp front with removable undercut blade; ⅛"
> standard, ¹/₁₀" on special order; Colt-Elliason fully
> adj. rear
>
> Features: Wide trigger, automatic slide-stop.
>
> Price: 4½" barrel .... $175.95.
>
> 6" barrel .... $178.50.

Domino SP602 & SP601: This is a very sophisticated pistol manufactured in Italy, designed primarily for the International Standard Pistol
Match, but equally suitable for American .22 matches of all sorts. The
SP602 is chambered for .22 Long Rifle cartridges, while the SP601 is
chambered for the .22 Short for use in International Rapid-Fire. Aside
from the differences necessary to produce reliable functioning with the
two cartridges, the guns are almost identical mechanically. The trigger
and sear mechanisms differ slightly, and the SP601 has a palm-shelf
stock appropriate to the kind of ISU matches for which it's intended.

The design is straight blowback, utilizing an alloy receiver and an unusual barrel configuration held to the receiver by a large-diameter stud
entering the front of the frame. This stud protrudes rearward from a
barrel shroud which also contains the steel barrel. Rotating a lock-lever
at the left front of the frame allows the barrel and shroud to be drawn
off, after which the bolt and the bolt housing may be removed. Probably the most unusual feature of the design is the magazine, which is
inserted *downward* through the open action, rather than upward into a
well in the butt. This design was chosen because it allows much greater
freedom of grip shape. One-piece wood grips are attached to a frame
stud by a screw from beneath. The Domino sights are precisely adjustable, and the line of sight lies very close to the bore's centerline.

Domino pistols exhibit excellent workmanship, are superbly accurate and handle quite well. The principal disadvantage is in their price—as with other fine European .22 target pistols. The Domino is currently near the bottom of the price range of the European pistols, and even so it costs nearly twice the price of the best domestic guns of the same general type.

DOMINO MODEL SP602 MATCH PISTOL

Caliber & magazine capacity:	.22 LR, 5-shot
Barrel:	5.5″
Length (overall):	11.02″
Weight:	41 oz.
Stocks:	Full target stocks; adjustable, one-piece; left-hand style available
Sights:	Match; blade front, open notch rear, fully adj.; sight radius, 8.66″
Features:	Line of sight is only $^{11}/_{32}$″ above centerline of bore; magazine is inserted from top; adjustable and removable trigger mechanism; single-lever takedown. Full 5-year warranty. Imported from Italy by Mandall Shooting Supplies.
Price:	....$499.50.

DOMINO SP601 MATCH PISTOL

Similar to SP602 but has different match stocks with adj. palm shelf; .22 Short only, weighs 40 oz., 5.6″ bbl.; has gas ports through top of barrel and slide to reduce recoil, slightly different trigger and sear mechanisms.

Price: ....$525.00.

Production-Line Guns for Competition

Hammerli M208

Hammerli M208 & M211: These two target .22 autoloaders have been offered for several years by the Swiss Hammerli firm (now a part of SIG). They differ only in that the 208 is equipped with an adjustable palm rest, while the 211 has conventional stocks with a thumb rest.

The design is mechanically simple, a typical blowback action with a short slide connecting to the underbarrel recoil spring by a forward-extending yoke. The barrel is rectangular in section, does not sport a rib, and is fitted with a raised ramp for interchangeable front sight blades. The rear sight is supported by a yoke attached to the rear of the frame, the inside of the yoke providing clearance for the slide to move. The rear sight is finely adjustable and the leaf carrying the sight notch may be readily interchanged to provide a notch meeting individual needs. The trigger is fully adjustable. This series was once offered with a vented barrel, chambered for the .22 Short, but is currently available only in .22 LR. Naturally, the .22 Short version was intended for International Rapid-Fire Matches.

This basic design is suitable for NRA-type .22 matches, and also for those International matches normally shot with a .22 LR auto.

HAMMERLI STANDARD, MODELS 208 & 211

Caliber &
cylinder capacity: .22 LR., 5 shot

Barrel: 5.9″, 6-groove

Length (overall): 10″

Weight: 37.6 oz. (45 oz. with extra-heavy barrel weight)

Stocks: Walnut; adj. palm rest on M208, thumb rest on M211

Sights: Match sights, fully adj.; interchangeable front and rear blades

Features: Slide-stop; fully adj. trigger (2¼ lbs. and 3 lbs.). Extra barrel weight available. Imported from Switzerland by Gil Hebard.

Price: M208 .... $510.00.

M211 .... $489.00.

Hammerli M230:   This is the successor to earlier .22 Short Hammerli pistols intended for International Rapid-Fire Matches. It is an entirely new design, sharing no parts or components with the M208-211 series already described. It consists of a light-alloy frame to which is fitted a massive rectangular barrel that may be removed by rotating a dismounting lever forward of and above the trigger. A very short, light breech block reciprocates inside a rear barrel extension. Finely adjustable target sights are fitted to the barrel and extension. There is no rib, but the inverted-V shape of the top of the barrel provides the effect of a sighting rib. The barrel contains a number of round, vertically positioned gas-escape vents in line ahead of the chamber, and they may be opened or closed to provide maximum recoil and velocity reduction compatible with fully reliable functioning with a particular lot or make of ammunition. The gun can therefore be "tuned" to the ammunition chosen. Only in this fashion can maximum recoil and muzzle-jump reduction be obtained while insuring maximum functional reliability.

The Hammerli M230 is designed purely for International Rapid-Fire competition, and represents probably the highest level of development of guns for this purpose. Because of its high degree of specialization, it is not suitable for any other form of competition.

HAMMERLI M230 RAPID FIRE PISTOL

Caliber &
magazine capacity: .22 Short, 5-shot

Barrel: 6.3", 6-groove

Length (overall):   11.6″

Weight: 43.8 oz.

Stocks: Walnut; M230-1 has standard grip w/o thumbrest; M230-2 has adj. grip

Sights: Match sights; Micro-click rear, fully adj.; interchangeable front-sight blade; sight radius 9.9″

Features: Gas-escape vents in front of chamber to eliminate muzzle jump; fully adj. trigger (5½ oz. to 10½ oz.) with three different lengths available; designed for International 25-meter silhouette program. Imported from Switzerland by Gil Hebard.

Price: M230-1 .... $495.00.

M230-2 .... $530.00.

High Standard: The High Standard company makes a number of very fine rimfire target pistols on its basic Supermatic design. Mechanically, the design is straight blowback with a rigidly attached but removable (interchangeable) barrel. The firing mechanism contains an enclosed rotating hammer, an adjustable trigger stop and, in most models, trigger adjustments for pull and travel. All are equipped with checkered wood stocks, a 10-shot, single-column, box magazine in the butt and excellent, fully-adjustable target-type sights. A wide variety of barrel lengths, weights and profiles is available, ranging from fluted-cylinder shape through solid tapered shapes and the slab-sided ribbed barrel found on the Victor variation.

Three types of rear-sight installation are found among the various models—the conventional, with the sight installed on the reciprocating side; the rib installation of the Victor wherein a barrel-mounted sighting rib carries the rear sight and extends back over the slide; and the frame-mounted installation wherein a large inverted-U yoke is attached to the frame to hold the sight rigidly so that the slide may reciprocate beneath it. The slide-mounted sight is the least desirable of the three inasmuch as it allows more relative movement of the sights than the other types.

Two butt configurations are available, the Standard and the Military.

High Standard Victor   High Standard Supermatic

The latter is intended to duplicate the dimensions and feel of the Colt GM pistol in order to eliminate problems that might develop in switching from the GM to a .22 during a full NRA-style match. A wide variety of accessories can also be had for these pistols, including muzzle brakes, magazine extensions, adjustable weights, etc.

High Standard .22 target pistols have achieved an enviable reputation for accuracy and reliability. They've overshadowed other American production-line guns in high-level competition. Even a .22 Short version is supplied for International Rapid-Fire.

HIGH STANDARD VICTOR

Caliber & magazine capacity:	22 LR, 10-shot
Barrel:	4½″, 5½″
Length (overall):	8¾″ (4½″ bbl.)
Weight:	43½ oz. (4½″ bbl., vent. rib), 43¾ oz. (solid rib), 46 oz. (5½″ bbl., vent. rib), 46¼ oz. (solid rib)
Stocks:	Checkered walnut
Sights:	Undercut ramp front, rib-mounted fully adj. click rear
Features:	Vent rib; interchangeable barrel; 2-2¼ lb. trigger pull; back- and front-straps stippled. Also available with aluminum solid rib.
Price:	Either bbl. length or rib $219.00

HIGH STANDARD SUPERMATIC TROPHY MILITARY

Caliber & magazine capacity:	22 LR, 10-shot
Barrel:	5½" heavy, 7¼" fluted
Length (overall):	9¾" (5½" bbl.)
Weight:	44½ oz.
Stocks:	Checkered walnut with or w/o thumbrest, right or left
Sights:	Undercut ramp front; frame-mounted click rear, fully adj.
Features:	Grip duplicates feel of military .45; front- and back-straps stippled; trigger adj. for pull, over-travel.
Price:	5½" barrel . . . .$185.00.
	7¼" barrel . . . .$195.00.

Ruger Mark I: The Mark I is a target version of the well-known Ruger Standard Model developed in the late 1940's as the first product of the then-new Sturm, Ruger Company. Essentially, it's the Standard Model fitted with a longer, heavier barrel and fully adjustable target sights. It shares the unique stamped and welded sheet-metal frame and tubular receiver of the standard model. The Mark I is not a sophisticated design, but the pistol is quite accurate and reliable, and ever since its introduction it has been the lowest-priced domestically made .22 rimfire autoloader that can be considered suitable for serious competition. Its retail price is barely half that of the cheapest of the more sophisticated designs.

As issued, the Ruger Mark I is suitable for all NRA-type .22-caliber matches and for many years it has served as the basis for very fine custom-built guns by several makers. It is an ideal gun for a shooter who is just getting into the game.

Ruger Mark I .22

RUGER MARK I TARGET MODEL AUTO PISTOL

Caliber &
magazine capacity: .22 LR, 9-shot

Barrel: 6⅞″ or 5½″ bull barrel (6-groove, 14″ twist)

Length (overall): 19⅞″ (6⅞ bbl.)

Weight: 42 oz. with 6⅞″ bbl.

Stocks: Checkered hard rubber

Sights: ⅛″ blade front; Micro-click rear, fully adj. Sight radius 9⅜″ (with 6⅞″ bbl.)

Features: Rear sight mounted on receiver, does not move with slide; wide, grooved trigger

Price: ....$94.50.

Smith & Wesson M41: This model arrived on the scene some years after World War II. It represented a long period of careful development and was intended to outperform Colt and High Standard designs. Due to excellent design and manufacture, it quickly became extremely popular for all sorts of .22-caliber competition, including International Rapid-Fire, for which a special .22 Short conversion kit was (and still is) supplied. With proper ammunition, the M41 has repeatedly proven itself capable of shooting groups under ½-inch at 50 yards.

The M41 design differs from other domestic .22 autoloaders in many ways. It utilizes a short slide connected by a long yoke to a recoil spring mounted beneath the barrel. The barrel is detachable (inter-

Smith & Wesson M41

changeable) and held to the frame by a protrusion on the hinged trigger guard; also, a rib extension integral to the barrel extends back over the slide and carries the fully adjustable rear sight. Firing is by an enclosed rotating hammer, and the trigger is adjustable. A detachable muzzle brake is supplied with the standard 7⅜-inch barrel; the optional 5½-inch heavy barrel does not accept the brake.

It is significant that the M41 is seldom "improved" or accurized by custom pistolsmiths and that relatively few accessories are available for it. It is a superb target pistol just as it comes from the factory—and this is all the more impressive when one considers that it's less expensive than the pistols offered by Colt or High Standard.

SMITH & WESSON .22 MATCH M41

Caliber &
magazine capacity: .22 LR, 10-shot

Barrel: 5½", heavy, w/o muzzle brake; 7⅜" with detachable muzzle brake

Length: 9"

Weight: 44½ oz. (5½" bbl.); 43½ oz. (7⅜" bbl.)

Stocks: Checkered walnut with modified thumbrest, usable with either hand

Sights: ⅛" Patridge front on ramp base; S&W Micro-click rear, fully adj.; sight radius, 8"

Features: ⅜"-wide grooved trigger; adj. trigger-stop; bright-blued, with satin-matted top.

Price: . . . . $172.00.

Unique D.E.S. 69

Unique D.E.S. 69: This is a recent design produced by a French firm, Manufacture des Arms des Pyrenees, near the Spanish border in the Basque country. Like most other European .22 target pistols, it was designed primarily for the International Standard Pistol Match but is also quite suitable for NRA-type .22 matches. It is fairly conventional in design, with a rotating-hammer firing mechanism, a fixed barrel and a short slide with forward-reaching yoke similar to that of the S&W M41.

It's unusual in appearance because a rear extension of the frame surrounds the hammer and supports the rear sight back beyond the limit of slide travel. This gives it a rather "open" appearance back there, as if a part had been lost. Another unusual feature is a dry-fire device incorporated into this frame extension. It is simply a threaded plunger which can be screwed forward over the cocked hammer to prevent the hammer from reaching the firing pin when the trigger is pulled. The hammer is manually cocked for dry fire, with its travel being limited by this plunger.

The D.E.S. 69 is, as of this writing, the lowest-priced of the European .22 rimfire target pistols available in this country.

CVA/UNIQUE D.E.S. 69 TARGET PISTOL

Caliber & magazine capacity:	.22 LR, 5-shot
Barrel:	5.91″
Length (overall):	10.63″
Weight:	35 oz.
Stocks:	French walnut, target style with thumbrest and adj. shelf; hand-checkered panels

Sights: Ramp front; Micro-click fully adj. rear mounted on frame; 8.66″ sight radius

Features: Meets ISU standards; comes in a fitted hard case with spare magazine, barrel weight, cleaning rod, tools, proof certificate, test target and two-year guarantee. Fully adj. trigger; dry-firing safety device. Imported from France by Connecticut Valley Arms.

Price: Right-handed . . . . $375.00.

Left-handed . . . . $395.00.

Walther Model GSP & OSP: The GSP is the latest and most sophisticated .22 rimfire autoloading pistol developed by the famed Walther works. It is unique, especially in appearance, in that it is the only .22 target pistol in the Western world which places the magazine forward of the trigger instead of inside the grip. Moving the magazine to this location eliminates the need for a grip frame and magazine well, thereby allowing almost complete freedom of grip shape and design. The magazine is otherwise conventional, and is removed and inserted from beneath.

The GSP features a separate firing mechanism that is easily removed as a unit and may be replaced by a special dry-firing mechanism which duplicates the live-firing mechanism in all other respects. The barrel is roughly rectangular in section, and is inserted (by means of a circular-section tenon) into an upper receiver housing. Both barrel and housing are locked to the light-alloy frame by a rotating lever forward of and above the magazine. A short, light, circular-section bolt reciprocates inside the upper receiver. Finely-adjustable sights are fitted, the front sight being on the barrel proper, the rear on the upper receiver housing. Even though the two sights are installed on different components, these components are locked securely together during assembly, so there is no relative sight movement.

The GSP pistol is also unique in that—at least as of this writing—it is the only available .22 rimfire target pistol that is readily converted to .32 S&W caliber so that it can be used in NRA-type centerfire matches. A conversion kit consists of barrel, upper receiver housing (with sights) and magazine—all of which may be installed on the frame in moments. With the .32 conversion unit installed, this becomes the Model GSP-C.

Walther GSP & OSP

It will accept only .32 S&W cartridges with wadcutter bullets seated flush with the case mouth.

In addition, there is the Walther Model OSP .22 Short pistol, intended purely for International Rapid-Fire. Mechanically the OSP is similar to the GSP except for internal modifications necessary to ensure proper functioning with .22 Shorts. The GSP has an almost glovelike, handfitting target stock; the OSP has the same type of stock but with an adjustable palm rest.

WALTHER GSP MATCH PISTOL

Caliber & magazine capacity:	.22 LR, 5-shot
Barrel:	5¾″
Length (overall):	11.8″
Weight:	44.8 oz.
Stocks:	Walnut, hand-fitting design
Sights:	Fixed front, fully adj. rear
Features:	Available with either 2.2 lb. (1000 gm) or 3 lb. (1360 gm) trigger. Spare mag., bbl. weight, tools supplied in Match Pistol Kit. Imported from Germany by Interarms.
Price:	.....................................$469.00.
	.32 cal. conversion unit................$309.00.

WALTHER OSP RAPID-FIRE PISTOL

Similar to Model GSP except .22 Short; stock has adj. free-style hand rest.

Price: ....$469.00.

SINGLE-SHOT PISTOLS

Hammerli M120: This is an unconventional design of .22 LR free pistol by Hammerli, an attempt to produce the required very high level of accuracy at lower cost. Traditional free pistols (for International Slow-Fire) have been of complex Martini-action design, and very costly to manufacture. The M120 utilizes a unique toggle-joint breech mechanism that opens to the left via a finger-lever situated on the left side of the tubular receiver. It is more or less as if the well-known Luger/Parabellum breech were laid on its side and operated manually.

The M120 is superbly accurate and, of course, fitted with the best of fully adjustable sights. That the design approach reduces costs is evident in the fact that the M120 is priced only about a third as high as the conventionally designed Hammerli M150.

Naturally, the M120 is suitable only for International Slow-Fire. It is barred from other slow-fire matches by restrictive rules.

HAMMERLI M120 TARGET PISTOL

Caliber:	.22 LR
Barrel:	10″, 6-groove
Length (overall):	14.8″
Weight:	44.1 oz.
Stocks:	Walnut; standard grip with thumb rest on M120-1, adjustable grip on M120-2
Sights:	Fully adj. Micro-click rear (match type); sight radius 9.9″ or 14.6″; interchangeable front sight blade

Hammerli M120

Features: New action operated by lateral lever; bolt fully encloses cartridge rim; target trigger adj. from 1.8 oz. to 12 oz.; trigger position adj. Imported from Switzerland by Gil Hebard.

Price: M120-1 ....$210.00.

M120-2 ....$240.00.

M120-2 Heavy Barrel (5.7″, 41 oz.) ......$240.00.

Hammerli M150: This is the latest refinement of the traditional Martini-type free pistol, intended only for International Slow-Fire competition. Its most distinguishing visible characteristic is a broad wood foreend placed well below and parallel to the slender barrel. The breech is opened and closed by a lever pivoted vertically on the left side of the frame. The very sensitive set-trigger is cocked by a separate lever; the trigger finger-piece is fully adjustable for reach and also for angle in two planes. The very precise rear sight rides on a frame extension at the extreme rear, actually back over the hand when the gun is grasped for shooting.

The Hammerli M150 represents the ultimate development of the traditional free-pistol type. It is very finely made and handfitted, and thus quite costly. Few but the finest slow-fire marksmen are capable of extracting its inordinately high degree of accuracy. The caliber is, of course, .22 LR, the only size allowed in the matches for which the M150 is made.

HAMMERLI M150 FREE PISTOL

Caliber: .22 LR

Barrel: 10.4″; 6-groove; free-floating

Length (overall): 15.4"

Weight: 42.4 oz.; up to 49.4 oz. with weights

Stocks: Walnut. Special anatomical design with adj. palm shelf

Sights: Match sights; Micro-click fully adj. rear with interchangeable blade; sight radius 14.6"

Features: Comes with fitted case. Martini-type action operated by lateral lever; straight-line hammerless ignition is vibration-free, with 0.0016-sec. ignition time. New set-trigger design fully adj.; low barrel and sight line; extra weights available. Imported from Switzerland by Gil Hebard.

Price: ....$675.00.

Thompson/Center Contender: Other centerfire single-shot pistols are available, but only the Contender is chambered in a sufficient variety of calibers (and quantity) to make it a suitable production-line gun for long-range metallic-silhouette matches. It is available factory-chambered for several rifle cartridges as well as most of the Magnum pistol cartridges. Consequently, it can be purchased as an off-the-shelf selection that meets the severe demands placed on a gun by the 200-meter stages of the silhouette matches.

The Contender is an unusual and quite simple design introduced about a decade ago. It contains very few parts, and it features quickly interchangeable barrels in a wide variety of calibers. It is essentially a break-open action with the barrel hinged to the frame a short distance ahead of the chamber. The hinge pin is simply pushed out (after removal of the fore-end, which holds the pin in place) and the barrel is lifted off. A barrel is installed by the same procedure in reverse order. The action is operated by pulling upward and rearward on a spur attached to the rear of the trigger guard; cocking of the hammer is done manually after the action is closed; closing the action places the hammer in the safe position.

While this gun is often heavily modified for metallic-silhouette matches, it is entirely adequate as it comes from the box if chambered for the .44 Magnum, .30-30, .30 Herrett or other cartridges possessing sufficient energy to knock over the 200-meter target.

Handgun Competition

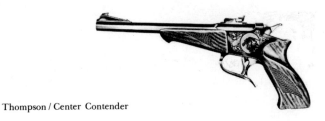

Thompson / Center Contender

THOMPSON/CENTER CONTENDER

Caliber: .218 Bee, .221 Rem., .25-35 Win., .30-30 Win., .22 S, L, LR, .22 WMR, .22 Rem. Jct, .22 Hornet, .22 K Hornet, .256 Win., 9mm Parabellum, .38 Super, .357/44 B&D, .38 Sp., .357 Magnum, .222 Rem., .30 Ml, .45 ACP, .44 Magnum, 5mm Rem., .45 Long Colt

Barrel: 8¾", 10", tapered octagon

Length (overall): 13¼" (10" bbl.)

Weight: 43 oz. (10" bbl.)

Stocks: Checkered walnut grip and fore-end, with thumb rest; right- or left-handed

Sights: Undercut blade ramp front, fully adj. rear

Features: Break-open action with auto-safety; single-action only; interchangeable bbls., drilled and tapped for scope. Engraved frame.

Price: Blued ....$155.00.

Extra bbl. ....$ 57.00.

.30 Herrett or .357 Herrett bull bbl. with fore-end, less sights ....$ 62.00.

Fitted walnut case ....$ 39.50.

.357 or .44 Magnum vent-rib, internal-choke bbl. ....$ 62.00.

12

Customized and Accurized Target Guns

Since the very beginning of organized pistol shooting in this country, marksmen have been suggesting ways to improve the accuracy and functioning of their guns by refining the mechanisms. Even Paine and Patridge had their guns worked over—that is, customized—at least to the extent of fitting new sights of their own design.

From those days forward, virtually all the parts of match revolvers and autos have been modified or replaced in the interest of improving scores. Such modifications have generally been in two categories, the first intended to improve the *mechanical* accuracy of the gun, the second to improve its handling qualities and thus the shooter's ability to *extract* the maximum of that mechanical accuracy. Merely honing or tuning a few parts to sharpen performance is generally called accurizing. More substantial changes—using a stock gun as the basis for a highly refined or specialized shooting tool—amounts to custom-building, or customizing. These changes have included almost everything imaginable. In the case of autoloaders, mainly the Colt .45 auto, they include complete replacement of barrel and slide; meticulous fitting of all recoiling parts to the minimum tolerances that are compatible with reasonably good functioning; specially dimensioned chambers and bores; specially designed and manufactured barrel bushings; cartridge-positioning plungers or other devices; barrel-positioning devices, and so on. In revolvers, accuracy-improving modifications are generally limited to replacement or refitting of barrels, usually with heavier, specially made tubes, and refitting and retiming of cylinders and cranes, sometimes with specially dimensioned chamber throats to match the barrel.

Efforts to improve *practical* accuracy began with a carefully honed and polished "trigger job," then moved on up through changes in the grip and frame to suit the shooter's hand; then special sights and ribs; trigger stops and shoes; stippling and checkering in the grip area; fixed and adjustable weights; ad infinitum.

Back in the 1930's and 1940's, the revolver—then *the* gun for center-fire matches—was often heavily customized into a more or less standard form. Most competitors shot single-action in those days, so the hammer spur was reshaped to facilitate smooth, rapid cocking without disturbing the shooter's hold. The most popular and highly developed such modification was the King "Cockeyed Hammer." The hammer spur was built up by welding and extended leftward (for a right-handed shooter), then ground down, reshaped and sharply checkered. A less common alteration intended to speed up hammer fall and thus reduce that critical period of time from sear release to primer ignition consisted of skeletonizing the hammer. Sections of the hammer were drilled and filed out, eliminating a substantial amount of weight and at least theoretically reducing lock time. The hammer was weakened in the process, and Lee Echols in his most enjoyable book, *Dead Aim,* tells how such a hammer sometimes broke with disastrous effects upon the shooter's peace of mind.

The gun was also usually fitted with the best adjustable target sights available at the time, often those made by King, and sometimes with a ventilated rib by that same maker. Ribs didn't have the reputation for indispensability then that they do now, but they were considered desirable, and King was the principal supplier.

Special barrels were seldom fitted in those days, but the throat might be carefully polished and the cylinder retimed to produce the maximum uniformity of alignment with the barrel. As a part of this process, the shooter might then spend hundreds of rounds and many hours of range time to determine the single chamber (of the six in the cylinder) that produced the best long-range accuracy; that chamber would be marked in one fashion or another, and in slow-fire matches every shot would be fired from that one chamber.

Last but by no means least, the single-action trigger pull of the gun would be very carefully worked over, the ultimate goal being a "breaking-glass-rod" type of let-off trimmed to the bare minimum weight allowed by NRA rules. Those shooters who could afford it might also employ a "short-action job" by King or one of the few other custom pistolsmiths. The modification involved extensive reworking of the lockwork, reducing hammer travel (from full-cock down) by as much as a third. This was in the interest of reducing both the time required to thumb-cock the hammer for each shot and the lock time mentioned in conjunction with skeletonized hammers. The short-action conversion normally eliminated the double-action capability of the lockwork, but this was of no consequence inasmuch as virtually all NRA-type shooting was done single-action.

All of this metal work would be topped off, of course, with a set of handmade custom grips matched to the shooter's hand, often made by Roper or Sanderson or some contemporary of theirs. Today, examples of their fine woodwork are almost collector's items.

A shooter with a custom-built revolver of the sort just described was considered to be equipped to the very best degree possible. Then, as now, such an extensively customized gun would represent an investment of several times the gun's original cost. And then, as now, it wasn't really possible to buy match-winning accuracy. The truly great shooters would win even when equipped with standard guns. On the other hand, even though such customizing might increase a shooter's scores by only two or three points, many handgunners figured those points were worth the cost.

Such customizing of revolvers is no longer common or popular, and the reason may well be that as the efficacy of certain modifications became apparent, manufacturers gradually added them to production-line target revolvers. Better target-type adjustable sights became standard on guns made by both Smith & Wesson and Colt. Smith & Wesson added ribs to the barrels of K-series revolvers early in the game and Colt added ribs after World War II. Wide target-type triggers became standard or extra-cost option items; actions were shortened and hammer spurs changed for easier cocking; and after World War II the manufacturers began to offer target-type stocks. Today a shooter can purchase revolvers that incorporate the majority of the features that were added by customizing the target revolvers of the 1930's.

However, during the early 1970's, police-match shooters began demanding features that weren't available on standard factory guns. Because of the unique nature of police matches, a particular form of customized .38 Special revolver has appeared. It would be difficult to say

Jim Clark is one of the most highly regarded pistolsmiths who specializes in accurizing and customizing handguns for match use. He tests every gun on his machine rest—as he is doing in this photo—and no job leaves his shop until it meets his stringent standard of accuracy.

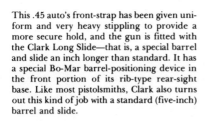

This .45 auto's front-strap has been given uniform and very heavy stippling to provide a more secure hold, and the gun is fitted with the Clark Long Slide—that is, a special barrel and slide an inch longer than standard. It has a special Bo-Mar barrel-positioning device in the front portion of its rib-type rear-sight base. Like most pistolsmiths, Clark also turns out this kind of job with a standard (five-inch) barrel and slide.

whether this gun evolved because of shooter demand or the shooter demand evolved because certain astute pistolsmiths developed the gun.

The "PPC gun" as it has developed to date is a strange-looking but efficient beast. It has the frame and lockwork of a Smith & Wesson K-series revolver more often than not, though the Colt Official Police or Python may be used. The original barrel and sights, sometimes even the cylinder as well, are removed. The barrel is replaced by a massive cylinder of steel measuring as much as a full inch in diameter and six inches in length. It is quite heavy, and frequently more weight is added by a square-section solid steel rib screwed securely to its upper surface.

This rib runs the full length of both frame and cylinder, and normally is very carefully fitted with the best-quality target-type adjustable sights—most often the Bo-Mar or Elliason. Naturally, in the case of the

S&W guns, the forward cylinder lock system is re-installed on the new bull barrel. To achieve the weight and muzzle-heaviness found to be particularly efficient in PPC shooting, some shops also install an "under-rib"—an additional length of steel bar (similar in dimensions to the upper rib) beneath the barrel. To the best of my knowledge, this under-rib was first devised by Jerry Stevens of Nu-Line Guns.

The massive barrel and rib combination places the preponderance of the gun's weight well forward, beyond the trigger finger, and thus tends to dampen jump, or the upward component of recoil. This aids in the most rapid recovery possible during the double-action shooting required in police matches. When the effect of the weight shift is combined with the minimal recoil of the very light-loaded cartridges used, jump becomes insignificant.

In conjunction with the barrel and sight work, the PPC gun's cylinder is very carefully timed, and in some instances chamber throats are reamed to match bore dimensions. And, without question, the PPC gun will have at least a double-action tune-up for the smoothest and lightest possible DA pull. Many shooters and pistolsmiths consider even this insufficient, and employ instead a conversion of the lockwork which eliminates the single-action capability and produces an amazingly smooth, light DA pull. Some pistolsmiths achieve this by removing the SA components of the hammer and very carefully polishing the surfaces and regulating the mainspring tension. Others, such as Fred Sadowski of Denver, modify the lockwork geometry and spring shapes and weights. Maximum efficiency of DA pull is generally achieved with these modifications.

The gun is finished off with a set of stocks designed specifically for double-action shooting. In some instances this requires the cutting away of the lower front corner of the butt frame to allow the shooter's little finger to fall where it feels best. Stocks are also relieved on the left side to facilitate use of one of the various quick-loading devices on the market.

This is the customized revolver of today, with its very specialized mission of producing maximum scores in double-action fire on the PPC silhouette target at ranges of 7, 25 and 50 yards.

The custom-built autoloading pistol began in the 1930's as simply a tightened-up .45 Colt Government Model. By the 1940's, this gun had developed in customized form to the point where it was invariably fitted with a careful trigger job and 4- to 4½-pound trigger pull. The barrel, slide and barrel bushing were very closely fitted together, and fitted equally closely to the frame so that there was the absolute minimum of clearances compatible with reliable functioning. Most of this was accomplished with the original parts by squeezing, bending, reshaping, welding build-up and painstaking handfitting and polishing. One accessory device, developed to improve the .45 auto's accuracy, was Berdon's so-called "mousetrap," a uniquely-shaped wire spring that aided in positioning the breech of the barrel consistently for every shot.

To that was added a set of the best target sights available or, in some instances, a set of much better fixed sights. A pre-war customized .45 auto was then complete in its usual form. The gun produced substantially improved accuracy, but by no means did it approach the results that can be obtained from today's customized .45 autos, which have been much more extensively modified.

To describe today's customized .45 (and .38-caliber conversions) better, I have chosen to use as an example the work of James Clark of Shreveport, Louisiana. Other pistolsmiths perform this type of work, but Jimmy's guns are widely known and he produces them in substantial quantities. (That other makers turn out excellent guns is evident in the fact that their works show up in the winner's circle at matches around the country, but we can't use them all as examples so we'll stick with Clark.)

He begins, of course, with a typical .45 auto, preferably in the best condition possible—and if a marksman wants the very best, the basis should probably be a new commercial gun. First of all, the firing mechanism is gone over completely and the trigger pull is regulated to the customer's specifications. If the gun is to remain in .45 caliber, then the trigger pull will be set at slightly over the weight required by NRA rules for that caliber. On the other hand, the gun may be intended for conversion to .38 Special for use in center-fire matches where a lighter pull is allowable. In that case, naturally, the customer will get the pull set in accordance with the rules and no lower than Clark has determined absolutely safe in the Government Model design. An adjustable trigger-stop will be installed and, if desired, a trigger shoe as well. The mainspring housing of the customer's choice will be installed (flat, arched or any in-between shape) and both it and the front-strap will be roughened for a more secure hold by stippling or checkering, according to the customer's wishes.

The key to accuracy in this design lies in the slide and barrel and their relationship to the frame. Clark begins there with a new commercial slide and a new match-type barrel made oversize in certain areas to permit perfect fitting. The barrel is first fitted to the slide, with the tang or hood fitted closely to eliminate any side-play and allow no fore-and-aft clearance when the locking lugs are fully engaged. The special bushing is handfitted tightly into the slide and with minimum clearance to the barrel. When all is fitted, there is no discernible relative movement between slide and barrel with the locking lugs engaged.

The slide is then fitted to the frame, with the absolute minimum lat-

Customized and Accurized Target Guns

This pistol, originally a .45, has been modified internally to handle the .38 Special mid-range wadcutter load. It has an extra-length barrel and slide, known as the Clark Long Heavy Slide, and is further weighted with a full-length Bo-Mar steel sight rib. All the added weight aids in damping recoil and jump.

eral and vertical clearance compatible with freedom of movement. Final lockup of barrel/slide/frame provides maximum accuracy, and this is obtained by actually altering the method of operation. The barrel link retains its function of unlocking the barrel from the slide during recoil, but the barrel lug is modified so that the barrel is lifted into final locked engagement by the lug camming over the slide-stop pin rather than being raised by the rotating link. This fitting must be done very precisely to produce maximum uniformity of vertical positioning of the barrel breech at the time of firing.

Sights of the customer's choice will then be installed. They may include a rib or an extended front sight mounted on a rail protruding beyond the slide muzzle to achieve the longest allowable sight radius.

Completed guns are thoroughly tested and given whatever additional tuning might be necessary to produce the degree of accuracy that Clark demands of his work. Guns are also tested for functional reliability with match ammunition, an essential factor if the shooter expects to get through a match without alibis.

Essentially the same gun can be produced in .38 caliber by utilizing a different magazine and barrel and such other modifications as are necessary to assure reliable shooting and handling of a standard, factory-loaded .38 Special wadcutter cartridge. The additional parts for this conversion from .45 to .38 are specially made for Clark and have an excellent reputation among shooters. (In fairness, I must repeat here that other pistolsmiths also produce excellent conversions, and I keep referring to Clark's work as an example—but by no means the exclusive example—of the best.)

With regard to .38 Special conversions of the Colt GM pistols, it should be noted that for many years Colt produced its own .38 Special version of the Gold Cup target pistol. It is a measure of the skill and ingenuity of custom pistolsmiths around the country that Colt finally discontinued this model, inasmuch as it was apparently not possible (at least economically) for the gun to be made to perform as well as good custom conversions. Thus we see the modern, customized .45/.38 autoloader emerging as a much more sophisticated gun than those of the early 1930's and 1940's.

Handgun Competition

This is a Ruger Security-Six, Clark-customized for PPC matches. It has a heavy, slab-sided six-inch barrel topped by a Bo-Mar sight rib. Note the protective wings flanking the front sight. The action has been smoothly reworked and a double-action trigger-stop installed. Custom grips have also been installed.

Here's a more usual PPC-match conversion, performed on the S&W K-38 (M14). It has a massive bull barrel, nearly an inch in diameter, topped by the original sights. The gun has been worked over internally to assure the smoothest possible double-action pull. This job was done by Fred Sadowski of the 300 Gunsmith Service in Denver.

In addition to the basic customized target .45/.38, Clark and the other makers routinely supply special variations, one of which is known generally as the "heavy-slide" gun and another as the "long-slide." The former simply adds weight to reduce recoil, while the latter utilizes a specially made slide and barrel one inch longer than the original. It is debatable whether the mechanical accuracy of a six-inch barrel is any better than that of a five-inch barrel, all other factors being equal. Nevertheless, the long-slide gun is highly regarded by top shooters.

It is apparent that the development of the customized .45 target autoloader has been continuous and with the same goal in mind from the beginning; it was conceived to produce better scores on numbered-ring targets over the standard National Match Course, and it remains so. The customized revolver was conceived for the same purpose but discarded as better autoloaders became available. The resumption of revolver customizing in the 1960's was for the purpose of producing maximum scores on silhouette targets (again with numbered scoring areas) mainly in double-action fire. Thus, when the so-called PPC revolvers began development, little use could be made of previous experience obtained with guns intended for bull's-eye shooting. In short, with revolvers, it's a whole new ballgame, while with autos the game has never changed.

All of this is not meant to imply that no other forms of revolver and autoloader customizing are done. Certainly they are, and the methods and goals are as varied as target shooting itself. Within the framework of NRA bull's-eye shooting, there are numerous variations in the customizing of autoloaders.

One that stands out for its sophistication and difference in appearance is the Pachmayr Signature conversion of the .45 auto. It involves

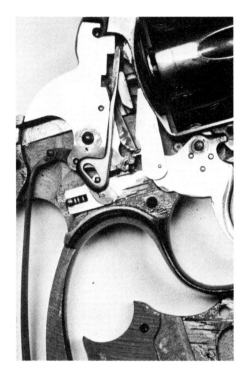

For police matches, a common customizing procedure is to alter a revolver to fire double-action only. This S &W M10 has had its lock-work extensively modified for that purpose by Sadowski. Note the modifications in the geometry of the mainspring, hammer and trigger.

extensive modification of the barrel link, substituting a wide, carefully shaped block of steel positions the barrel vertically by coming to rest solidly against a prepared seat in the frame. The barrel is held in the slide at its muzzle by an unusual hemispherical bushing that rotates in a special housing to permit the angular movement necessary for locking and unlocking. At least theoretically, this permits closer fitting of the barrel than the traditional method employed by Clark and others. Most unusual and most visible in the Pachmayr customizing job is the fitting of a specially shaped steel yoke that wraps around the frame ahead of the trigger guard and exerts upward pressure on the underside of the slide through V-grooves to center the slide laterally and eliminate vertical play with respect to the frame. This yoke can be adjusted in minute amounts to achieve just the desired tightness between slide and frame that is compatible with functional reliability. It is secured by a special replacement slide-stop and pin.

Revolvers, of course, are customized for other purposes, but probably the most common is the fitting of a longer and heavier barrel for long-range shooting as in game-silhouette competition. While this can't be considered a "standard" customizing procedure, several makers fit Ruger single-action .44 Magnum revolvers with a heavy, straight-taper or cylinder bull barrel 10 inches long. The goal differs somewhat from

This relatively low-cost conversion by Sadowski for PPC competition is a heavy-barreled S&W M10, altered to fire double-action only and fitted with Pachmayr Presentation grips and a Bo-Mar rib carrying combat-match sights.

other target customizing in that the additional barrel length is provided so that maximum velocity can be extracted from a given load. The increase in sighting radius is really secondary. And whereas recoil is seldom a problem with the light loads used in bull's-eye shooting, these long-range customizing jobs often include a recoil- and jump-reducing device such as the Mag-Na-Port. The very heavy recoil of the maximum loads used makes the use of a recoil-damper quite desirable.

The average shooter might think that customized guns would seldom be encountered or really needed. However, it must be kept in mind that when factories produce in large quantities they cannot devote time and effort to individual handfitting and testing that is essential for maximum accuracy. Certainly when Smith & Wesson manufactures one of its .38 pistols for target use, that gun is more carefully attended during the various processes than, say, a run-of-the-mill double-action revolver. And this additional attention is reflected in the price. But, just as stock automobiles may be tuned and modified by specialists, so can the average target autoloader or revolver.

Consequently, there are few *serious* target shooters who have not either attempted to improve their scores by using a customized gun or have at least wished they could afford one. Obviously, all of this careful handwork is not to be had cheaply. These days it is not unusual to invest $500 or more in a gun that originally retails for as little as $170. Whether the improvements in accuracy and handling are really worthwhile can only be decided by the individual shooter. When only a couple of points or a couple of extra X's separate you from first place in a prestigious tournament, that slight difference in score might well be considered a bargain even at several times the price.

13
Tuning for Maximum Reliability

The most accurate gun and ammunition in the world cannot produce winning scores unless its functional reliability closely approaches 100 percent. This means the gun, with the chosen ammunition, must perform *unaided* all eight steps of the functioning cycle following each shot, and must continue to do so without cleaning or special attention (except in the case of muzzle-loaders) for a period sufficiently long enough to allow the completion of the longest match likely to be encountered.

The rules for some competitions, particularly the NRA National Match type, allow for a few gun and ammunition failures without necessarily penalizing the shooter. The "alibi rule" specifies that within certain limits a competitor may elect to refire a string of shots that is interrupted by a gun or ammunition malfunction. This is a wise rule, because there are circumstances under which a normally reliable gun or ammunition can fail, circumstances that cannot be predicted accurately and cannot be absolutely eliminated. An example would be the breakage of an extractor or firing pin, or a legitimately defective cartridge that fails to fire. However, at least when I was active in competition, quite a few shooters relied on the alibi rule to compensate somewhat for guns that were not truly reliable. They entered shoots with guns that they *knew* were not capable of working through the match without a malfunction. In some instances this was done in the interest of accuracy. Feeling that a gun set-up unusually tight would be just a tiny bit more accurate, some shooters were willing to accept reduced functional reliability. Then there was also the fact that the highly tuned and modified target guns of 20-odd years ago were not as well developed as those of today, and they often lacked the functional reliability we now demand. And of course, there were shooters whose carelessness reduced the reliability of their guns.

Those shooters banked on their ability to refire any given string of five shots and not produce a lower score. Unfortunately, the pressure of firing an alibi string is greater than that encountered in firing the string originally. I cannot buy the presumption that the alibi rule compensates for reduced functional reliability. Over a period of time or number of matches, I feel certain that a gun of less than ideal reliability will reduce scores.

Reliability of an autoloading pistol, centerfire or rimfire, depends first and foremost upon a specific range of recoil energy being produced by the ammunition. Any gun is designed for proper functioning with ammunition producing recoil energy that falls within minimum and maximum limits. Beneath the minimum, insufficient power is generated to cycle the system, and above the limits, parts are overdriven and both wear and breakage are accelerated. The average gun of a given make and model is intended to function reliably with the average factory-loaded ammunition of the proper caliber. A particular lot of ammunition producing the minimum recoil impulse should cycle the average gun, but may not cycle a gun that is roughly fitted or finished and thus offers more frictional resistance.

During design and development of a gun, the weights of recoiling parts, frictional loads, spring forces, etc., are balanced against the recoil impulse of the cartridge to produce reliable functioning. The parts are fashioned with this in mind if the gun is being designed for an existing cartridge. If a new cartridge or load is being designed for an existing gun, the same effect is accomplished by building into the cartridge the necessary recoil to ensure proper functioning.

Generally speaking, target loads for autoloaders produce somewhat less recoil than standard service ammunition; and guns that have been modified and accurized for target use do not usually have the freedom of parts-movement found in a service gun. Therefore, in target work, the combination of gun and ammunition sets critical limits for reliable functioning.

Tuning a target gun for maximum reliability with a given cartridge and load requires first that the load produce sufficient recoil. For that reason, the standard factory target load must be used as a norm or

Tuning for Maximum Reliability

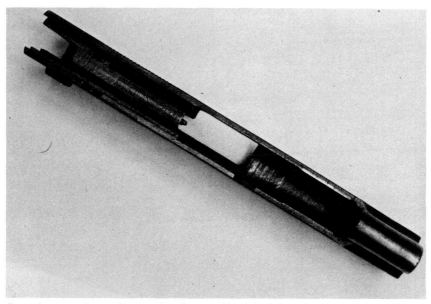

Even when a good magazine is used and ammunition is loaded to the correct recoil impulse, an autoloader is susceptible to functioning problems if the moving parts are impeded by excessive friction. An important place to look for signs of such trouble is the underside of the slide. This bottom view of a slide shows rough machining burrs which increase friction. Behind the firing-pin tip, you can see a long, bright streak, indicating substantial rubbing against the tip of the disconnector and against the top cartridges in the magazine. This area should be polished smooth. In addition, the breech face should be smooth and free of dirt; the extractor claw must be smooth and properly shaped so that it won't dig into the cartridge case and slow it down; and the tension of the extractor spring must not be so heavy that undue energy is needed to push a cartridge up.

point of departure. The only centerfire target loads suitable for auto-loaders are the .38 Special mid-range wadcutter and the .45 ACP loaded with 185-grain semi-wadcutter bullets at reduced velocity. The following discussion is based on the use of those two loads in pistols of typical Colt/Browning design and in the S&W M52. Generally speaking, the problems encountered in obtaining the maximum functional reliability remain the same with other makes and models.

The most common failures involve the feeding, chambering, extraction and ejection stages of the functioning cycle. Feeding depends first on the slide being driven sufficiently rearward for the breech face to pass beyond the rear of the magazine well and allow the top cartridge in the magazine to rise in front of the breech face. Excessive friction among any of the recoiling parts, and between the slide and other parts, can reduce the rearward travel. Friction between the top cartridge and the magazine and the underside of the slide, or between the disconnector and the slide, or excessive cocking force (force which the

This is the underside of a well-tuned Government Model. It has been polished smooth where it rides over the disconnector and top cartridge. To reduce friction still further, a slight bevel has been filed at the bottom of the breech face to assist in camming down the disconnector as the slide moves forward after recoil. The disconnector notch at the rear has also been polished smooth, and so has the portion of the slide and firing-pin stop that ride over the hammer to drive it to full-cock.

slide must impart to the hammer to drive it to full-cock) can also re-duce this rearward travel. An excessively powerful recoil spring, or the spring within a recoil buffer, or difficult extraction can also reduce slide travel. Another common cause is simply the accumulation of dirt and grit between recoiling parts.

If the slide of an autoloader does not travel far enough to the rear to pick up the next cartridge from the magazine, begin by thoroughly cleaning and properly lubricating the gun. If that doesn't do the job, check the chamber for any roughness or hard, rough powder fouling. Anything that roughens the interior of the chamber will increase the force needed to draw out the empty case, and this can slow down the slide. After that, check every recoiling part and every part contacted by a recoiling part for roughness, burrs or other causes of excessive fric-tion. One area often overlooked is the mainspring, particularly in Colt guns. If excessive dirt builds up around the mainspring inside its closed housing, cocking will require more effort, and thus the slide will be slowed down as it forces the hammer back. Roughness inside the hous-ing, where the spring can rub on it, can also cause this sort of problem. The best way to ensure that the mainspring is not at fault is to disas-semble the housing, polish the hole in which the spring rides, then de-burr and clean everything thoroughly before reassembly. Often the cocking force can be reduced by several pounds in this way. Some pis-tolsmiths also shorten the mainspring a bit to reduce cocking effort, but this can lead to misfires and is not recommended.

Of course, smoothing the portion of the hammer face that is ridden over by the slide, as well as that portion of the firing-pin stop and slide which contacts it, will also reduce cocking force. Any contact between

Carefully inspect the lips of every magazine to be used. There must be no burrs or sharp edges to dig into a cartridge case. A bit of filing and polishing here can prevent friction that increases the energy required for feeding and chambering.

the hammer strut and the grip safety or other part also increases cocking force, and should be eliminated. Up front, any kinks in the recoil spring can reduce slide travel by causing additional friction when they rub against the barrel, slide or frame. If a recoil buffer is installed, its spring may be too stiff and thus reduce slide travel a bit.

In any event, assuming you've taken care of all those things so that the slide does move fully to the rear, feeding next depends upon the slide moving *forward* with sufficient force and velocity to strip the top cartridge from the magazine lips. If the lips are of a proper configuration (as they came from the factory) and have been polished free of burrs and roughness (which *usually* exist on new magazines), then relatively little force is required to strip the cartridge. Feed lips should always be carefully checked for these defects, and any that exist should be corrected. The velocity and force with which the slide moves forward is determined primarily by the strength of the recoil spring. A badly deteriorated or bent spring or one that has been reduced in length may not supply sufficient force for proper feeding. Difficulty is occasionally encountered in balancing the spring so that it is not too powerful to permit full rearward recoil travel but powerful enough for smooth feeding on the counter-recoil stroke. This problem can be partially overcome by the use of a recoil buffer; the spring inside the buffer is fully compressed as the slide travels rearward, so it adds its own thrust to that of the recoil spring as the slide starts forward. This spring is compressed only during the last, short portion of slide travel, so it does not interfere with initial rearward slide acceleration. Conse-

By the time the cartridge enters the chamber, it must be fully seated in the slide breech face. To minimize the energy requirement, the extractor should be under just enough pressure to hold the cartridge in position as shown, and the cartridge should move into that position with minimum effort.

quently, the two springs together provide greater initial forward slide acceleration than the recoil spring alone, thus making more energy available for feeding. Often this can make the difference between mediocre and perfect feeding.

As the cartridge is driven forward, it soon pops up out of the feed lips and passes vertically across the slide breech face, moving under the extractor at the same time. Any burrs or roughness that impede this travel help reduce slide velocity and energy and have an obvious effect on feeding reliability. Burrs may be found on the underside of the extractor claw; when present, they tend to dig into the cartridge case and prevent its proper alignment. Careful use of stones and needle files eliminates this problem. An excessively strong extractor spring can have somewhat the same effect. Roughness on the slide breech face can also impede cartridge travel and reduce slide velocity. Careful polishing of the breech face, with particular attention to any burred areas around the firing-pin hole, reduces this problem. When everything about the extractor and slide breech face is right, you should be able to press a cartridge upward, under the extractor and into position with the primer centered over the firing-pin hole, without any undue effort; yet the extractor should be snug enough against the case to hold it in that position. In other words, when you push a loaded cartridge up across the breech face and under the extractor, the cartridge should remain in that position without additional support when the slide is held horizontally.

After being stripped from the feed lips, the cartridge will strike the feed ramp. In .45 caliber, the bullet nose, at approximately 6 o'clock,

Tuning for Maximum Reliability

As the cartridge moves foreward, its nose strikes the feed ramp. A one-piece ramp is used in the Browning (right) and S&W pistols. This design interferes least with smooth passage into the chamber. The edges of the chamber mouth at left are square and sharp—untuned, so to speak. On the center barrel, the lower half of the chamber mouth has been radiused to remove the sharp shoulder. On the one at right, the entire mouth area has been radiused and polished. Radiusing improves feeding by eliminating the possibility that a case mouth or bullet will snag on an edge. This tuning refinement and the others described in this chapter aren't generally needed in service pistols (or they would be factory-provided) but target loads can make them quite important.

will strike the ramp somewhat below the chamber mouth and be deflected upward. The amount of this deflection may range from just enough for the bullet nose to enter the chamber, up to the point where the bullet nose actually strikes the underside of the barrel tang or the 12 o'clock portion of the chamber wall. If there is excessive roughness on the feed ramp or a perceptible gap or overlap between the two portions of the ramp, the nose of the bullet may be caught momentarily, reducing slide velocity to the point that insufficient energy remains to chamber the cartridge fully. Careful polishing of the feed ramp and elimination of any gaps or overhangs or sharp edges will eliminate this problem—though great care should be taken to see that no significant changes in ramp shape or angle are caused. Rough ramps and other

Handgun Competition

The Colt-type feed ramp has two parts—the top portion cut in the barrel, the lower portion in the frame. Any irregularity between the two parts can rob energy from the moving slide and reduce the certainty that the gun will go fully into battery. Or worse, it can snag a bullet nose. At right is a typical feed ramp, just as it came from the factory. At left is a modified ramp, smoothed and widened, and with the chamber mouth radiused, all to increase feeding reliability.

defects in this area are much more likely to cause trouble with lead bullets than jacketed ones, and with light loads than full charges.

Individual guns will vary a good deal in the amount the cartridge is deflected upward by its initial impact against the feed ramp. If the amount is slight, as the cartridge enters the chamber it may scrape heavily across the sharp-angled transition from feed ramp to chamber wall. This is especially true if there is roughness in the extractor or slide breech face which retards upward movement of the case head. In new guns, this transition is usually sharp, sometimes even possessing a slight "wire edge." Careful polishing, just enough to break the sharp edge and lightly radius the transition without removing any significant amount of metal, will eliminate the problem. Longitudinal scratch marks on the case from about 4 o'clock to 8 o'clock, ending abruptly along a curved line, are a sure indication of this problem.

If the nose of the cartridge is deflected too high, it may hang momentarily on the underside of the barrel tang or chamber wall, causing the slide to push the head of the cartridge *down* and jamming it solidly. Again, this is often caused at least partially by roughness in the slide breech face or too much extractor tension. The head of the case must move up smoothly and quickly under the extractor so that the case head is not pushed downward as the bullet nose hangs up. Aside from that, smoothing the underside of the barrel tang will help. However, when some guns display this particular malfunction, nothing less than a change in bullet shape or overall cartridge length will cure the problem. Fortunately, there are variations from make to make in .45-caliber bullet shapes, and there is sure to be one that will work in any given gun.

Assuming that the cartridge has at least begun to enter the chamber and is thus being driven forward by the slide, the case may still scrape against the sharp edges of the chamber mouth. This usually isn't serious, though it can slow down the slide enough to prevent its going fully into battery. This problem is solved by careful polishing and slight radiusing of the right and left edges (between feed ramp and tang). It is more often encountered with high-performance loads than with factory-loaded target ammunition.

Once the cartridge is aligned with the chamber and entering smoothly and is still being driven forward by the slide, there should be no further chambering or locking problems—unless the actions to this point have slowed down the slide so much that it lacks sufficient momentum to lock up fully in battery. If the gun is new it may have been fitted up just a little bit too tightly in the locking area, in anticipation that the first few hundred rounds fired will "break in" all of the related surfaces, after which functioning will be better. If your gun almost locks up properly—only about $^1/_{16}$-inch or less from full battery position—yet the slide feels as if it is wedged solidly shut, then this is probably the only trouble.

The simplest way I know to correct this is to drive the slide the rest of the way into battery with either the heel of your hand or a small rubber mallet. Then fire the cartridge. Do this with every shot as long as the slide keeps stopping slightly out of battery and you'll note that after 50 rounds or so it begins to approach full battery position after firing. Once broken in a bit more, it will lock up fully into battery without any difficulty. If this sounds like a crude way to correct the condition, just remember that the only alternative is to start filing and grinding those surfaces critical to final lockup—and if you do that, you are likely to take off too much metal and destroy some of the accuracy that the pistolsmith went to such pains to build into the gun.

Extraction and ejection remain to be checked. This is best done with a single round in the chamber and an empty magazine in place. Fire the gun and note whether or not the empty case flies clear of the gun. Normally it will, but if it does not, note also whether the slide-stop engages and holds the slide to the rear. If not, obviously the problem is that the slide is not moving sufficiently far to the rear. That leads right back to the first point of this discussion—the methods of assuring complete rearward slide travel. A gun that extracts and ejects perfectly when clean but does not when dirty will often have some roughness in the chamber. This may be the result of etching or pitting, or it may be built-up powder fouling. Light etching or rust-pitting can be polished out, and hard powder fouling can be removed with fine steel wool wrapped around a dowel or rod spun at low speed in a portable electric drill.

Occasionally, extraction is correct and slide travel complete, yet the case is not ejected. This can be due to a broken or too-short ejector, but these are not likely occurrences. It can also be due to a broken or missing firing-pin spring or a bent firing pin, either of which will allow the firing-pin nose to remain imbedded in the primer as the gun unlocks. The pin nose then shears through the primer as the barrel moves downward in unlocking, jamming the case tightly in the slide breech face. Burrs around the firing-pin hole can also cause this, and the appropriate corrective action is obvious.

Probably the most common failure during extraction and ejection is the well-known "smoke-stack" fired case, jammed mouth-up between the slide breech and the barrel tang. This is caused by only partial ejection, the slide carrying the fired case back only to the point where it is barely touched by the ejector. With such light contact, the ejector simply rotates the case slightly, without enough force to pivot it about and clear of the gun. The result is that the slide moves forward, still carrying the tipped case, and jams it against the barrel. Though often not recognized as such, this is the result of insufficient rearward slide travel, and should be treated accordingly.

That just about covers the feeding, chambering, extraction, and ejection problems that are most common. However, malfunctions do occur in other areas of the gun. One that is encountered with fair frequency in highly tuned target guns is that of "hammer follow-down." This becomes evident when, after a shot is fired, you note that pressure on the trigger will not fire a second shot and that the hammer has not remained at full-cock but is resting on the safety notch or in the fully down position. This may also be accompanied by the unintentional firing of one or more subsequent shots, like a machine gun. When the latter occurs it is known as "doubling," even though more than two shots may be fired. Doubling can be especially dangerous since it catches the shooter totally unprepared and can cause loss of control of the gun before firing ceases.

Follow-down or doubling may be caused by insufficient sear engagement or incorrect sear angles. This may be the result of incorrect original fitting (more or less likely if a shooter has been working over the trigger pull himself). It may also be caused by a sear nose or full-cock notch surface that has been badly worn or chipped. In either case, the sear nose initially catches the full-cock notch and holds the hammer back as the slide goes forward. However, the hammer is held back only by the slightest margin, and when the slide slams fully into battery the jar and vibration of the impact causes the hammer to override the sear nose and fall. As it falls, the hammer *might* be caught by the safety notch engaging the sear, or it might continue all the way down to strike the firing pin and *sometimes* fire the cartridge in the chamber. The intercept notch is intended to catch the hammer before it can strike the firing pin, but it may not do so if the sear nose is badly chipped or worn.

Correction of either of these conditions falls within the domain of the expert pistolsmith, and as a rule it should not be attempted by the home gun tinkerer. If the job must be done at home, the only practical and safe approach is the installation of brand-new hammer and sear, or the same parts fully reconditioned by a competent pistolsmith.

The condition of insufficient sear engagement or incorrect sear angle is generally produced by inexperienced attempts to regulate the trigger pull. This is a very meticulous job and not to be attempted by the average gun tinkerer. This type of work is covered in the chapter on accurizing, and should be attempted only under the conditions described there.

One other malfunction sometimes affects the use of a target gun. Occasionally the slide-stop may fail to engage and hold the slide rearward after the last shot has been fired from the magazine. This really doesn't present a serious hazard to one's scores but it can be irritating; its major disadvantage is that the range officer sees your gun still in battery and assumes that you have not completed firing. This misunderstanding is easily corrected, but if the gun were functioning correctly it would never arise.

Functioning of the slide-stop depends first upon the magazine follower and spring forcing it upward, and second upon the slide moving sufficiently rearward that the lug on the stop can engage the appropriate cut in the slide. It is possible that the slide is traveling rearward sufficiently to produce proper feeding, chambering, extraction and ejection, but not quite far enough to be caught solidly by the slide-stop. The solution is, of course, either to extend slide travel a bit rearward or else cut forward the engaging surface of the slide-stop sufficiently to compensate for the reduced slide travel. A second cause of this problem is a bent magazine follower that fails to elevate the slide-stop sufficiently; this may or may not be accompanied by a magazine spring too weak to overcome the spring-plunger slide-stop detent and move the stop upward. Straightening or replacing the follower solves the first problem; replacing the magazine spring and/or freeing up slide-stop movement solves the second.

Of course, other mechanical malfunctions, breakages and failures of one sort or another may occur occasionally in any handgun that is used extensively. But a gun of target quality will not normally display those other malfunctions unless abused or very heavily used. The problems and corrections described above are those most commonly encountered and thus the ones that deserve special attention in ensuring that you will have 100 percent functional reliability during any match. This is exclusive of problems that might be generated by the use of hand-loaded ammunition (or the wrong factory loads). Ammunition problems are discussed in the chapter on handloading.

14

Accurizing Autoloaders at Home

Almost every pistolero eventually decides that he ought to be able to improve the accuracy of some old clunker .45 auto. Probably more guns have been ruined by such impulses than have ever been improved, but many a Government Model pistol has had its group size halved or quartered by the patient, careful ministrations of an owner working only with hand tools in his spare time. There isn't really a great deal the average shooter can do to a revolver to increase its accuracy, nor can he harbor much hope that he will be able to improve a reasonably good .22 rimfire auto. But when it comes to the .45 autoloader, almost anyone can successfully complete a fair number of operations that will improve performance.

It's sometimes difficult to decide just where to start, but I think it's safest to break the various jobs down into two categories—those that will improve the mechanical accuracy of the gun itself and those that will improve the shooter's performance by helping him to use that mechanical accuracy fully. Changes in sights and trigger pull are examples of the second category, while careful fitting of barrel and slide are examples of the first.

Even an ordinary military-contract pistol can be sufficiently improved for match shooting by accurizing procedures performed in a home workshop. Slow, careful work and attention to detail can result in targets like this one, showing a score of 99-6X.

It almost goes without saying that one should begin with a reasonably good gun. While it's certainly possible to improve a battered derelict, a great deal of time and effort will be saved by starting with a serviceable gun. An acquaintance of mine once chose the doggiest-looking .45 auto he could find—it looked like it had been rusting away underwater while serving as a trot-line weight—and he tuned it to maximum accuracy without changing its external appearance. He won a lot of range bets with that old gun, but the average tinkerer is neither as skillful, nor as sneaky as that fellow was.

No great supply of tools and equipment is needed to do a pretty fair job of accurizing a serviceable .45 auto. You'll need a small assortment of needle files, a couple of larger fine-cut flat files, a small machinist's hammer, abrasive cloths in assorted grits, low-temperature silver solder

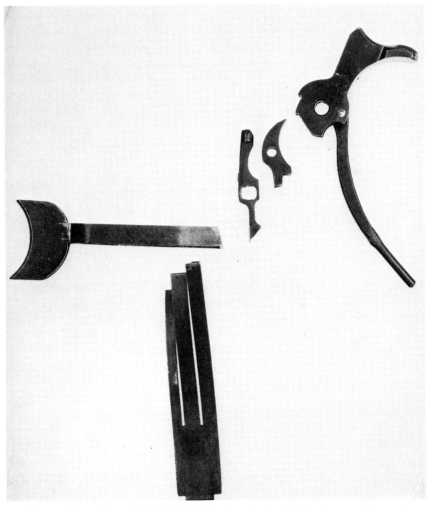

All of the small internal parts should be checked closely and rejected if they show excessive wear, burrs or pitting. Pay special attention to the sear spring, noting whether it has been bent in a previous effort to improve trigger pull or functioning.

Match up the stipped slide and frame—after making sure the grooves are thoroughly clean—and note how much looseness exists. As a rule, the fit will be quite loose.

and steel shim stock, a good propane torch, assorted hard Arkansas stones, cleaning and preserving materials and molybdenum-disulphide lubricant, some machinist's blue (candle soot will substitute), a center-punch and a few pin punches, and (not absolutely necessary) an electric hand-grinder such as the Dremel Moto-Tool. For many operations, parts of the gun must be held rigidly, so you'll also need a sturdy bench vise with padding for the jaws and a bench or stout table to which it can be bolted solidly. You may find you need a few other odds and ends as a job progresses, but I suspect they will be items already on hand or available cheaply at the nearest discount store.

You'll probably be working with a used gun. Begin by stripping it completely—removing every part from its neighbor—and laying all the parts out where they can be examined closely. Scrub all parts thoroughly, removing any oxidized grease and oil, dirt, old rust, etc., and check them closely for wear, damage, or abuse. For example, a sear spring that shows evidence of having been bent or rebent in the past is best discarded and replaced. An extractor with a worn hook or little spring left in its shank should also be replaced, and a bent firing pin is certainly anathema. Unless the barrel is in new condition, it should be set aside and a replacement obtained—of the best quality you can afford. The old barrel may serve quite well in another gun for plinking, but unless its interior appears virgin, it seems a waste of effort to attempt including it in an accurizing job. Probe all the recesses of the slide and frame, using small brass or plastic scrapers and worn-out bore brushes, if necessary, to make certain all foreign material is removed. It would be foolish to install a new, smoothly polished disconnector if its seat is half-clogged with oxidized oil and rust.

Ideally, circumstances and finances permitting, you should obtain a brand new match-grade barrel with its own fitted bushing. This will represent the major expense—it can easily cost $40 to $50. I've had excellent results with Bar-Sto stainless-steel barrels with collet-type bushings, and they fall in that price range. They are made with excess metal in certain areas to permit precise fitting. At the other end of the scale, you may simply obtain a new military-type barrel and bushing at about a third of that cost, but more work in fitting will be required. A plain-steel match barrel and bushing will fall about midway between those two extremes of cost.

While waiting for the new barrel to arrive, you can fit the slide to the frame. Place the slide on the frame and notice how loosely it fits. You can probably wobble it a significant amount from side to side, top to bottom, and even angularly. This is because the matching grooves and tenons that hold the slide to the frame are loosely fitted. Looseness isn't necessarily bad in a service gun, for it contributes to the .45 auto's great

Using protective jaws or wood blocks, clamp the stripped frame tightly in a vise. It's a good idea to add wood blocks underneath in order to support it vertically.

reputation for reliability under severe conditions (some looseness being necessary if a slide is to ride over mud, jungle foliage or desert sand that can easily infiltrate the works). However, any play between slide and frame is transmitted to the barrel and will reduce accuracy because it allows the barrel to be positioned slightly differently for each shot. The grooves in the frame can be vertically narrowed somewhat by peening, thus limiting vertical play of the slide. At the same time, the lower portion of the slide can be squeezed together, eliminating sideward play.

Begin on the frame. Clamp it tightly in a sturdy vise, using shaped wood blocks to help hold the frame without distorting it, and keeping the upper surface level. If a suitable measuring instrument is available (I use a dial-indicator vernier caliper) measure the width of the grooves in the frame and record that dimension. Take your machinist's hammer and carefully but firmly peen the top of the frame on both sides the full length of the groove. Space the blows uniformly, each overlapping the previous one by about half, and don't strike more in one area than another. The blows must be firm, but not so stiff that they form significant dents. After once up and back on each side, again measure the groove width. If there is no measurable decrease, you aren't strik-

You can avoid removing the stock-screw bushings by drilling clearance holes for them in the protective vise jaws.

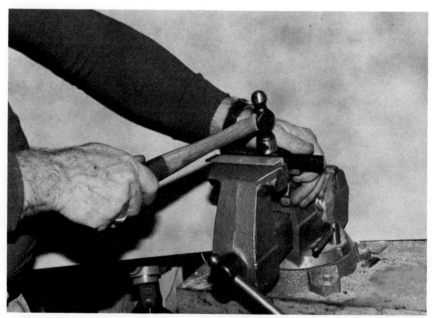

Carefully peen the upper surface of the guide ribs, reducing their width and the width of the grooves underneath.

ing the metal quite hard enough. Once you've produced a measurable narrowing of the groove, you'll notice that a slight increase in width has also been produced as the metal peens outward under the hammer blows. This occurs only at the upper edge of the frame, so doesn't really have any effect. Carefully file off any burrs produced in this manner, then slip the slide onto the frame. Move it fore and aft a few times to get the feel. You should be able to notice less vertical play than before the peening. Remove the slide and continue peening the top of the frame until it takes substantial effort to force the slide onto the frame. In fact, at this point, you'll find a rawhide or plastic mallet necessary to drive the slide on. Make certain that this new tightness is not resulting from burrs on the upper edge of the frame; keep them cleaned off so that any tightness you feel is definitely produced by narrowing of the guide grooves.

Once you've eliminated vertical looseness in the slide by peening the frame, it's time to squeeze the slide in a bit to take up lateral play. This requires a sturdy vise with clean, smooth jaws that are reasonably parallel. Carefully position the slide in the jaws, only to the depth of the top of the groove in which the rib on the frame rides. Make certain the upper edges of the vise jaws are parallel with this groove. Apply pressure carefully until you can *feel* the lower edges of the slide being squeezed very slightly together. Don't overdo it or you may crack something. Once this first slight yielding is felt, try the slide on the frame. You should note some reduction in lateral play. Squeeze it in a bit more until the slide is quite tight on the frame and requires vigorous assistance from the mallet to move through its full travel.

At this point, coat the sliding surfaces with machinist's blue and then drive the slide fore and aft. Remove the slide and note the high points on the receiver, which will show where the blue is wiped off. These high points can be stoned down lightly or they can be worn down by simply driving the slide back and forth a few dozen times with light oil between it and the frame. Don't, at this time, attempt to obtain a free-running fit. That comes later as the barrel is fitted.

For the time being, you can now forget about slide-to-frame fit and concentrate on installing the barrel properly. Let's assume you've bought a new match-type barrel and bushing. The bushing should already be closely fitted to the barrel muzzle, so begin by trying the bushing in the slide. It should be quite tight—so tight, in fact, that you'll need a bushing wrench to rotate it into the firing position. If the bushing seems reluctant to enter the slide at all, polish out the burrs in the bushing seat, then tap the bushing into place with a soft hammer and rotate it into firing position with the wrench. Do *not* attempt to make this a loose fit in the interest of easy disassembly. The bushing should

Align the slide so that the vise jaws don't extend above the upper edge of the guide groove. With the vise handle, apply pressure smoothly, firmly and cautiously, alternately squeezing the slide and trying it on the frame until lateral looseness has been substantially eliminated.

be quite tight in the slide, and it can be "worn in" to this point by simply rotating it back and forth a few times with the wrench.

Remove the bushing from the slide, insert the barrel and re-install the bushing over the barrel. Push the breech of the barrel upward and rearward toward the locked position; the oversized barrel tang will *probably* prevent the barrel from seating. The tang on most match barrels is made oversized to allow careful handfitting to the slide at this point. If necessary, very carefully file the sides of the tang so that it can enter the slot above the breech face. Don't overdo this, for proper side-to-side fit is essential to correct barrel positioning. When this is done, file the rear face of the tang until the barrel can just barely be forced into engagement with the locking ribs in the slide. The rear face of the tang should bear hard against the breech face with the locking ribs engaged. Break the edges of all the filed surfaces to a very slight bevel, and then you can consider fitting the slide-and-barrel unit to the frame.

The barrel should have been supplied with a link and link pin, and this is the link to be used in trial assembly. Note first whether the existing slide-stop pin will pass freely through the bottom hole in the link;

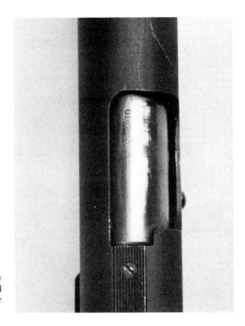

With the locking ribs on the barrel properly engaged in the roof of the slide, the barrel tang should fit quite closely in the slide breech.

it may be a bit loose. Also check the fit of the stop pin in the holes in the frame. If there is any looseness here, it will be wise to have the stop pin built up by hard chrome plating, then very carefully reaming or polishing the holes to a close fit on the pin. If you have access to a supply of low-cost, military-surplus .45 auto parts, you might be able to sort through slide-stops and obtain one with a slightly larger-diameter pin, which will eliminate the need for building up the original. Consistent shot-to-shot positioning of the barrel depends to some extent on very close fit of the pin in both frame and barrel link. With that taken care of, assemble the barrel-and-slide unit to the stripped frame and insert the slide-stop.

The slide is still tight on the frame, so urge it forward, using the mallet if necessary, until it is halted by the barrel. At this point, note carefully whether the barrel is fully up and engaged with the locking lugs in the slide, and also whether the rear of the slide is flush with the rear of the frame. You may find that the slide is halted slightly out of battery and the locking lugs are not fully engaged. If this occurs, it will be because the barrel tang is still just a tiny bit long. To correct the condition, use machinist's blue or soot on the rear of the tang to mark the high spots, then very carefully dress it down until the slide can be urged fully into battery with a modest rap of your plastic mallet.

It is time now to determine how deeply or fully the locking ribs on the barrel engage their corresponding recesses in the slide roof. Re-

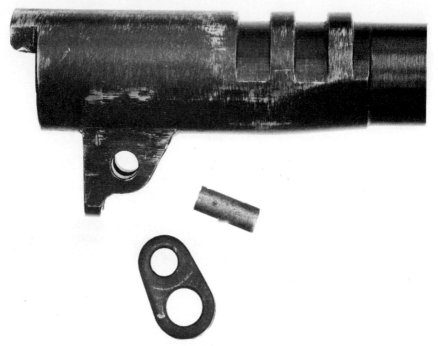

A match barrel will normally come with a new link and pin, but if a standard barrel is being used, a long link and new pin should be purchased.

move the barrel and coat this area with machinist's blue or soot; then put it back on and urge the slide fully into battery. Remove the barrel and check the front face of the locking ribs. The depth to which the coating has been removed represents the depth to which they engage the slide. Theoretically, full-depth engagement is best, but anything over 50 percent is acceptable. Also check to determine whether bearing and engagement are uniform from side to side. If one side bears and the other does not, very carefully trim the high part of the barrel lug until engagement is uniform all the way across.

If engagement is not sufficient, fit a longer barrel link—that is, a link with greater distance between the centers of its two holes. Links are available in several lengths, and it's best to be prepared for the job by buying a set of three. Greater depth of engagement is produced by installing a longer link; however, this may also require refitting of the rear of the barrel tang.

Now it's time to work in the tightly-fitted parts. Reassemble the slide and barrel to the frame with the recoil spring and its related parts in their places. Then, by hand, draw the slide fully to the rear and let it

Accurizing Autoloaders at Home

A standard military or commerical barrel bushing can be made to fit much more tightly in the slide by dimpling its outer surface, as shown. This can be done with a sharp center punch. It won't last as long as a new match bushing, but it's a great improvement over the original loose fit.

run forward—if the recoil spring is strong enough to overcome the tightness. If it won't run forward, urge it on with the plastic mallet. Draw it all the way back and repeat. Keep this up until the recoil spring will drive the slide into battery, or at least very nearly so, every time. If the spring drives the slide to within $^1/_{32}$-inch or so of full lock-up, that's good enough at this point.

It's possible to go ahead with the rest of the work before test-firing, but I prefer to fully assemble the gun at this time and test-fire it with 50 to 100 *ball* cartridges. Before doing so, though, you should clean all of the oil, grit and metal chips off the mating surfaces of slide and frame; then apply molybdenum-disulphide grease, sparingly but uniformly, over those entire surfaces. Reassemble the entire gun and retire to the range with ball ammunition. Be sure to take along tools, especially the plastic mallet. Load up and fire. After the first rounds, the slide should be cycling normally without assistance. Head back for home, completely disassemble the gun, clean it thoroughly, and proceed with the rest of the operations.

However, you may have elected to go the cheaper route and use a new military or commercial barrel and bushing. In this instance, the bushing will be a much looser fit in the slide, probably so loose that it requires tightening. It will also be loose enough on the barrel to require tightening there if really first-class accuracy is to be obtained. These problems can be handled, but you'll be better off to obtain a so-called "tight bushing" from Micro or one of the other suppliers. However, to use the issue bushing, first make it tight in the slide by slipping it over a piece of steel rod clamped tightly in the vise, then dimpling the entire

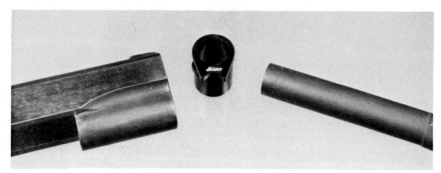

The best (and longest-lasting) solution to the bushing problem is to buy a new match-quality bushing such as the one pictured here, made by Micro.

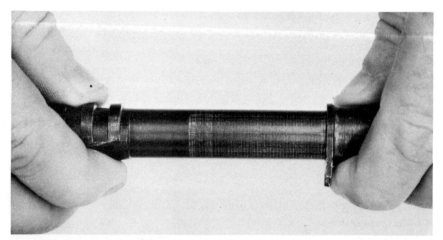

The tight bushing should be carefully fitted to the barrel muzzle, preferably by lapping.

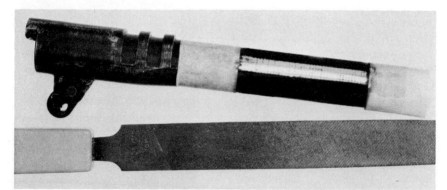

Though the bushing has to fit snugly at the muzzle, clearance must be provided rearward to allow the bushing to pass freely over the barrel during functioning. Ideally, this is done by grinding part of the barrel to a smaller diameter. However, you can accomplish the same result at home by careful filing (after masking the muzzle area) and then polishing the filed surface with strips of abrasive cloth.

slide-engaging surface with a center-punch. Do this uniformly all over the surface, setting the punch against the bushing and rapping it smartly with a hammer to raise burrs deliberately. These burrs increase the effective diameter of the bushing and make it a tight fit in the slide. Once they've been raised, force the bushing into the slide and work it around as before until it can be removed with a bushing wrench but remains quite tight.

The tight fit obtained in this way will not last nearly as long as if an oversized bushing is used; the dimples occupy only a small portion of the bushing surface and they will wear down rather rapidly. The interior of the bushing may also be tightened upon the barrel by careful dimpling, but you'll be better advised to take the barrel to a plating shop and have the first ¼-inch of the muzzle built up with hardchrome plate about .003- to .005-inch. Make certain that the plater doesn't allow any of the chrome to get on the inside of the bore and that he fully understands that *only* the first ¼-inch of the exterior is to be built up.

This should make the muzzle oversized for the bushing, so it must now be lapped to fit. This is best done in a drill press, holding the bushing in a vise on the press table and guiding the barrel by a mandrel in the chuck. The barrel muzzle is coated with oil and fine abrasive, and the barrel is slipped up over the mandrel, then lowered into the bushing by lowering the spindle. Power *must not* be used, the barrel being rotated in the bushing simply by hand rotation of the press chuck while light downward pressure is maintained. This is a slow, tedious process, but it produces an excellent fit of the barrel in the bushing. Continue the lapping process until the barrel protrudes through the bushing. Clean off all the abrasive and the two parts are ready for fitting to the slide.

If you can afford to use the tight Micro bushing, you'll save all that punch work and also the plating operation. First the tight bushing must be fitted to the slide. It will be substantially oversized, and you may have to lightly file or polish its outer surface before it can be forced into the slide and rotated (as already described). I prefer to dress it down to the point where it can be seated to full depth by only moderate raps of a plastic hammer, yet remain tight enough so that it can just barely be rotated by a bushing wrench. Removal can be a little difficult with it in this condition, but that's the price willingly paid for a tight fit. The internal bushing diameter will be too small to allow the barrel to enter. However, before fitting the barrel to it, mask off the barrel and reduce its diameter about .010-inch by careful filing from the front locking lug forward to the masked area.

Once the muzzle is fitted tightly to the bushing, additional clearance is required rearward of that point so the bushing can pass freely over

Handgun Competition

On a standard barrel, the tang will probably fit loosely in the slide. The only way to correct this is to have the edges of the tang carefully welded up, then dressed back down to the proper profile and a close fit. This barrel is missing a locking lug, having been shortened for use in a combat conversion of the GM. Its tang and lug have been built up by welding but not yet dressed down.

the barrel for normal functioning. After the overlapping file cuts, polish the reduced portion bootblack-fashion with strips of abrasive cloth to produce a smoothly rounded surface. Measure the inside diameter of the bushing and the outside diameter of the barrel muzzle; if there is more than about .005-inch difference, obtain a simple expansion reamer and carefully open up the inside diameter of the bushing until it is only .003-.005 inch smaller than the barrel. Then proceed to lap the barrel muzzle into the bushing as already described.

Now the rear of the barrel must be fitted to the slide as described for a match barrel; however, there is no excess material on the tang to permit this. Production replacement barrels are made small enough in this area to fit any slide on any gun, and thus cannot fit tightly enough in this area to provide best accuracy. The only way to provide the tight fit is to first have the sides and rear of the tang built up slightly by welding, then file to fit. This is not a casual welding job that can be done by the local farm-machinery mechanic. It requires a light touch with a small torch, and really should be done by a first-class heli-arc welder. After the weld has been applied, most of it can be filed off, gauging by eye the amount that must be left to allow fitting the tang tightly to the slide. After that, the procedure is exactly as already described.

As an alternative—in the event you simply can't obtain the quality of welding needed—*steel* shim stock can be silver-soldered to the rear and sides of the tang. Use feeler gauges between slide and barrel to determine the amount of build-up needed; then cut small pieces of steel shim of slightly greater thickness and very carefully silver-solder them in place. Afterwards, the fitting procedure is as described above, and the balance of the barrel-fitting operation remains exactly the same as described for a match barrel.

At this point, you've probably decided that the use of the standard replacement barrel is more trouble than it's really worth. I'm inclined to agree because the time, effort, and expense involved in welding, plating and fitting the bushing more than make up for the greater cost

Accurizing Autoloaders at Home

At left is a standard barrel. At right is a barrel with the tang and lug welded up and then filed to approximately correct dimensions, prior to final fitting.

This accessory, known as a group-gripper, is easily installed and—as explained in the text—probably achieves greater accuracy improvement for its cost than any other.

of a match barrel-and-bushing set. This isn't to say you can't produce a first-class job with a standard barrel, but it involves so much effort and cost that you're really better off beginning with a plain-steel match barrel or, at somewhat greater cost, a Bar-Sto stainless-steel barrel with its very fine collet-type bushing.

However, there is yet another alternative that involves a standard barrel. First a tight bushing must be fitted, after which two bolt-on accessories can be used to insure precise barrel positioning without welding and handfitting. The first item to be installed is known as a "group-gripper," and it replaces the standard barrel link and recoil-spring guide. A stout leaf spring is fitted into the new guide—the group-gripper—and it bears upward on a lug formed as part of a special link. Thus, when the gun is in battery, there is considerable pressure on the link, insuring that the barrel is forced into full contact with the slide and that its vertical position is consistent from shot to shot. Of all accuracy-raising accessories available for the GM pistol, I consider the group-gripper the most productive.

A barrel-positioning accessory that substantially improves accuracy is the Bo-Mar Accuracy Block. It can be obtained as part of a full length sight rib, as shown, or as part of a shorter rear-sight base. The block fits inside a recess in the rib or base and is adjustable vertically, forming a positive stop to upward movement of the rear of the barrel. This ensures uniform vertical positioning from shot to shot. Often, the use of a long link is required in conjunction with this device. The block is easily installed, necessitating only the drilling and tapping of holes in the top of the slide.

The second device, intended to serve the same purpose as the group-gripper, is known as an "accuracy block." Manufactured by Bo-Mar, it's a rectangular block that is screwed to the top of the slide; it has a short leg which protrudes downward into the barrel-tang recess, where its position is regulated by attaching screws to provide a positive stop to upward barrel travel as the gun goes into battery. Even when the group-gripper is used, the addition of this positive stop improves the consistency of barrel position, because the locking lugs themselves really do not provide quite so positive a limit to upward travel. With the accuracy block in place, the spring of the group-gripper works in opposition to the block, insuring absolute uniformity of vertical barrel position.

Installation of the accuracy block requires only that two holes be drilled and tapped in the top of the slide (behind the ejection port) to accept the installation screws. The block should be clamped into position, then a hole-fitting center-punch used to mark the location of the screw holes on the slide. After that, simply drill and tap the holes, deburr them and attach the block.

Another method of positioning the barrel breech vertically is often used by custom pistolsmiths. It consists essentially of building up and reshaping the underside of the barrel lug so that it cams off the upper rear portion of the slide-stop pin. This takes the locking load off the barrel link and pin, substituting a much larger surface. Some custom barrels are made with excess metal on the barrel lug to allow this sort of fitting. But if the job is to be done on an ordinary barrel, the first step is to have the lug welded up carefully. Excess weld is then filed out of the slot so that the link can move freely. The sides of the weld are filed down toward the original lug surfaces, but the weld may be left a bit wider for a close fit in the frame recess.

Then the front of the welded area is carefully filed and ground so that the S-curve will ride up over the slide-stop pin as the slide moves into battery. This will require much slow, careful fitting—with many trial assemblies. Ideally, the lug should ride smoothly up over the pin, forcing the barrel to the top of the slide as far as it can go; then, with the slide in battery, the lower portion of the curved lug surface will bear down on the pin, wedging the barrel tightly into the slide roof. Of course, the rubbing surfaces must be polished quite smooth, and lubricated with M-D. This system requires that the barrel link be fitted rather loosely, for now it serves only to pull the barrel down and unlock it. If fitted tightly, it might oppose the camming action of the reshaped barrel lug and cause jamming or excessive wear.

That's about all you can do to improve the fit of barrel/slide/frame. The points covered are those which are most important to the purely mechanical accuracy of the pistol. A gun properly prepared, as described to this point, will shoot just as well from a machine rest as one that has all the other refinements we'll mention later. From this point onward, any modifications are intended primarily to improve functional reliability with light target loads and—by improving such details as sights and trigger pull—to enable the shooter to better take advantage of the mechanical accuracy.

Sights are an excellent place to start. The issue sights of both military and commercial versions of the GM pistol leave a great deal to be desired. While it is possible to shoot first-class scores with fixed sights of the proper design, the initial targeting of them can be a terrible chore,

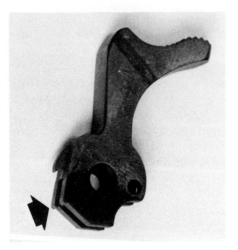

If the hammer's sear notch (full-cock notch) is no more than .040-inch deep, sear engagement can be reduced by stoning at the front of the notch. In an unusually deep notch, however, this will allow the sear nose to be struck by the lip of the intercept notch as the hammer falls, resulting in damage to the sear. One way to reduce sear engagement with a deep notch is to insert a pin and dress it back until proper engagement (no less than .020-inch) is obtained. For shooters not equipped to do the rather difficult drilling job, a simpler method is to soft-solder shim stock at the rear of the sear notch and dress it down to obtain proper engagement.

and thereafter the shooter is limited to a single load unless he wishes to employ Kentucky windage and Tennessee elevation.

Traditionally the GM pistol has been prepared for target work by fitting a sophisticated, micrometer-adjustable rear sight to the slide, along with a matching blade or ramp-and-blade front sight. These sights are not terribly expensive; a good set is available for about $20 to $25. However, installation cost can easily run this up to more than $50. As explained in the chapter on sights and sight installation, the job can be accomplished at home, but the amount of filing, hacksawing and other dirty work makes it quite a chore. At the risk of being accused of heresy, I am going to suggest that a sight-and-rib combination represents a much more practical approach for home installation. Bo-Mar makes a very fine unit of this sort, consisting of a full-length rib with a proper blade installed up front and the working portion of the very fine Bo-Mar target sight let into appropriate cuts at the rear of the rib. This unit is ideal for home installation, mainly because the complete job requires only the drilling and tapping of four holes in the top of the slide. You don't even need a drill press for this operation, provided you're careful and patient. Once properly located, the holes can be drilled with a hand-held electric drill or even with a geared breast drill if nothing else is available. The additional weight of the rib (usually around 5 ounces, depending on the model) smooths out recoil, cuts down muzzle jump and aids feeding.

Other sight options and the mechanics of their installation are covered in the chapter on sights. Functional reliability, especially with light target loads, is absolutely essential for good match performance, and

Installation of a trigger shoe doesn't actually have a measurable effect on trigger pull, but by spreading the pressure over a larger area of the shooter's finger, it permits better control and can make the pull feel lighter.

this is another topic covered separately and in detail. See the previous chapter for ways to ensure maximum reliability.

Trigger pull can be exceedingly important. It must be completely controllable, of the proper weight, smooth and crisp. Yet the modifications required to accomplish this must not cause malfunctions such as hammer follow-down or doubling. Neither can the trigger be allowed to affect safety in any other way.

Essentially, trigger pull depends on the proper relationship of sear nose to full-cock notch and on a proper balancing of spring forces and frictional loads within the system. The usual approach of the home mechanic is to take out the sear and hammer, then spend hours working over the engaging surfaces without much regard to the other parts and factors involved. I prefer to begin at the other end of the system, saving the hammer-sear relationship for last. As a matter of fact, it's often possible to achieve a vast improvement in trigger pull without ever touching the sear nose and full-cock notch.

The job starts with eliminating as much friction as possible between the moving parts. The long-yoked trigger of the GM pistol rides in two grooves inside the frame. These grooves are often quite rough and heavily burred. Clean them up as smoothly as possible with small files, removing all burrs and sharp edges in the process. For a really super job, finish by polishing the grooves with a piece of hard Arkansas stone glued to a handle long enough so the stone can be pushed the entire length of the grooves. Also deburr the edges of the slot where the trigger protrudes up front. Then polish and deburr the trigger yoke so that it slides smoothly in those grooves without any hesitation or rough

A simple trigger-stop can be fashioned by drilling and tapping a hole through the lower part of the finger piece and turning in a screw whose tip will bear on the magazine catch. For such a stop to operate uniformly, the magazine catch must fit very closely in its hole in the frame. An alternative stop system can be fashioned by drilling a hole in the lower part of the trigger guard and threading in a screw to limit the trigger's rearward movement.

spots. There probably will be substantial lateral play, and this should be taken out by expanding the width of the yoke so that its sides contact the grooves very lightly. The usual method is to simply spread the yoke near its center. Unfortunately, this produces a single point of contact on each side, leaving the yoke free to wobble sideward. The sides should be spread, but must remain parallel at the same time, so they make long contact with the grooves and thus prevent side-play. If you can't seem to obtain this by bending, solder steel shim stock on the outer sides of the yoke and then polish it down until the unit fits and moves properly.

At the same time, check to make certain the yoke does not make contact with the sides of the magazine to be used in the gun. If it rubs on the magazine, pull weight will vary from time to time—especially when magazines are changed—and you may even encounter trouble with the trigger not returning fully forward after each shot. Eliminate any existing contact by polishing the inside of the yoke as well as the outside of the magazine in the area over which the yoke passes. Blue or soot will reveal the high spots to be trimmed or polished.

During all this you will probably notice there is considerable vertical play in the trigger finger-piece. To eliminate it, first smooth and polish the upper and lower portions of the trigger guard against which the ends of the trigger slide. Afterward, the play can be removed by building up either or both ends of the trigger with weld or soldered shim stock. This build-up is then filed and polished to slide smoothly without excessive vertical play. An alternative method, applicable only to the old-style solid-steel trigger, consists of drilling a vertical hole in the top of the trigger, then placing in it a short length of nylon rod which protrudes about $1/16$-inch. The tip of this nylon rod is dressed down until it makes very light contact with the frame as it slides, eliminating vertical play. You can probably think of other ways to eliminate vertical play, but these two seem the most practical to me.

Polish the angled rear surface of the trigger yoke smooth, making certain there are no burrs on its upper or lower edges. Then polish the corresponding surface on the foot of the disconnector where the two meet in normal functioning. Check the rest of the disconnector and remove any burrs or serious roughnesses. Follow this by carefully deburring and cleaning the vertical hole in the frame in which the disconnector rides. Again, if any really severe roughness is noted in this hole, polish it out as best you can—*without* enlarging the hole significantly.

Deburr the rest of the interior of the frame wherever it is possible for it to be contacted by moving parts; this especially includes the areas of the sear and hammer. Assemble the sear and hammer to the frame with their original pins and note whether they wobble on their pins and whether the pins are snug in the frame. Originally these parts were made for easy, tool-less assembly by troops in the field, so they are generally loose. Any angular displacement of sear or hammer on the pin will affect trigger pull. If looseness is evident, make new oversized pins from hardened drill rod, reaming the holes in the frame so that at least

Handgun Competition

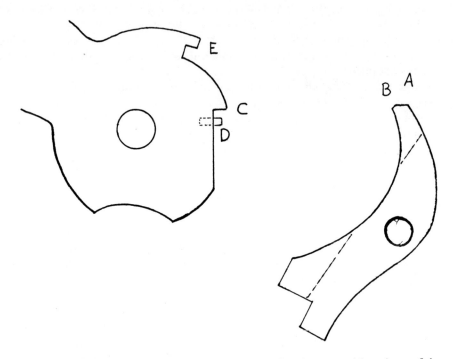

These drawings (not proportioned to scale but for clarity) show the sear at right and part of the hammer at left. The primary angle of the sear is at Point A, the secondary angle at B; the latter eliminates a sharp, weak edge that could chip or crumble. The hammer's full-cock notch (C) can be reduced in depth by inserting a pin (D) and stoning its tip back until the desired engagement is reached. Point E is the safety notch.

slight pressure is required to seat them. Carefully polish out the holes in both sear and hammer so that they will rotate freely but without wobble on the oversized pins. Check to determine how much side clearance exists between frame and hammer and sear. Again, lateral movement here can have a small effect on trigger pull. If there is significant clearance, it can be eliminated by placing small disks pierced for the pin on both sides of the two parts. These disks should be cut from steel shim stock of the appropriate thickness, carefully flattened and deburred, then held to the respective parts by a very tiny amount of cyanoacrylate adhesive. Alternatively, use thin disks of Teflon, held to the part for assembly by a small dab of grease. Fit is correct when both sear and hammer can rotate through their normal arcs freely without lateral play.

Install the manual safety and make certain that in the disengaged position it does not place any drag on sear or hammer. Sometimes there will be burrs on the engaging surface which can interfere with free sear movement; remove them. Check the grip safety for the same reason;

occasionally this part will be shaped and dimensioned so that the lug, which gives it its function, rubs somewhat on the other moving parts even when disengaged. If this occurs, file the offending area until there is absolutely no contact when the safety is depressed.

Personally, I prefer to do this and then drill the grip safety and frame for a loose pin which will hold it in the disengaged position. It serves no really useful purpose in match work, and by locking it out of action, I eliminate one more factor that can affect the uniformity of my hold on the gun. The pin is held in place by the grips and is easily removed when I wish to restore the grip safety to action.

Check the old sear spring carefully. I much prefer to begin this sort of job with a new spring, even though old ones are more often than not quite serviceable. If there is evidence that any of the limbs on the old spring have been bent before, you'll be far better off to replace it. At the same time, check the fit of whichever spring you'll be using in the frame and pay particular attention to the way the left limb fits. I've encountered many instances where the notched and bent upper end of that limb was burred. Consequently, it was crowded to the left where it could rub the frame, and thus its action was impeded. If either the right or left limb rubs the frame, grind down its outer edge a bit to provide clearance, or peen one end or the other of the frame slot in which the foot fits so as to rotate the entire spring slightly to clear the frame. Lightly bevel and polish the contact surfaces where the upper ends of the limbs rub on the parts they actuate.

Make certain also that the inner edge of the protrusion on the tip of the left limb is not exerting sideward pressure on the sear. Another point regarding the sear spring is often ignored—the tightness with which it's held against the frame by the mainspring housing. Even if there is considerable clearance between the spring and the underside of the housing, the spring will be kept in its proper location. However, unless the housing bears down solidly on the spring, it can "float" a bit, and this will affect the consistency of the pressure the various limbs exert on their respective parts. The easiest way to make certain sufficient pressure is exerted on the spring is to dimple the underside of the housing with a sharp punch in such a location that the dimples will bear on the spring about ¼-inch above its lower end. Make the dimples fairly large, then attempt to seat the housing over the spring; if the housing will not go, dress the dimples down a bit with a file. If there is still too much clearance, enlarge the dimples or form new ones.

Consistency of mainspring pressure will affect trigger pull. This can be ensured only if the mainspring is free and unimpeded inside the housing, and only if the hammer strut moves freely and does not rub against any other part of the gun. Procedures with regard to these two points have been included in the chapter on functional reliability.

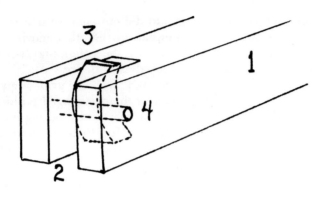

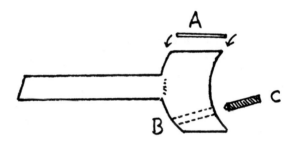

The isometric drawing at top represents a typical sear jig with the sear positioned in it as it would be in the gun. The jig body (1) is slotted (2) to accept the sear (3), which is held by a pin (4). With the sear rotated to the right, the sear nose is positioned so that it will be cut at the proper angle by a stone moved across the jig's flat top. It can then be repositioned and the secondary angle can be stoned in the same manner. In the drawing at bottom, vertical trigger play is eliminated by soldering shim (A) to the top (or bottom) of the finger piece. A trigger-stop is installed by drilling and tapping a hole (B), centered on the magazine catch, and turning in a screw (C). The screw is adjusted to control the magazine catch and halt the trigger just as the hammer begins to fall.

When all of these operations have been completed, try the trigger pull. You'll probably be gratified to note that it's much smoother and consistent. Pull weight will probably feel a bit lighter, because all the excess friction and interruption have been removed. Overtravel will probably still be excessive, and any problems in sear engagement will certainly still exist. It is now time to correct any problems in that particular area—assuming, of course, that the pull is still unsatisfactory.

It's virtually impossible for a modestly experienced pistolsmith to properly polish and angle the full-cock notch and the sear nose entirely free-handed with stones. Some people place the parts in a small vise, positioning them very carefully so that a stone guided by the top of the vise jaws will produce the correct angle. This is better than working free-hand, but is by no means as accurate as using a jig. Sear and hammer jigs are available, and are not always terribly expensive. Since jigs differ in type and method of operation, I'll cover them only in general terms. Beginning with the sear, note in the drawing the angles and width of surfaces that must be produced. Keep in mind also that those surfaces on the sear nose must be perfectly parallel to the corresponding surfaces in the hammer notch. If not, you'll get only partial bearing on one side or the other, multiplying the friction and the contact forces (which are very great and capable of chipping both the nose and the notch). This is also the reason to eliminate wobble of either part on its pin.

Incidentally, no matter how perfect the jig might be, any lack of parallelism between the holes in the hammer and sear or between the hammer and sear pins will cause partial engagement. Once both hammer and sear are properly stoned, the engaging surfaces should be coated with machinist's blue, the parts installed in the gun, and the sear nose heavily engaged in the hammer notch. Then remove the parts and examine the surfaces to determine if full-width engagement is present. The areas of actual engagement will have the blue wiped off, so they are easily seen, especially with a magnifying glass. If contact proves to be uneven, it will be necessary to shim the parts to a slight angle in the jig and restone the surface until full-width engagement is produced.

Back to the jigs. The sear jig is made so that the sear is placed in a slot and secured there by a pin. The jig is dimensioned so that the sear nose falls just above a flat guide surface. A special stone is then laid across the hardened surface of the jig, over the sear nose, and applied gently until all of the sear material above the jig surface is removed. When the stone rides flat upon the jig, the sear nose is cut at the proper angle. The sear jig is normally provided with stops or shims so that the sear can be placed first in position to cut the primary angle, then rotated somewhat to cut the secondary angle. These angles are shown in the sketch, emphasized somewhat for clarity. The secondary angle is necessary to prevent chipping of the rear edge of the nose. If this angle were eliminated and the entire nose cut only at the primary angle, there would be a sharp, weak edge at the rear which would crumble and eventually become rounded from the pressure of the front edge of the hammer notch as the sear clears. The secondary angle allows a smooth transition at this point without damage and also causes the hammer to cam the sear forward. In this fashion, the secondary sear angle also prevents the sharp front edge of the hammer notch from crumbling. All too many gun tinkerers ignore this secondary angle entirely, either because they don't know its purpose or because they don't recognize its importance.

The inexpensive sear jig I've been using is made by Martin and is supplied with two special stones. They are of square section and considerably larger than what is normally available. One is an artificial stone of relatively coarse grit for initial trimming of the nose, while the other is used to produce a very smooth finish on the surface. Some individuals have such a passion for highly polished engaging surfaces that they use a flat brass lap loaded with rouge to put a final polish on the sear nose. I don't think this is at all necessary, but the lap can be used with the jig exactly as are the stones. Even when the jig's guide surface is quite hard, care must be taken to ensure that the stones do not wear away that surface at an undesirable angle. The stones should always be applied in such a fashion that any reduction of the guide surface will be parallel to the original surface. Careless use can cause the guide surface to be cut away and deformed in relatively short order, but if care is taken the surface will last for many, many sear jobs. If it should eventually become out-of-true, it can be restored very quickly by surface-grinding the worn area.

Jigs also exist for stoning the sear notch in the hammer. They work in essentially the same fashion, but there's an added problem in that great caution is needed to avoid deepening the notch as its engaging surface is cut. After all, the stone cuts on all of its sides. While it is being applied to the engaging surface, it is very easily brought into contact with the adjoining surface of the hammer—and will cut that away as well. The result is a sear notch far too deep for proper functioning.

Once the engaging surface of a typical sear notch has been cut to the proper angle and smoothed, the depth of sear engagement must be regulated. This should not be reduced below .020-inch, and may be as much as .040-inch and still produce a good pull if everything is carefully fitted and polished. If the notch is not too deep—not more than .040 inch—then the depth of sear engagement can be regulated by cutting away the front edge of the notch. It is absolutely essential that the front edge of the notch in its final form be perfectly parallel to the peak formed by the primary and secondary angles on the sear. If this parallelism does not exist, one side of the sear nose moves out of engagement with the hammer notch before the other, greatly increasing contact pressures on the still-engaged side for an instant. This greatly increases the probability of chipping or galling.

When engagement depth is regulated in this fashion, the rear face of the sear nose and the corresponding area of the hammer against which it comes to rest should be clean, smooth, free of burrs. If not, there is the possibility that the depth of engagement—and thus pull weight—will vary slightly from shot to shot. These areas must also be kept very clean; any grit or debris that accumulates there will reduce sear-engagement depth, possibly to the point of hammer follow-down or doubling.

If the hammer notch is too deep, engagement depth must be regulated in another way. Traditionally, this has been done by drilling a $^1/_{16}$-inch hole into the hammer below the notch, then driving a drill-rod pin into this hole, allowing it to protrude $^1/_{32}$-inch or so.

This pin becomes the surface against which rearward sear movement is halted. The pin is carefully filed and stoned shorter until the desired depth of sear engagement is produced. Unfortunately, drilling this hole in a hardened hammer can be frustrating for the home mechanic. Hammers vary a good deal, and probably the only way to be certain you can drill the hole is to purchase an expensive cobalt drill. This type of drill is very fragile, so a drill press and very solid setup is necessary to avoid breaking it. The better custom pistolsmiths simply anneal the hammer, drill it normally, then reharden it after the pin is in place. One seldom finds a furnace in a gun buff's home that is suitable for this purpose, so that is pretty much out of the question. As an alternative, I have on occasion simply soft-soldered brass shim stock to this area, then filed it back until sear-depth engagement was correct. In theory this might be a sloppy way to do the job, but it seems to work perfectly well.

Once both sear and hammer have been properly stoned and engagement has been set up close to .040-inch, assemble the gun completely and cock the hammer. Now weigh the trigger pull. It should be smoother and lighter than before, and should break clean and crisp. The weight may be as much as five pounds, though I'd expect it to be less. Cock the hammer again, then exert as much forward pressure on the hammer spur as possible with your thumb, and at the same time pull the trigger. Repeat this two or three times; the increased engagement pressure will cause the sear nose and the hammer notch to burnish one another, smoothing out minor surface irregularities and producing a smoother and sometimes lighter pull. Weigh the pull again. If it is still too heavy—keeping in mind that anything under four pounds might constitute a safety hazard and cause doubling—you may reduce the depth of sear engagement in small increments until the desired pull is achieved. Do not, however, reduce sear engagement to less than .020-inch; to do so makes doubling or follow-down likely.

When all of this is accomplished, the result is a first-class trigger pull, with one exception—there will be substantial trigger overtravel. This can be eliminated only by installing some sort of trigger-stop. By far the simplest type of stop is that included in a trigger shoe. A shoe also offers the added advantage of greater finger contact, making the trigger-pull *feel* smoother and lighter, even though it is not. Such shoes are available from several makers at relatively low cost, and they constitute the cheapest form of trigger-stop. The stop is incorporated into the shoe by simply adding a rearward-pointing socket-head screw, threaded into the shoe proper. Once the shoe is installed, you simply turn the screw in until its tip contacts the frame behind the trigger, very minutely, after hammer release. Some shoes contain a clamp screw to lock the position of the stop screw so that its adjustment will not vary with use; with those that do not have such a clamp, a small drop of Loc-Tite should be applied to the screw to prevent its shifting from firing vibrations. The shoe proper contains a slot which fits over the trigger, and it is held in place by a pair of tiny clamp screws. In my experience, these screws often do not hold the shoe as strongly as needed unless dimples to receive their points are drilled or ground in the sides of the trigger. Even then, it is often difficult to keep the screws tight. I prefer instead to drill small holes completely through the shoe and trigger, then insert small roll pins to tie the two parts solidly together. (Of course, this creates an inconvenience when removing the trigger, because the pins must first be drifted out.)

You may not want to use a trigger shoe, or your fingers might not be long enough to handle the additional trigger reach created by it. In that case, a different type of stop will be required. The next simplest is a set-screw threaded into the trigger and adjusted to bear on the magazine catch. This type is not difficult to install at home, and it saves the substantial price a pistolsmith would charge for the job.

With the trigger and magazine catch in place, carefully mark the front face of the finger piece where a screw must enter to make contact with the magazine catch; also scribe on the side of the trigger the path the screw must take. Then, remove both parts, and drill a small hole from front to back through the finger piece, following the scribed line. Tap this hole to a convenient size, keeping it small enough so that the finger piece is not cut nearly in half by the hole, and turn in a headless socket-type screw that is long enough to reach the magazine catch with the trigger in its rearmost position. Install both parts back in the frame, then adjust the screw so that it contacts the magazine catch solidly at the instant after the hammer is released. Keep in mind that you do not want the head of the screw protruding from the trigger; trim it as necessary from the other end. When all is properly regulated, a drop of Loc-Tite on the screw will keep it from shifting. If you don't like the screw hole in the face of the finger piece, an alternative is to thread a similar screw into the bottom of the trigger guard to make contact with the rear of the trigger. In some respects, this installation is simpler and quicker than running the screw through the trigger to the magazine catch.

That about wraps up the basic procedures for accurizing the GM. Virtually all of them may be adapted to other Browning-type pistols;

and many of them can be applied to copies and near-copies of the Colt .45. Guns in this class would include the Llama, Star, Argentine-made copies, etc.

Some other guns, such as the Browning Hi-Power, require considerable modification of the procedures to suit their mechanical design. For example, in the Browning there is no separate barrel bushing, so to achieve maximum accuracy it is necessary to bore out the muzzle of the slide and make and fit a bushing similar to the threaded unit employed by Custom Gun Shop. The Browning trigger system is also much different in that the separate sear lever engaging both trigger and sear must be individually fitted to eliminate all play between those two contacts.

Regardless of the gun you might wish to accurize—excluding a few unusual types such as the Luger and the Walther P-38, which aren't generally used as target guns except in military competitions that allow the shooters no choice—a close examination of the design will usually suggest ways in which to adapt the procedures I've described. Of course, dozens of other alterations might be included in an accurizing job. But generally speaking, they are more cosmetic than functional, though some do improve handling and control. A number of these operations will be covered in the chapter on gunsmithing.

15

Home Gunsmithing

It's difficult to separate "accurizing" from the broader term "gunsmithing" (or "pistolsmithing"). The word "accurizing" is most often used to describe those gunsmithing operations that are directly related to a gun's inherent mechanical accuracy (such as the fit of slide, barrel and barrel bushing) or improvements related to the shooter's ability to extract that accuracy (such as the weight and smoothness of trigger pull) —the kind of operations described in the previous chapter. Obviously, many other operations are less closely related to mechanical accuracy— or aren't related at all. Some of them, for example, improve a gun's handling qualities or meet a shooter's individual needs. There are also minor repairs or alterations that can sometimes restore accuracy or other aspects of good performance when deterioration has been caused by wear or damage. These operations, grouped under the general title of gunsmithing, form the subject of this chapter. Many of them can be performed at home and with relatively few tools by anyone who takes the time to learn.

Nicks or dents in the barrel muzzle of any gun, and similar deformations at the mouth of revolver-cylinder throats, can cause a gun to go sour. This is why barrels are generally *crowned,* so that the actual edge of the bore lies rearward of the muzzle surface. The protruding metal

The muzzle of a revolver or auto should be examined closely for any burrs or nicks that intrude into the bore, where they might mark or damage an exiting bullet. Flat muzzles like this one are particularly susceptible to such trouble, which can usually be corrected by crowning or counterboring.

protects the rifled edge from impact. The chamber-throat mouth has no such protection, being of necessity flat across the face to permit a proper fit with the barrel breech. However, the front portion of the frame does provide a good bit of protection.

Examine the area closely, preferably with a magnifying glass of at least 4X power, for any burr or turned-over metal that intrudes into the bore so that it will mark the bullet at its exit. A very small intrusion may not affect accuracy, but a large one will gouge a deep groove the full length of the bullet, not only disturbing it at the critical point of barrel exit but possibly unbalancing it as well. It matters not whether the intrusion is in a land or a groove, the effect will be the same. A typical burr can be removed by very careful use of a scraper and/or small needle file. However, it's easy to remove too much metal, creating an interruption in the smooth perimeter of the bore, and that can also reduce accuracy. If the burr is large, it is best to simply remove about half of it with scraper or files, then recrown the muzzle. Recrowning is also the best bet if the burr is very small.

A gouge or nick intruding into the bore will allow a tiny jet of powder gas to escape as the base of the bullet clears the muzzle. This can result in a groove being cut in the matching portion of the bullet base as high-pressure gases wash away bullet material in that area. This can unbalance the bullet or even tip the bullet slightly as it leaves the muzzle. Either effect will reduce accuracy. Generally a nick will not extend so far into the bore that it cannot be removed by recrowning; however, if it intrudes more than about .020-inch, the entire muzzle should be cut back and recrowned or, if that isn't possible, counterbored.

A large, round-headed brass screw will do a creditable job of crowning or recrowning a muzzle. Coated with fine abrasive and oil, it's rotated against the muzzle to grind a neat bevel at the mouth of the bore, removing minor nicks and burrs. A figure-eight movement should be imparted to the screw while grinding.

Crowning isn't as difficult as one might think. Most gunsmiths simply cut the crown with a shaped tool in a lathe. In early times, the inner edge was usually finished with a brass ball spun against the muzzle with a coating of fine abrasive and oil. The spinning ball produced a muzzle edge perfectly right-angled in relationship to the bore. You'd have a hard time finding a muzzle-crowning ball today, but large brass-headed wood screws will do the job as well. Of course, the screw must be of a round-head type. Select a clean, new screw at least a little larger in diameter than the bore; it really should be at least half again as large. This screw can be chucked in a carpenter's hand brace since it should not be rotated very fast, but a variable-speed electric drill set at its slowest speed will do the job faster. Plant the barrel muzzle-up in a padded vise, then coat the head of the screw with oil and fine abrasive powder.

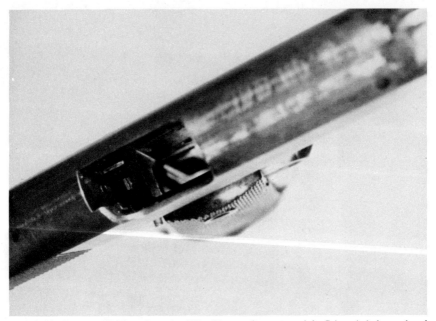

Look at this photo very closely and you should be able to see burrs around the firing-pin hole, produced by extensive firing or dry-firing. Such burrs should be carefully filed or stoned flush with the surrounding surface.

At one time, common valve-grinding compound was used, and if you can't find any smaller-sized grit the finest grade of that material will do. Start the screw-head spinning against the muzzle, applying hardly any pressure, and at the same time rotating the opposite end of the brace or drill in a circle several inches in diameter. This rotation keeps the sharp edge of the muzzle from wearing a groove in the screw-head. Wipe the muzzle clean and check it frequently, and you'll soon see a new surface being ground around the edge of the bore. When this surface reaches deep enough to completely obliterate the nick or burr, the job is finished. You might want to give it a little more class by polishing it with fine abrasive cloth and oil on the ball of your thumb, but this is by no means necessary. Make certain all grit and oil is removed from the barrel, both inside and out, before shooting the gun.

Deep damage at this point can be corrected only by shortening or counter-boring the barrel. Shortening usually isn't practical in center-fire autoloaders, and in revolvers it might mess up the front sight installation. Consequently, I prefer counter-boring. This job is beyond the home pistolsmith's abilities unless he has a well-equipped bench lathe. It's necessary to carefully chuck the barrel, centering it with a dial indicator, then bore out the muzzle deeply enough to remove the damage and to a diameter of $^1/_{16}$-inch or so greater than the bore proper. Then deburr or lightly crown the new muzzle surface and the job is finished.

Similar damage to the mouth of a chamber throat is not so easily repaired. The cylinder cannot be shortened to remove damage without the extra cost and effort of setting the barrel back. This would make it a major gunsmithing operation. Neither can the mouth of the chamber be crowned or counterbored. To do so would greatly increase the amount of gas that escapes at the barrel-to-cylinder gap. The only method left is to very carefully use a scraper and files to remove any intruding metal. The ideal procedure is to remove the bulk of the metal, then make up a hardened and polished rod or mandrel that will just barely fit into the chamber throat. This rod is forced into the throat, pushing the displaced metal back into its original location. (This method is also used to remove chamber-mouth burrs from .22 rimfire pistols; such burrs caused by excessive firing-pin protrusion combined with dry-firing.) If there is any serious damage to the mouth of a chamber throat, you'll probably be better off to replace the cylinder than to attempt repair.

Extensive firing will sometimes produce burrs around the firing-pin hole in both autoloaders and revolvers. This is most common in revolvers having the firing pin affixed to the hammer, but it can occur in almost any design. It results when a hard firing pin bears upon the edges of the hole in the relatively soft metal of the slide face or recoil shield, slowly peening that metal forward. Given enough time and enough firing, the firing-pin hole will be surrounded by a sharp, rough edge protruding beyond the flat surface. This does not reduce mechanical accuracy, but it can interfere with functioning. In a mobile-barrel auto, the burr becomes imbedded in the primer; dragging through the soft brass during unlocking, it robs the slide of recoil energy needed for proper cycling. In revolvers the burrs also become imbedded in the primer and may impede rotation of the cylinder.

This is one of the easiest problems to correct. With a flat needle file, trim the burrs off flush with the surrounding surface. Remove file marks with a stone or a Flexi-Grit strip or abrasive cloth. In a revolver, make certain the surface around the hole is polished smoothly to reduce friction against case heads as the cylinder rotates.

As burrs at the firing-pin hole are produced, the hole itself becomes enlarged. This can eventually result in primer-cup metal extruding back into the gap around the pin, and it will cause the same functional problems as the burrs. It can be corrected either by installing a larger-

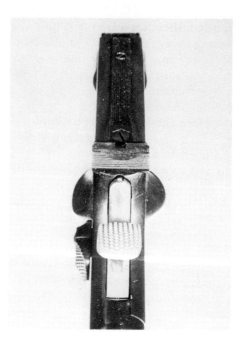

The rear-sight leaf may develop side-to-side looseness in its base. This is easily corrected by peening the leaf to slightly greater width so that it will be held more tightly. Fore-and-aft looseness has far less effect on accuracy but can and should be corrected—either by building up the lower portion of the leaf to the greater thickness or by peening the base to narrow the slot.

diameter firing pin or by drilling out the recoil shield or slide face and installing a closely-fitted bushing. Installation of a bushing is strictly a professional pistolsmithing job and should not be attempted by the shooter unless he is a well-equipped machinist.

Loose sights are the bane of accuracy. The most common problem is looseness of the sheet-metal element of the rear sight—the leaf containing the square notch. New leaves cost little, and they are usually not difficult to install. Unfortunately, a factory-made replacement will often fit no better than the original. To eliminate all looseness, it is probably best to remove the old leaf and determine just what areas are causing the problem. Usually widening the bottom of the leaf will help, as will reshaping the retaining notches with needle files. Widening is easily accomplished by laying the leaf on a steel block and carefully peening the lower portion. This can be done with the rounded end of a small machinist's hammer, but you're more likely to avoid striking the wrong area if you use a punch that can be guided more accurately.

After the leaf is carefully fitted in regard to width, building up the thickness so that it just barely enters the base will also help a good deal. If only a very small increase is needed, simply flow on a layer of silver solder. For greater build-up, sweat shim stock over the bottom of the leaf. Steel shim is probably best, but brass is easier to handle and I feel it is entirely satisfactory. If you can measure the amount of increase

Home Gunsmithing

needed, then it is a simple matter to select shim of the proper thickness and thus avoid a lot of filing. When finished, the leaf should move smoothly in windage but show no looseness.

Rear sights also sometimes develop lateral play in the portion that moves vertically in a notch or slot in the base. There must be sufficient clearance here for smooth elevation adjustment, but the fit must be close enough so the sighting element doesn't wobble sideways. The simplest way to correct this is to peen the edges of the slot in the base very carefully to reduce its width slightly. By alternate peening and filing, you can obtain a fit that eliminates all play and yet does not interfere with elevation adjustment. Depending on sight design, side-play can also sometimes be reduced by replacing the original pivot pin with a very carefully fitted one of larger diameter. Often the sighting element is loose enough on the original pin (which is fitted tightly in the base) so that it can wobble sidewards. The fit of the pin should be close enough to prevent play, yet allow smooth rotation during elevation adjustment.

Looseness in the rear sight may sometimes be traced to springs that are a bit too weak, or excessive dirt and grease interfering with movement. It's best to install new springs, but stretching them a bit may improve their action. And, of course, complete removal of all dirt, grit and excess oil and grease will help a lot.

Front sights usually don't cause much trouble—except, possibly, in the old Colt models that incorporate elevation adjustment into the front sight. It's doubtful that many of those are still in target use. Among other guns, trouble probably arises most often with the Colt Government Model and several copies of it. Original sight-blade installation is by means of a stud on the bottom of the blade seated in a hole in the slide and riveted over the inside. This often loosens, allowing the blade to wobble and eventually fly off. The only certain repair for this is to clean the joint area thoroughly, then flow silver solder into the joint. Simply re-riveting the stud has never been satisfactory, in my experience. However, re-riveting the stud and applying a cyanoacrylate adhesive might do the job. These modern, quick-setting (60-second) adhesives have remarkable holding power.

Revolver front sights often consist of a separate blade pinned into a slotted base either formed integrally with the barrel or brazed to the barrel. If the brazed joint fails, I strongly recommend sending it back to the factory or to a competent pistolsmith for repair. The average torch artist will ruin the bore by using too much heat and/or allowing scale to form there. If the blade simply becomes loose in the base, drive out the original pins and ream the holes for larger ones while the blade is clamped very tightly against the base. Then install new pins, and if

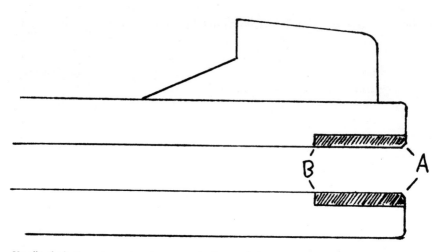

Usually, the best way to repair a deep gouge in the muzzle is to counterbore it to a depth beyond the gouge. This should be left to a competent pistolsmith or machinist. The shaded area (A-B) is removed, making B the true muzzle surface even though the outer barrel profile remains unchanged.

you lack faith in that, apply a tiny drop of cyanoacrylate to the joint where it will be sucked in by capillary attraction and reinforce the installation. Other sight work is covered in the chapter devoted to that subject.

Accuracy can be reduced by overzealous cleaning with a hard or abrasive cleaning rod. Revolver barrels are invariably cleaned from the muzzle because of their design and construction, and autoloaders are frequently cleaned the same way to avoid the disassembly necessary to work from the breech. In any event, as mentioned in the chapter on care and maintenance, excessive contact of the cleaning rod against the edges of the muzzle will produce funnel-shaped wear that can reduce accuracy. This type of wear is accelerated by the use of an aluminum or plastic-coated rod that has picked up dirt and grit. Aluminum is particularly bad, because its soft surface becomes impregnated with all sorts of foreign material, causing it to act almost like a file. Avoid this by using a cleaning-rod guide, but if your gun has already suffered damage, repairs may be needed to restore its accuracy.

In its early stages, this type of wear will be most evident in rounded or beveled land edges right at the muzzle. If the rod is making contact there, it will naturally fall into a groove between two lands, and—depending on its diameter—will rub the corners of adjacent lands and possibly the center of the groove between them. An advanced case of this type of wear can be seen with the naked eye, but you'll be more likely to recognize it with a magnifying glass at its early stages.

If the wear is extensive, barrel replacement is probably the only answer; the barrel can't be counterbored deeply enough to get rid of all of the wear, and shortening it the required amount may not be possible. If the wear isn't too bad, though, extending no more than ¼-inch down the bore, counterboring is in order. This may not be possible with thin-walled barrels such as the .45 Government Model, but otherwise it generally works out well. Once carefully set up in the lathe, the muzzle is bored out deeply enough to eliminate all the cleaning-rod wear, to a diameter of about ¹/₁₆-inch over bore diameter. (There is no reason the counterbore diameter can't be greater, if the barrel is large enough.)

Ideally, all the chamber throats of a revolver should be of identical diameter—but often this is not the case. All other factors being equal, a throat larger or smaller than the rest will cause bullets fired from it to deviate slightly from the path of the others. Because of many interacting factors, an over- or undersized throat may shoot either tighter or looser groups than the other chambers. This is just one of the reasons why many revolver shooters use only one chamber when shooting slow-fire. They have determined by test and experience that when the gun is used as a single-shot with that chamber only, it will produce its tightest groups.

To determine throat diameter, first make certain all throats are absolutely clean and free of lead. Then, either upset an undersized lead slug in each throat and then push it out or push an oversized slug through from the rear. Mark each chamber and the slug from it for identification, then measure the slug carefully with a micrometer. One measurement isn't enough; measure the slug at least twice at right angles; three or four equal-spaced measurements are better yet. The diameter of the slugs will indicate the diameter of the individual throats, and while three or four of them will probably run virtually the same, you'll likely find at least one that is several thousandths larger or smaller.

The most consistent accuracy is produced from a revolver if the throats are then carefully hand-reamed so that all are brought up to the diameter of the largest. Some custom pistolsmiths do this as a routine matter when rebarreling a revolver; one I know even uses barrels of slightly oversized groove diameter so that he will be able to ream the throats to uniform diameter without exceeding groove diameter by a significant margin.

If you can obtain a proper reamer of the correct diameter, you can ream the throats without much trouble. The best type of reamer to use is one piloted in the *chamber*—that is, with the pilot behind the cutting portion, and of a diameter to fit the chamber. The reamer should have a very short shank and be fitted with a tap-wrench or other handle.

Handgun Competition

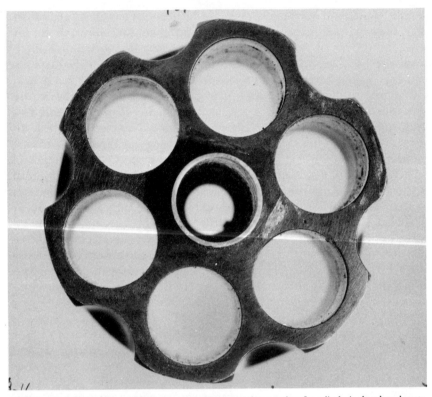

There's no practical, economical way to repair damage at the mouths of a cylinder's chamber throats. Perhaps the best solution is to replace the cylinder. Next best is to have it shortened at the front by a competent machinist (if the damage doesn't extend too far into the throats), after which the barrel must be set back to produce the correct barrel-to-cylinder gap. The length of the cartridge limits the shortening of the cylinder, but generally very little shortening is needed.

Turn it slowly by hand with a light feed pressure. Use plenty of cutting oil, *never* back up the reamer, and keep the chips cleaned out so that they cannot pack under a cutting edge and score the finish or cause the reamer to cut oversize. If the reaming is done carefully with a new, sharp reamer, the throat finish will be quite satisfactory. If it does appear a bit rough, light lapping—using a cast lead lap and J.B. Bore Polishing Compound—will smooth it up without measurable enlargement.

No matter how perfectly a gun's grips fit the shooter's hand, the slightest amount of looseness will cause some shots to go out of the group. No matter how mechanically accurate the gun might be, any relative movement between the grips and the gun may open up groups to an alarming degree. Even a very small amount of loosehess will affect accuracy by preventing smooth transfer of the recoil impulse to the shooting hand, and this effect is inconsistent and irregular. Without smooth, consistent recoil transfer, that portion of jump which occurs before the bullet leaves the muzzle will vary. The result is larger groups.

No matter how closely grips are fitted in the beginning, natural expansion and contraction of the wood due to changing humidity and temperature will cause periodic looseness. This will eventually cause some wear, with the result that the grips cannot be kept tight at all. Absorption of oil and perspiration also play a part in these changes.

The simplest and best method of correcting grip looseness is to hog out wood at key points (corners and front and rear of the frame), fill these gaps with glass-bedding compound, then re-install the grips and allow the compound to cure thoroughly. Care must be taken to prevent the grip plates from becoming bonded together, and also to prevent bonding to the frame. It's best that all recesses in the frame be filled with modeling clay, and that all metal likely to come in contact with the bedding compound be thoroughly but sparingly coated with release compound. It is especially important that any undercuts in the frame or any surface irregularities into which the epoxy might flow are completely filled with modeling clay. Allowing for this, an even better and more secure fit can be obtained if a small bead of epoxy is laid on the wood so that it will flow over the interior edges of the frame and thus form a shoulder which fits down inside. Applying this requires a good deal of care to prevent locking the wood to the metal. In order to prevent the two grip halves from being glued together, thin plastic film— or as a substitute, aluminum foil—should be placed between them wherever they meet.

After the epoxy is thoroughly cured, the grips should be removed and the epoxy trimmed wherever it might interfere with the movement of the mainspring or other internal parts. Once a set of grips is properly bedded to the frame in this fashion, it is unlikely that they will ever loosen. However, if that should happen, simply adding a couple of small spots of epoxy in the loose areas will again cure the problem.

You may encounter a revolver that is perfect otherwise, but has a rough barrel throat. By rough, I mean that the original reaming job left annular rings and grooves which scrape material off the bullet as it passes into the bore. Generally when this occurs, lead deposits build up in the throat. Lead here will deform bullets as they enter the barrel, certainly reducing their accuracy and in some instances actually causing wild fliers. Removal of lead is covered in the chapter on care and maintenance, but here we are concerned with smoothing the throat so that the tendency for lead to accumulate will be reduced if not completely eliminated. A custom pistolsmith would use a special reamer for the job, but this is pretty much beyond the home mechanic. Instead,

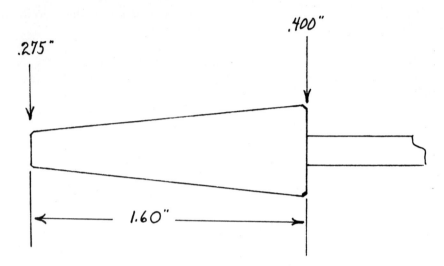

To polish a rough forcing cone in a revolver and thus reduce leading, a lap on a brass rod can be lathe-turned to the dimensions shown. The lap is coated with oil and very fine abrasive, then rotated slowly in the chamfered portion of the barrel breech. Take great care not to remove too much metal.

use a brass or bronze lap that can be turned on a miniature lathe such as the Sherline or Unimat. The lap should be shaped so that it can be used on almost any caliber from .32 upward. It's best to make it full length for this reason, but if you intend to use it only on a particular caliber, it can be shortened up front so long as the small end remains under bore diameter.

Before the lap can be used, the barrel must be removed. It might be possible to build a complex fixture for doing the job with the barrel in the frame, but it certainly wouldn't be worth the cost and effort. Taking out a revolver barrel is relatively simple, provided one uses care and doesn't overstress the relatively weak frame. The job requires a very strong and heavy vise, and a set of hardwood blocks carved to fit the barrel very closely. There is always the chance that the barrel might rotate in the blocks. Integral eccentricities such as ribs and underlugs present no problems in this respect, but if the barrel happens to carry a soldered or screw-attached rib or other protrusion, rotation might break it loose. Be especially watchful for this. Also, make certain there is clearance beyond the blocks for the front sight; any slippage of the barrel could easily bend or break off the sight. The closer the blocks fit, the less likely the barrel is to turn in them; however, powdered rosin or some similar frictional material (even sugar works well) can be dusted over the barrel to reduce the probability. An alternative to wood blocks, and one less likely to allow the barrel to slip, is the casting of lead blocks around the barrel. Such blocks should be cast in two halves, building up a form around the barrel from wood and clay.

Clamp the barrel between the blocks in the vise, turning it up as tight as possible. Before proceding farther, make certain that any extra barrel-securing devices—such as the cross-pin used on Smith & Wesson models—have been removed. I've seen more than one barrel and frame ruined by a removal attempt made without driving out a pin. Shape a stick of hardwood or some soft metal such as aluminum to fit into the cylinder recess in the frame. If metal is used, be sure to cover all contact areas of the frame with a couple of layers of masking tape; this is probably not needed with wood, but still not a bad idea. While holding the stick or bar in place, rap the end sharply with a hammer to loosen the frame from the barrel. A sharp but relatively slight impact will break the threads loose much more easily than steady pressure. I've seen the application of steady pressure bend the frame without starting the threads, while a light blow broke loose the same threads without causing any damage whatever. The frame is rather easy to bend because of its light construction up front, so special care is needed. Once the frame is loose on the barrel, it may be turned off easily. First, however, be sure to make a small index mark on the frame and barrel to facilitate retightening to the proper point when you put the barrel back on.

Of course, if the gun in question is a Dan Wesson (not Smith & Wesson) this is all unnecessary. The Wesson barrel can be removed (or interchanged) by hand, using only the simple tools supplied with the gun.

Now you can begin to clean up that barrel throat. Coat the conical section of the lap with very fine abrasive and oil. Advance it into the barrel throat, keeping it carefully aligned with the center line of the barrel, and spin it at the slowest speed of a variable-speed electric drill, or by hand with a carpenter's brace. It must be rotated slowly. Keep it aligned with the barrel and check frequently to see how much roughness is being removed by the abrasive. Redistribute the abrasive and oil occasionally on the cone where it appears to be wiped off by contact with the barrel, but also remember that abrasive imbedded in the surface of the brass will continue to cut slowly, even though the bulk of it appears to have been wiped away.

Don't overdo it. Don't expect to produce a completely smooth throat. If you carry the operation that far, the throat will be much oversized at the rear and will cause excessive bullet upset as the projectile enters the barrel. This will reduce accuracy as severely as the condition you're trying to correct. Just continue the lapping until the worst of the reamer marks are removed. If you were able to obtain abrasive grit fine enough, the new throat surface will be as smooth as necessary. How-

If a revolver barrel does not turn tightly enough into the frame when reassembled, the rear face of the barrel shoulder (arrow) must be moved down by peening the outer edge very lightly.

ever, if it looks too grainy and rough, smooth it up a bit more by wrapping the finest-grit abrasive cloth around the lap and spinning it very slowly in the throat.

With the throat smooth, it's time to re-install the barrel. Provided you made a small index mark on both frame and barrel before disassembly, this will present no problems. Clamp the barrel again between the blocks in the vise and turn the frame on as far as possible by hand. Then insert the bar, and by light hammer taps on its end, turn the frame up until the index marks are perfectly aligned.

It may be that the barrel was rather loosely fitted in the beginning, so that when the index marks line up the frame and barrel are not tight. You want a tight, "crush" fit of the barrel shoulder against the frame. If this is not obtained, the barrel may work loose with extensive firing. So, if the frame turns on the barrel too far, remove it and carefully peen the edge of the barrel shoulder with a light hammer. Use only very light blows and make certain the hammer face is smoothly polished. When peening is done this way and blows are thickly overlapped, the surface will not be noticeably distorted. Try to keep the peening as uniform as possible, completely around the perimeter of the shoulder. Now try the frame on the barrel and you should discover that the shoulders meet ⅛- to ¼-turn before the index marks can line up. From that point onward, use the bar and hammer to bring the marks together.

Even though you have aligned the index marks as accurately as possible by eye, there is a strong possibility they might be a tiny, tiny bit off. Consequently, it will be wise to re-zero the gun. At the very least, you will want to check the zero before doing any serious shooting.

You may have a gun whose bore has been damaged or has become pitted or rusted by neglect. You might also have a problem I have seen with some degree of frequency—that of a bulged barrel caused when a powder charge was left out of a handload and the primer drove the bullet only a little way into the barrel, after which another shot was

When a new barrel is fitted, the proper barrel-to-cylinder gap must be established. After the barrel is fitted into the frame, the rear face of its breech is carefully filed forward until the cylinder will close properly and a uniform gap of .003-.006-inch is attained.

fired producing a bulge at the point where the first bullet had lodged. (The shooter is fortunate indeed if a bulged barrel is the worst result.) It is possible to fit a new revolver barrel at home with no more equipment than already mentioned. Removal of the old barrel is exactly as described above—except that you won't have to be quite so concerned about keeping it from slipping in the blocks. Slippage will ruin the finish, but if you're going to throw the old barrel away it really doesn't matter. It will matter a lot, though, if you let the new barrel slip!

Make a trial assembly by turning the frame onto the new barrel as far as possible by hand and then tapping it gently snug against the barrel shoulder with the hammer and bar. Note whether the index marks (if any are present) approach each other more closely than ⅛th of a turn. If there are no index marks, you'll have to take the gun out of the vise and check visually by way of the front sight. If the barrel turns up to approximately ⅛th-turn from proper alignment, continue tapping on the bar, perhaps occasionally backing it off a half-turn and starting over, until alignment is correct. If the frame turns on too far, resulting in a loose assembly when the barrel is aligned, peen the barrel shoulder as already described.

If the barrel will not turn up within ⅛th-turn of alignment, it may be necessary to very carefully cut the shoulder back. This must be done with a small, safe-edge pillar file—and extreme care must be taken to ensure that the same amount is removed from the shoulder all the way around. It's very easy to allow the file to tip a bit and thus give the shoulder a slight forward angle, rather than being kept perfectly square as it should. Pay particular attention to this. File off only a small amount, then trial-fit barrel and frame; continue this until the two turn up within ⅛th-turn of alignment. At that point, finish the job as before and barrel installation is complete.

Now, assemble the stripped crane and cylinder to the frame, and you will doubtless discover that the barrel tenon extends too far to the rear to allow the cylinder to close. Replacement barrels are made deliberately long so that the barrel-to-cylinder gap can be properly regulated. Note how much of the barrel must be removed, then mask all the adjacent areas of the frame with tape and begin filing the rear face of the barrel forward. Do this with a fairly wide safe-edge file, and take particular care that you don't angle or cant the barrel face. Continue this, along with trial fitting, until the cylinder will just barely close. At this point, begin checking with feeler gauges as you file forward, working upward until a uniform gap of .006-inch is produced. Once you've achieved this gap and it is absolutely uniform from side to side and top to bottom, all that remains is to deburr the inner and outer edges of the barrel face and the job is finished.

When installing a new barrel, the opportunity presents itself to clean up the front face of the cylinder. A gun that has been fired extensively might show some pitting or etching around the chamber mouths, or there might be slight nicks or other damage to the edges of the mouths. After first making certain there is sufficient excess length of the barrel tenon to compensate for this, you can have an expert machinist very carefully make a light cut across the front face of the cylinder. This cut should remove roughness or pitting, and should also correct any out-of-square condition. That is, it's entirely possible that the cylinder face is not at exactly right angles to the center line of the cylinder. A good machinist can discover this and correct it when he cleans up the front of the cylinder. Once the cylinder face is cleaned up, you need only deburr the chamber mouths and regulate the barrel-to-cylinder gap as already described.

At some time you might discover that a barrel whose accuracy has dropped off a bit has developed a slight roughness in the bore. This might be very fine pitting resulting from galvanic action with copper fouling (from jacketed bullets) or the roughness might simply be a thicker-than-usual coat of bullet-jacket fouling. This is most likely, of course, to occur in the .45-caliber Colt Government Model pistol because jacketed bullets are used in it extensively. However, jacketed bullets and full-charge loads are also used in revolvers in some forms of competition, so the problem isn't peculiar only to autoloaders.

Your first reaction to such a problem might very well be to simply replace the barrel. Sometimes this is necessary, but often a simple polishing or lapping of the bore will restore accuracy—if not entirely, at least to an acceptable degree.

Two methods are available. The first is the simpler one, involving the use of a very tight-fitting patch coated with a polishing material known as J-B Bore Polishing Compound. It is important that the patch fit the bore very tightly, and that the compound be used sparingly and spread uniformly over the entire surface of the patch contacting the bore. This can be accomplished with several patches forced through the end of a slotted rod, but I prefer to wrap a double layer of patch around a tight-fitting brass-bristle bore brush. This provides more uniform contact and pressure and reduces the possibility of tearing or jamming patches in the bore. A viable alternative is the use of a dowel about ¾ of bore diameter with a double layer (more if needed) of patch material glued around one end.

Regardless of the implement used, the bore should always be polished from the rear, which means it should be removed from the gun. The barrel should be clamped rigidly in a vise, and some sort of stop should be placed directly ahead of the muzzle so that the polishing head (formed by those patches) does not exit. If the muzzle is rough clear to the very end, it will be necessary to position this stop about a quarter of an inch from the muzzle; however, if the muzzle is not rough, I prefer to place the stop right up against the muzzle. Then, during polishing, the balance of the bore will be very slightly enlarged while the muzzle will not. This produces a slight "choke" at the end, and there are many who feel this is advantageous to accuracy.

Apply the bore polishing compound, insert the polishing implement from the breech and make about a dozen full-length strokes, taking care to keep the rod aligned with the bore. Even though contact with the chamber mouth in an auto probably won't do any harm, I'm sure best results will be obtained if the rod is kept straight. Wipe the bore clean and dry and examine it carefully. If the fouling and/or roughness is not removed, give it another dozen strokes. Check again, and repeat until the bore looks smooth. From time to time it will be necessary to add polishing compound to the patches, but don't overdo this. The smallest amount that will produce visible polishing is the proper amount to use. This will, of course, enlarge the bore slightly, and it will also slightly round the edges of the lands. The amount of bore enlargement produced will probably not make a larger bullet necessary—but if it does, that's still a cheaper solution than fitting a new barrel.

Once the bore appears to be well polished, you'll need to run some accuracy tests on it. If it doesn't shoot better, then your time has been wasted and a replacement barrel is indicated. However, do enough shooting to make *certain* that this is true before giving up. Some times a polished barrel will require development of a new load or a change in factory loads before producing its best accuracy.

A more difficult method of cleaning up the barrel consists of running a cast-lead lap in it with very fine abrasive flour. This method is less likely to round off the edges of the lands. The lap is made by fixing the barrel upright in a vise, then inserting a cleaning rod from the breech, with notches filed on its end to grip the lap, and a wad of patches positioned about 1½ inches below the muzzle. With the bore lightly oiled, the muzzle is warmed up to 200 degrees or so and molten lead is poured in around the exposed end of the cleaning rod. When the lead has solidified, the lap is pushed forward a bit, any irregularities are trimmed off the end, and the barrel is repositioned in the vise so that the cleaning rod can be moved back and forth. Then the lap is pushed most of the way—but not all—out of the muzzle and is coated with light oil and the finest abrasive flour you can obtain. A stop is then fixed just ahead of the muzzle, and the lap is manipulated in the same manner as the bore-polishing rod was worked.

It will not require many strokes for the lap to wear down and become slightly loose. When this occurs, remove it and melt it off the rod. Clean and dry the bore and inspect it to see how the polishing is progressing. If it appears to be not enough, cast a fresh lap and begin again. When the barrel appears to be significantly improved in smoothness, it's time to reassemble the gun and check it for accuracy. There usually isn't any way of predicting whether it will shoot better or worse after this treatment, so it may be that you'll have to replace the barrel after all. However, I feel that lapping is successful often enough to make the investment in time and effort worthwhile.

Primer ignition is another factor that influences accuracy. You might at some time discover that accuracy has fallen off—especially vertical spread—and that there is no explanation for it. When this occurs, very carefully check the condition of the firing pin and its amount of protrusion. In most autoloaders, firing-pin protrusion is almost unlimited —that is, the pin can protrude as much as ½-inch and is halted only by contact with the primer. In revolvers, firing-pin protrusion is limited mechanically. As parts wear, and particularly if the nose of the firing pin has become corroded or damaged, protrusion may be reduced so

Adequate firing-pin protrusion is needed for positive, uniform ignition, and so is a properly shaped firing-pin nose. Here, protrusion is adequate but the pin has become deformed and must be replaced.

much that ignition is not consistent. A sure sign of this is shallowness of the firing-pin dents in the primers. However, firing-pin protrusion should be measured. Force the pin forward to the maximum mechanical limit of its travel, then measure the amount of protrusion. This should fall between .060- and .080-inch, and my personal preference is for the latter. Within those limits, the greater the protrusion, the less chance there is of a deeply seated primer receiving an inadequate indentation. If protrusion is not sufficient, replace the firing pin and regulate its protrusion to a bit less than .080-inch. At the same time, make certain the firing-pin nose is hemispherical and polished very smooth. (Chisel-shaped points are for rimfires only, and have no place at all in a centerfire gun.) Once you've obtained positive and consistent indentation of the primer, you have ensured more consistent ignition and burning of the propelling charge—and that means more consistent velocity and reduced vertical spread.

Of course, there are many other gunsmithing operations that can be said to affect accuracy. Entire books have been devoted to the subject—including a book by me, entitled *Pistolsmithing* and published by Stackpole. If you plan to do much more of this work than I've described here, you ought to buy a reference volume to guide you. Your favorite bookseller should be able to help you out in this respect.

16

Handloading .38 and .45 Match Ammunition

Serious pistol shooting costs money. As this is written, .38 Special match cartridges cost about $9 per carton of 50, or 18¢ *per shot*, and .45 ACP match cartridges cost $13 per carton, or 26¢ *per shot*. The 180 shots of a conventional centerfire 2707-aggregate NRA match would cost $39.60 (for 90 rounds of .38 and 90 rounds of .45). That doesn't include the expense of many, many times that number of rounds fired in practice to prepare for a single match.

If you're buying sufficient quantities of ammunition, you can shop around and do a good deal better than standard retail prices. But all the same, the cost of shooting a season with factory-loaded ammunition is substantial. However, ammunition prices needn't present the barrier they might seem to at first glance. Anyone who handloads his ammunition can shoot cartridges costing a tenth, or *less,* of the factory-load price. A handloader saves his fired cartridge cases, then reprocesses them himself, adding new primer, powder, and bullets to produce a cartridge that is fully as good for the purpose as those that he might buy at the local gun shop.

Actual savings depend on the amount and price of equipment that the shooter is willing to purchase, and whether he's willing to perform every operation himself. If he has lots of time, he can get by with a

The basic handloading tool is a C-type bench press such as this low-cost Pacific model. It's shown with a cup-type catcher for spent primers and a semiautomatic primer-feed. The catcher keeps the floor clean. The primer-feed device works well enough, but the author prefers to use a separate priming tool.

loading outfit costing hardly more than $150, but if time is quite limited, he'll need high-speed equipment that might cost as much as $700 or $800.

First, let's suppose you have plenty of free time, a small space to work, are willing to do the maximum amount of work by yourself, but don't want to make a large investment. You'll need a conventional C-type, bench-mounted loading press. Such presses can be had new for around $35, though you can easily spend two or three times that much for fancier models—which you don't really need. To go with the press, you'll need a set of dies (with shell holder) for both .38 and .45 caliber. Two sets of dies will cost from $25 to $35, depending on brand. When it comes to dies, you'll be far better off to buy the best. The resizing die in particular should be of a tungsten-carbide type. For a few dollars extra you can obtain an automatic primer-feed which attaches to the loading press, but if you have nimble fingers (to handle primers), I doubt that it's really worth the cost.

The press and dies serve to resize and reprime the fired case, and to assemble the other components into completed cartridges. You'll also need a means of placing the proper powder charge in the case. Small but very reliable and accurate "pistol-type" powder measures with non-adjustable metering drums can be had for as little as $10 or $12. A measure set up for .38 and supplied with a spare metering chamber or drum for .45 will be entirely adequate. By using this type of measure, you avoid the necessity for a $30-or-so investment in a first-class powder scale that is needed for safe use of an adjustable powder measure.

All that remains now is equipment to cast, size and lubricate lead bullets. An electric melting pot of adequate capacity for casting several hundred bullets an hour can be had for as little as $35 to $40, but it's better to pay about two and a half times that price for a more durable and larger-capacity unit that will make casting much more convenient and rapid.

Then you'll need a multiple-cavity bullet mold for target-type bullets in each of the two calibers. Unless you intend to cast thousands of bullets per week, there's no reason to buy molds with more than four cavities. This will allow you to drop four bullets with each filling of the mold, without the labor of handling the very heavy and bulky molds containing up to 10 cavities. A pair of four-cavity Lyman molds (low in cost and of excellent quality) for the .38 wadcutter bullet and the 185-grain .45 semi-wadcutter will cost you about $25 each.

A lubricator-sizer is necessary to true up the cast bullets, bring them to exact diameter and roundness, and force lubricant into their grooves. While there are several more economical lubricator-sizers available, I opt for the most costly, the semiautomatic Star machine. The Star greatly reduces the number of operations by simply pushing the bullet straight through the die and automatically ejecting it downward without any additional effort. Only a few hundred bullets per hour can be processed through the less-costly tools, and at the expense of much greater effort—while I have been able to process 1,500 bullets per hour through a Star tool without any great fatigue. However, if you must go the cheapest route, you'll have entirely satisfactory bullets.

Cast-lead bullets will seldom be as uniform in weight, diameter and concentricity as the swaged type made by the factories. There are several reasons for this. First, the individual cavities of multiple-cavity molds are seldom precisely identical; the molten metal enters the cavity only under its own weight, and this is not always sufficient force to overcome trapped air bubbles or to fill out all the edges and corners; shrinkage sometimes produces invisible cavities in the bullet case; the alloys from which the bullets are made will not be entirely consistent from batch to batch. And there are other reasons. Really expert bullet-casters are sometimes able to produce bullets that are as consistently uniform and accurate as swaged bullets. In order to do this, they must take special pains at every stage of the process (including the sizing and

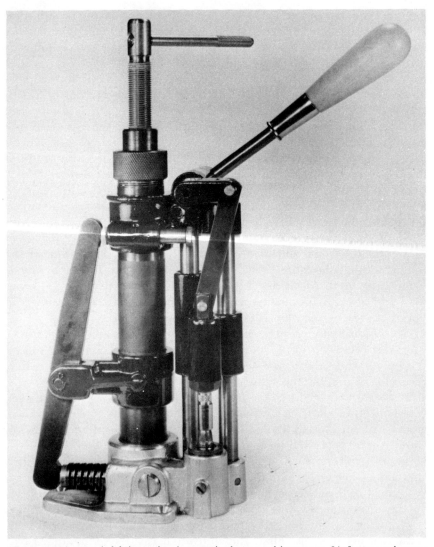

This Star semiautomatic lubricator-sizer is expensive but a good investment. It's fast to use because the bullet is sized and lubricated as it's pushed straight through the die to fall out at the bottom.

lubricating) and this slows output down tremendously. Factory-made bullets are formed in a die from a short length of lead wire subjected to as much as 50 tons of pressure. This compresses the lead very heavily, eliminates the possibility of any voids, eliminates any eccentricity due to mold-half misalignment—and the dies are so constructed so as to "bleed off" any excess lead and, therefore, any excess weight. Swaged

Handloading .38 and .45 Match Ammunition

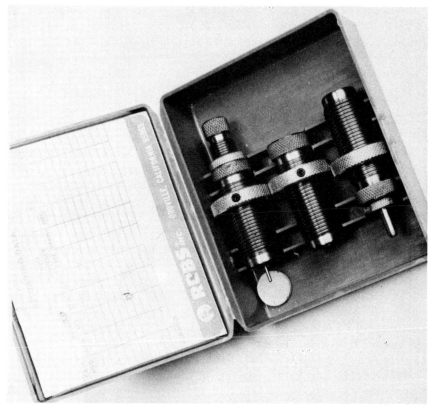

Here's a typical three-unit set of loading dies, made by RCBS. At left is a neck-expansion unit which also decaps. The resizing die is at center. At right is a bullet-seating die which will crimp either simultaneously or separately.

bullets are therefore more uniform than cast bullets. And that means they're more accurate, all other factors being equal.

You can, however, combine cast-bullet economy with swaged-bullet quality. First you cast, size and lubricate the bullets to the best of your ability, then put them through a swaging operation that compresses the bullets and bleeds off any excess weight. For this you need a swaging-die set and a heavy-duty press. The press may be a reloading press such as the RCBS Rockchucker, or it may be a bullet-making press such as the Mity-Mite manufactured by Corbin.

After sizing and lubricating—and it is absolutely necessary that all of the lubricant grooves be completely filled—the bullets are placed in the swaging die and the die is adjusted so that, even with the lightest of the bullets, at least a very small amount of lead is extruded through the bleed hole. This is a tiny hole in the die body through which lead can flow when sufficient pressure is brought to bear upon the bullet. Before sufficient pressure is generated to bleed off lead, all voids that might be inside the bullet are closed by that pressure. Then, when excess lead bleeds off, the finished bullets are of extremely uniform weight. Precise shape will also be more uniform, inasmuch as every bullet goes through the same die. However, if the lubricating grooves are not completely filled, the unfilled portions will be filled by lead displaced under the swaging pressure; and this will produce more lead at that particular point of the bullet's surface than at the opposite point, with the result that the bullet will not be balanced. That is, its center of gravity will not be coincident with its centerline. Thus, if the grooves are not entirely filled with incompressible lubricant, the swaging operation can make the bullets less accurate rather than more accurate.

Given a cast bullet of nominally 148 grains' weight, proper adjustment of the die to produce uniform weight may very well result in a finished weight of only 145 grains, or even less. Within a given batch of cast bullets being swaged, you can be assured of uniform weight only when at least a small amount of lead is extruded through the bleed hole. Any bullets that do not extrude will be of less than full weight and should be either discarded or reserved for plinking. However, simply ramming the press handle hard over, so that lead bleeds off, and then jerking it back to extract the bullet from the die will not insure proper weight. The press handle must be moved uniformly from one bullet to another, and it should remain in the fully extended position for the same amount of time for each bullet. If you adjust the die extra-tight and ram the handle hard up, you'll note that lead doesn't start extruding from the bleed hole until the handle comes to rest, and that the extrusion may continue for several seconds afterward. Lead is virtually incompressible under those conditions, but it does flow. The extrusion that continues after the handle has come to rest is not due to the lead itself, but to distortion of the die and the press frame, brought about by the tremendous pressures being generated. Therefore, a bullet swaged by a quick, hard movement of the press handle and then ejected immediately will be longer and larger, as well as heavier, than one that is allowed to remain in the die until lead extrusion stops. It might take several seconds for the lead and die to completely stabilize after the handle is thrown over on a given bullet. This could slow the operation down a great deal, so uniform bullet weight and dimensions should be obtained by throwing the handle over smoothly and not too fast, then allowing it to remain there for a uniform period of time before opening the die to eject the bullet. Only experimentation will tell you what this time interval should be for your particular bullets and equipment.

Handloading .38 and .45 Match Ammunition

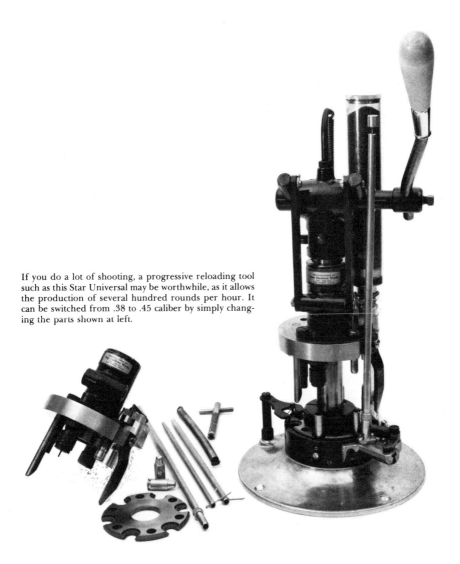

If you do a lot of shooting, a progressive reloading tool such as this Star Universal may be worthwhile, as it allows the production of several hundred rounds per hour. It can be switched from .38 to .45 caliber by simply changing the parts shown at left.

Hollow-base .38 bullets are generally credited as being the most accurate. Yet it is exceedingly difficult to cast perfect bullets of this type. When hollow-base bullets are required, as for serious matches, I've found that it's far more practical to swage them from solid-base cast bullets. A conventional solid-base W/C, such as the Lymann #35891, can first be cast, sized and lubricated, then inverted and placed in the swaging die. By "inverted," I mean that the base punch, which forms the cavity in the bullet, must contact the bullet nose. This is because the lubricating groove close to the original base of the bullet might other-

These cast bullets illustrate flaws that can reduce accuracy. The bullet at left was tipped as it went through the sizing die, and the sized bearing surface is therefore not concentric with the nose. The mold block that cast the right half of the center bullet was elevated slightly, so that it doesn't quite match the left half. At right is a bullet that went through sizing eccentrically, and the narrowing grease grooves indicate that more of its surface was removed on the left than on the right. As a result, the bearing portion is eccentric in relation to the nose, and the bullet is out of balance.

wise cause distortion as the punch enters the bullet. The nose extends much farther beyond its lubricating groove, so there is much less likelihood of this problem if the bullet is inverted.

Of course, there are additional small items and accessories you will find convenient if not necessary: a work bench, obviously; containers for all the components and for loaded ammunition; durable plastic ammunition boxes to take to matches; loading blocks, and perhaps other items that will occur to you as you get more deeply into the game. However, most of the items just mentioned can be scrounged or made out of scrap, and good cartridge boxes are quite cheap.

At the other end of the investment scale, there are semiautomatic, progressive-type, loading tools (actually loading *machines*) which perform all loading operations at rates of up to 800 cartridges per hour with a single operator, or substantially more if a friend is available to keep the hoppers and the feed-tubes filled with components. The epitome of such tools is the Star Universal Progressive reloader, which may be set up for either .38 or .45 caliber, as needed. Complete with the conversion kit, the price at this time is a bit over $600. It's easy to spend several hundred dollars more for accessories to increase the speed and convenience of the Star tool, but the only one I consider essential is the Hulme Automatic Case Feeder, priced at $65. I consider this accessory necessary to achieve the 800-rounds-per-hour speed.

With this sophisticated equipment and an adequate supply of all components, one weekend of fairly spirited effort can produce at least 5,000 loaded cartridges, perhaps as many as 10,000. If time is of considerable importance and value to you, then this may be the route to go. One or two weekends of loading will take care of an entire season's needs.

However, the progressive loader won't do a thing to eliminate bullet casting, sizing and lubricating. When I was loading large quantities of ammunition, I spent long, cold, dreary winter weekends and evenings casting, lubricating and sizing bullets that wouldn't be needed till spring. Then, when it came time to start loading ammunition for the coming season, I had an adequate supply of bullets sitting on the shelf.

If you don't have the time or inclination to make bullets yourself, there are other sources. There are numerous "custom casters" around the country, and as of this writing they will furnish cast, sized and lubricated bullets in .38 and .45 caliber for as little as $15 to $18 per thousand. When shipping is included, this increases your ammunition cost by nearly 2¢ per cartridge but the total still represents a very substantial saving over the price of factory loads.

Unfortunately, the casting and packaging methods used by many custom casters result in a product that isn't quite good enough for match use, and might leave a bit to be desired in accuracy for serious practice. Until a particular supplier proves to you that his bullets deliver match accuracy in your gun, you'd better not depend on it. There's an alternative, more costly source of bullets. All the major independent bullet manufacturers offer a series of match-type, lubricated-lead bullets of superb design and highest quality. Prices range from about $35 per thousand for .38 W/C up through about $47.50 per thousand for .45-SWC, and more for some others. Those prices are approximate retail as this is written. Many shooters handload ammunition with these factory-produced bullets for match work and top-line practice, while using home-cast or custom-cast bullets for general practice. Using factory bullets in your handloads will increase the cost of .38 W/C cartridges to a bit less than 4¢ each, and around 5¢ each in .45 caliber. This can certainly be justified for matches (which constitute the smallest percentage of actual shooting).

With tools and equipment selected, let's get on with the actual loading operation. First you must have fired cases, clean and free of grit or abrasive corrosion. Ideally, those cases should be of the same make and of the same manufacturer's lot. This will hardly ever be true, but no matter what conglomeration of fired cases you've scrounged, it will not be too difficult to segregate them by manufacturer. This is not because cases of one manufacturer are less accurate than another. But makes do differ, and if loads in different makes of cases are fired in the same

Factory-swaged bullets like these are almost invariably more uniform in dimensions and weight than home-cast bullets. As a rule, therefore, they are more accurate.

string, the group may be enlarged due to the different centers of impact.

Ideally, cases within the same batch should all be the same length. This will never be true, so use a case-length gauge to identify those that are too long or too short. Pass each case through the gauge and segregate those which do not fall within minimum and maximum limits. The reject cases can be used for plinking or other purposes, but abnormal lengths will produce vertical stringing on target.

With cases segregated, wash or tumble them to clean thoroughly. If you wash them, give them time to become absolutely dry before resizing. If you're using a tungsten-carbide sizing die, the cases may be processed completely dry; however, if you use conventional hardened-steel dies, the cases must be lightly lubricated. This is done by moistening a large towel with a small amount of case-sizing lubricant, then rumbling

Handloading .38 and .45 Match Ammunition

Cartridges to be resized should be clean, free of corrosion and lightly lubricated. You'll probably detect a few small dents among these .45 ACP cases, but nothing significant.

the cases in the towel so that they pick up a very minute amount of the lubricant. Without lubricant the cases will seize and gall in ordinary steel dies; they will not only look bad from scratches and scraping, but will ruin the die in short order. On the other hand, T-C dies are so hard and smooth that this will not occur.

Depending on the resizing die you're using, the fired primer may be punched out during sizing, or during neck expansion. It doesn't really matter which, so long as you adjust the decapping stem and pin to positively eject every primer, and to enter the flash hole centrally without catching on the edge and turning up burrs that might interfere with consistent ignition. Note carefully whether the resizing die reduces the rear portion of the case body down very nearly as small as the unexpanded portion immediately in front of the rim. When starting out with a new die, try the first few resized cases in the chambers of your guns to make certain the case is being reduced sufficiently to enter freely without interference. With some of the more economically priced T-C dies, pay particular attention that the mouth of the T-C insert doesn't scrape the case and turn up burrs; make certain also that it doesn't reduce the case to a diameter *less* than the portion immediately ahead of the rim. If the die creates either of these conditions, it is defective and should be returned to the maker, with an explanation of its faults and with one or two of the cases showing the results of the defect. I've encountered more than a few of the cheaper T-C

The author seats primers in a separate operation with a bench-type priming tool. The one shown here was made by Lockmiller, a company that has been absorbed by RCBS.

dies that reduced the case too much or had sharp edges on the mouth which gouged the case. Resized cases should also be free of any readily visible, longitudinal scratches or striations. These seldom appear when a T-C die is used but are often generated by a plain-steel die that has picked up tiny particles of grit from use; the grit becomes imbedded in the working surface of the die and scratches each case as it is forced in.

As can be seen, a good tungsten-carbide die possesses great advantages. It eliminates the need for lubrication, it virtually eliminates case damage, and it is of itself free from the damage that careless use produces in ordinary steel dies. A T-C die may well last for resizing a million cases, while a steel die can be ruined or worn out after resizing only a fraction of that number. Cases also tend to last longer (that is, for more loadings and firings) when resized in a T-C die; frictional loads and work-hardening are less severe than with steel dies.

Repriming the case is quite simple, from a mechanical viewpoint. However, inconsistencies in seating primers can produce variations of ignition, which in turn produce increased variations in velocity—and those variations increase the vertical spread of the shot group. If you're using a progressive-type tool such as the Star, the seating of primers is closely controlled by the design and adjustment of the tool. As the tool is shipped from the factory, it will seat primers with approximately the same degree of consistency as is done by the commercial ammunition manufacturers. That is quite acceptable. If you're using one of the bench-type presses, the most accurate method you have for regulating seating is the "feel" of the handle. Depending upon the mechanical advantage of your particular press (and the less the advantage, the better the feel), you can ease the primer into the pocket in the case head until it can actually be felt to touch the bottom of that pocket. In this position, with the anvil actually bearing slightly on the bottom of the pocket, the primer offers the most consistent resistance to the impact of the firing pin, and therefore will give the most consistent ignition.

If you seat it too deeply or with too much pressure, the anvil will be forced up into the cup, and perhaps the cup itself will be distorted by the head of the priming punch, and the pellet of priming compound will be fractured or otherwise damaged. The result will be less consistency of ignition and therefore less vertical accuracy on target. If the primer is not seated to the proper depth, that is, barely flush with the head of the case but with a fair amount of space between the anvil and the bottom of the pocket, it will yield to firing-pin impact, being driven toward the bottom of the pocket, and this produces a softening of the firing-pin blow which varies from shot to shot and causes similar variations in ignition, velocity and accuracy.

Admittedly, the variations produced by primer seating are slight, but they do exist and can definitely enlarge a group. The amount of enlargement may not be of much importance in practice, but if it costs only one point in an important match the price is too high. For that reason, some shooters load their practice ammunition in the normal fashion but they prime cases to be used for serious matches as a separate operation in a separate tool. This does slow down the operation, and may prevent the loading of those cases in a progressive tool. But considering the small amount of ammunition actually fired in matches, the added inconvenience isn't all that great. A small bench-type priming tool such as the RCBS will allow you to seat primers separately with a very high degree of uniformity. The mechanical advantage of the tool is rather low, and it is quite possible with a little practice to seat primers by feel so that they contact the bottom of the primer pocket very consistently. In this condition they will produce maximum accuracy.

Seating of primers may take place before or after the mouth of the case is expanded and flared. What I've said doesn't change, regardless of the sequence.

You may have heard or read a good deal about the use of Magnum primers in handgun loads. Well, there is no advantage whatever to be gained with Magnum primers in light target loads. The small charges of easily ignited powder recommended here are *best* ignited by Standard

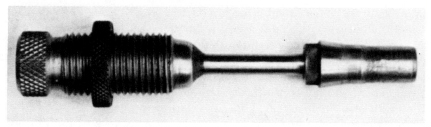

An expander such as this opens the case mouths to the diameter necessary to provide a good grip on the bullet. The plug may or may not contain a decapping pin, depending on the model. The tapered portion of the plug flares the case mouth for easy starting of bullets. The cylindrical portion may require shortening for auto cartridges.

pistol primers—the proper .38 size being Small Pistol, and the proper size for .45 being Large Pistol. Generally speaking, any of the major primer makes will produce entirely satisfactory accuracy. Much is said about the ability of one make or another to produce better accuracy in rifles, but I have yet to prove to my own satisfaction that any handgun-and-ammunition combination performs better with one make of primer than another.

The mouth, or neck, of the case must be expanded from its resized diameter to an internal diameter that will ensure that it grips the bullet with the proper tension. Maximum consistency of powder combustion and velocity is achieved when the force required to push the bullet from the case is exactly the same for each shot. This force is known as "bullet pull." It affects the rate at which the powder charge is consumed, and therefore affects the velocity given to the bullet. If there are wide variations in bullet pull, there will be corresponding variations in velocity. With normal cases and bullets of normal hardness, the inside diameter of the expanded case mouth should be approximately .003-inch less than bullet diameter. This means that the bullet must further expand the case as it enters. This neck expansion should continue only to the depth in the case to which the bullet will be seated. Consequently, the plug furnished with your die set should be of .354-inch diameter for use with .357-inch bullets. If for some reason you use some other bullet diameter, then the expander plug should be changed accordingly. Plugs are not costly and can be ordered in any practical diameter, though it is usually easier to begin with one that is a hair oversize and polish it down carefully.

Inasmuch as the bullet is larger than the inside diameter of the case neck, the very edge of the case mouth must be flared or given a slight funnel shape so that the soft lead bullet can enter without deformation. Expander plugs are made with a short conical section that opens up the case mouth to produce this flare. Unfortunately, this conical portion is

Handloading .38 and .45 Match Ammunition

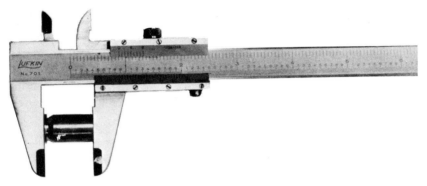

In the absence of a cartridge-length gauge, a vernier caliper can be set for the maximum length desired. A case that passes through its jaws properly is acceptable.

usually quite some distance above the end of the full diameter of the plug. The plug is adjusted vertically to give the proper amount of flare. The lower portion of the plug should be reduced in diameter so that the case is opened up only to the point reached by the base of the bullet. You can do this yourself by slow and tedious polishing, or you can have it done on a toolpost grinder at a machine shop. As a last resort, simply order a special expander to meet this need. Adjust the expander plug to produce only the minimum amount of flare that will allow the bullet to enter without being shaved by the sharp edges of the mouth.

Because there will be some variation in case length, the plug must be adjusted for flare on the shortest case. Of course, it will then produce excessive flare on the longest case, but you can live with this. You can't get by with the short cases being insufficiently flared and therefore mutilating bullets, causing them to strike well out of the group. Adjust the amount of flare so that the bullet can be just barely started by hand. *Any* amount of flare work-hardens the case mouth, and this will eventually result in longitudinal cracks and splits after a good many reloadings and firings. The greater the amount of flare, the sooner the splits will develop and the more destructive their effects will be. Cases flared only the minimum necessary for bullet entry may last for 20, 30 or more reloadings before the mouths crack; cases flared excessively may split after only four or five loadings. Once the case mouth has developed cracks or splits, it is no longer capable of holding the bullet with sufficient tightness or consistency, and accuracy will be reduced. Keep in mind also that really excessive flare of the case mouth will prevent the case from entering the bullet-seating die.

Once the cases have been prepared to this point, only inserting the powder charge and seating the bullet remains. Fortunately, target loads have been so highly developed that you needn't experiment with pow-

Small charges of fine-kernel powder may be placed in the cases fast and easily with a pistol-type measure like this, held in the hands and moved over the cases, which are held in loading blocks.

der charges. It has long been established that 2.7 grains of Hercules Bullseye powder will produce superb results in the .38 Special cartridge with a 148-grain W/C bullet of either solid-base or hollow-base design. This is virtually the only bullet in those two forms used in the .38 Special. However, there are bullet options in the .45, and this makes more than one powder charge necessary to cover the competitive uses. In .45, 4.0 grains of Hercules Bullseye is fairly standard with a 185-grain semi-wadcutter bullet, while a charge of 4.2 grains of Bullseye powder is slightly more effective with a 200- or 210-grain SWC bullet. For those individuals preferring to use a target load approximating the recoil and velocity of the service ball load, a 225-grain bullet requires 7.2 grains of Unique powder. This latter load is necessary to practice for the National Trophy Matches which must be fired with military ammunition issued on the range.

In any event, powder charges are placed in the case in the same manner. I have found the fixed-charge, pistol-type measures already mentioned to be most efficient and accurate for this purpose. Much has been said about the desirability of weighing charges on a sensitive scale, rather than dropping them from a volumetric measure. However, this has validity only with much larger charges than those in light target loads. In our range, 2.7 grains to 4.2 grains, weighing is generally no more accurate—often less—than the use of a good volumetric measure.

So purchase a basic measure from any one of the better makers, with metering drums for the charges you wish to use. Verify that each of these drums will actually drop the precise amount of powder for which it is marked. Often they do not. It may be necessary to modify the metering cavity until it drops precisely the amount of powder desired. Be-

Handloading .38 and .45 Match Ammunition

This Pacific Pistol Measure is a good type of powder measure (also supplied by other manufacturers) for target loads. It employs a fixed-charge bar.

fore attempting modification, you'll require access to a very accurate scale. I use an Ohaus Dial-O-Grain, which is far too costly to be justified for this purpose alone. Most likely you can locate a friend who has an accurate scale, or you might simply go to your local pharmacist (if he's friendly enough and you don't owe him too much money) and enlist his aid. If the metering chamber drops a powder charge too heavy, obviously the volume of the chamber must be reduced. I have found it practical and convenient to do this by placing a small amount of five-minute epoxy in the bottom of the cavity. The surface must be thoroughly clean and dry so that the epoxy adheres tightly, and you must use *more* epoxy than you believe is necessary. Then, after the epoxy is thoroughly cured, carefully scrape it away until the volume of the cavity is such that it drops exactly the right charge. If, on the other hand, the metering chamber throws charges that are too light, it must be enlarged. This is best done, or at least easiest, with a twist drill of very nearly cavity diameter. You don't even need a drill press or other

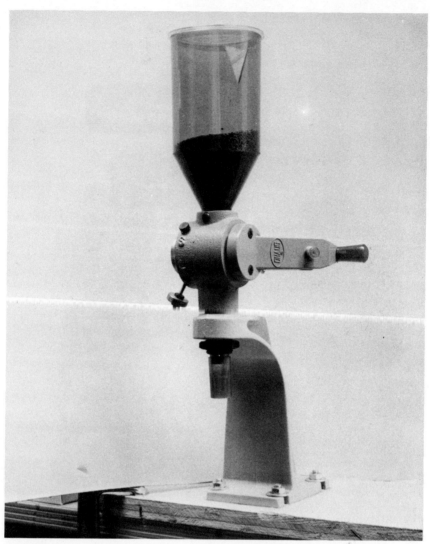

If a small metering chamber is used, a rifle-type micrometer-adjustable powder measure like this Ohaus D-O works well with small charges of pistol powder. However, a powder scale is needed for setting such an adjustable measure.

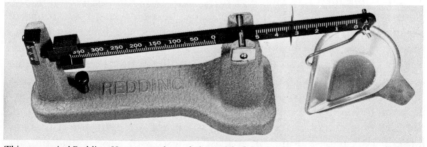

This economical Redding-Hunter powder scale is typcial of the simple, economical beam-type balances that can be obtained.

There are bullet molds for casting single bullets or up to 10 at a time. The single-cavity Lyman model at right is adequate for most users, and the four-cavity model is the largest the author recommends.

power; simply clamp some form of handle or knob on the drill and twist it by hand while bearing down just enough so that it will cut thin chips from the bottom of the chamber. Go lightly and check frequently, continuing until the chamber drops precisely the charge you want to use.

You can't simply weigh one charge dropped by the measure and assume that it will always throw exactly that amount. Inevitably, there will be some charge-to-charge variation. In order to eliminate this effect when changing metering-chamber volume, drop 10 charges—manipulating the measure as consistently as possible. Then weigh the entire 10 charges and calculate the average charge weight. This average weight is the reference point for any adjustment of metering-chamber volume.

The charge-to-charge accuracy (known as "extreme spread") in, say, 10 charges dropped by any measure is far more dependent on the consistency and uniformity with which the measure is manipulated than on measure design or the fit of parts. Practice operating the measure, with the reservoir filled with powder, until you are operating it as consistently as possible. There is no need for this practice to be wasted—use the practice to place charges in cases for plinking or practice ammunition. Just make certain that by the time you load any ammunition for serious matches you are quite expert in operating the measure uniformly.

With the measure properly prepared and the proper powder in it, fill a loading block with prepared cases and then carefully drop one (repeat, *one*) powder charge into each case. If the emphasis upon "one charge" seems superfluous, rest assured that it is *not*. The powder charges used in mid-range target ammunition are so small that they occupy only a fraction of the case volume. It's entirely possible to place two, even three powder charges in a case if you're not very exacting

After the powder has been dropped in the cases, each one must be inspected visually for missing charges or double charges.

and observant. Even though a double or triple charge of powder *might* not destroy the gun, it will certainly overstress it, and might produce minor damage that reduces accuracy. And until you've fired a double charge during a serious match, you cannot visualize what it will do to your mental state. I guarantee that it will ruin any chance you might have had of producing a worthwhile score.

After having measured a charge into each of the 50 or so cases, move the loading block under a good light source and visually examine the powder level in each case individually. Any double charges or absent charges should be readily visible. However, if you do not trust your eyesight to determine whether the proper charge is in each case, make a simple plug gauge of the type shown in the diagram. It can be made of metal, of sections of hardwood or of plastic dowel. Simply place this powder-charge gauge over the mouth of each case, with the outer portion resting solidly thereon, and note the amount of inner rod that protrudes upward. Protrusion beyond the zero line indicates an excessive or multiple charge, while less protrusion (the zero line not visible) indicates an underweight or missing charge. Visual inspection is by far the quickest and most convenient, and most handloaders that I know soon develop a very acute visual perception of non-standard powder levels. Thus, very few people use a gauge. Let your self-confidence be your guide, for a missing charge will tie up the gun and I've already described what a multiple charge can do.

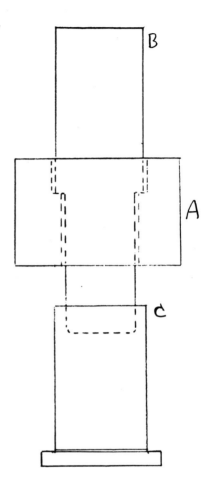

This drawing shows how to use the powder-charge gauge described in the text. The bottom of the plunger (B) should rest on the powder when the body of the gauge (A) is seated on the case mouth (C). Make a mark on B so that it will be flush with the top of A when the powder charge is correct.

With a loading block containing properly charged cases, the time has come to put the bullets in place. Carefully start a bullet into the flared mouth of each case. Press the bullet in tightly, but don't use too much force. Bevel-base bullets enter easily and wedge snugly in place with very little effort. Flat-base bullets have more of a tendency to tip in one direction or another. If tipping occurs to any great extent the bullets theoretically should be started in perfect alignment with the case—that is, with the bullet centerline coincidental with the case centerline. As a practical matter, this is very difficult to achieve, so just align them by eye and don't worry about it.

For the best results, bullets should first be seated to the proper depth in the case, and then the case mouth should be crimped on the bullet as an additional operation. Seating and crimping can be combined, but when this is done the case mouth digs into the bullet during the last ¹/₁₆-inch or so of bullet travel and may shave off a thin ring of lead which can cause problems. In autoloaders, this ring of lead may interfere with proper chambering and headspacing. (It may do the same in a revolver, but not to as great an extent.)

Set up the seating die by first screwing it into the press until it contacts the shell holder, then backing it out one full turn. Lock the die in that position and then adjust the seating stem (which should fit the nose of the bullet quite closely) so that when the case is run fully into the die, the bullet is forced into it to the proper depth. Then, when this has been accomplished on all of the prepared cases, back out the bullet-seating screw several turns so that it *cannot* contact the bullet when the cartridge is run completely into the die. From this point, turn the die successively farther into the press in small increments until all of the flare in the case mouth is removed by the squeezing action of the crimp portion inside the die. Adjust the die to produce slightly more crimp, then lock it in that position and complete crimping all the cartridges.

There are two schools of thought regarding the crimp that produces maximum accuracy in lightly loaded target ammunition. Actually, numerous tests have been conducted, and there seems to be no discernible accuracy difference between the "roll" and "taper" crimp. Both produce superb accuracy, and any differences that have been discovered are probably due more to variations in the operation than to the difference in the types.

All the same, a taper crimp is to be preferred on the .45 ACP inasmuch as it ensures somewhat greater uniformity in the headspacing of the case in the chamber. This cartridge headspaces by the case mouth coming to rest against a shoulder at the front of the chamber. If a roll crimp is used, particularly a heavy roll crimp, case contact with the chamber shoulder is less solid and less uniform than with a taper crimp. Personally, I've also found that there is likely to be greater variation in a roll crimp than in a taper crimp. By virtue of the long, conical taper in a taper-crimp die, the cartridge is self-centering in the die as the crimp is formed, while forming of a roll crimp sometimes allows the case to lean slightly and thus produce more crimp on one side than the other. A roll crimp die that does not fit extremely close upon the neck portion of the cartridge case will almost invariably produce an eccentric crimp, and there is reason to believe that such a crimp reduces accuracy, at least to some extent. For all of these reasons, I prefer a taper crimp in both .38 and .45 caliber, regardless of whether the ammunition is to be used in a revolver or autoloader. However, this preference is limited to light target loads and does not apply to Magnum-type loadings for hunting or defense.

Very little crimp is needed in .38 caliber when used in revolvers. Assuming a bullet diameter of .357-inch and a case-mouth diameter of .354-inch after expanding, crimp reduction $^1/_{16}$-inch below the case mouth of about .005-inch appears to be quite adequate. A slightly tighter crimp seems to do no harm, but the greater the amount of crimp, the fewer loadings may be had from a given case before its mouth begins to crack from work-hardening.

A greater amount of crimp is generally required on the .45 ACP. The bullet nose receives a considerable impact as the cartridge is driven from the feed lips against the feed ramp to be deflected into the chamber. If the bullet is not held quite tightly, this impact may drive it deeper into the case. This rearward bullet shift may not only cause a failure to feed, but it reduces the case volume and thus causes a given charge of powder to produce greater pressure, consequently greater velocity, and, as I've said, vertical stringing on target. For this same reason, it is especially important that the expander plug enter the case no more deeply than the point to be reached by the base of the bullet. In fact, it may be advantageous in some guns to expand only to a point $^1/_{32}$- to $^1/_{16}$-inch *above* the point reached by the bullet base. Then, when the bullet is seated, it is rammed solidly against the slight shoulder remaining at the bottom of the expanded portion. This shoulder supports the bullet more solidly against feeding impact.

Combined with seating the bullets solidly against the bottom of the expanded portion of the case, I generally taper-crimp .45 cases to produce about .008- to .010-inch reduction in diameter $^1/_{16}$-inch behind the case mouth. Seldom if ever is a bullet pushed back during feeding when this is done.

Occasionally you may wind up with a batch of cases whose walls are thinner than usual at the mouth. When this occurs, a standard resizing die may not reduce the diameter sufficiently for the case to grip the bullet tightly enough. In this event, the expander plug will enter the case mouth without any significant effort. The only solution is to either discard the cases or obtain an *undersized* sizing die which will reduce them a greater amount and produce the proper after-expansion inside diameter. The cases can also be salvaged by using larger-diameter bullets, reserving such loads for shooting where accuracy isn't so terribly important. You'll not notice the difference in plinking.

You may also occasionally encounter .45-caliber cases that do not grip the bullet tightly enough, even though sized and expanded to the dimensions given. They are simply too soft at the mouth. When that occurs, the cases may be usable by expanding the necks to a *smaller* diameter or by using an undersize resizing die. Expander plugs are cheaper than dies, so I usually just polish a standard expander plug down, about .001-inch at a time, until a point is reached where the case will grip the bullet tightly enough. Of course, as this is done, it is possible to reach a point where the plug no longer expands the case. When that happens, you can discard the cases or get an undersize sizing die.

Still other factors sometimes are considered worth extra effort when maximum accuracy is demanded. Inasmuch as .45 ACP cases headspace upon their mouths, length can be a factor in uniformity of ignition. An extra-short case will hold the primer farther from the firing-pin tip than a long case. If you could depend on the case being held tightly forward so that its mouth seated solidly upon the chamber shoulder, this would not be important. Firing-pin protrusion is more than enough to ignite primers consistently under those conditions. Unfortunately, you can't depend on that. A short case may simply be lying there, its mouth as much as $1/32$-inch from the chamber shoulder. A great deal of the firing-pin energy is then absorbed by driving the entire cartridge forward to contact the headspacing shoulder before the primer is actually ignited. By this time, the firing-pin blow is much lighter than normal, and thus an ignition and a velocity variation will be produced. This can be reduced somewhat by carefully selecting your longest .45 cases and reserving them for match reloads. It can also be reduced by having a barrel especially chambered somewhat short, then trimming a batch of cases so that they fit the shortened chamber precisely. This presents problems, though, because the gun—or at least the special barrel—will not accept any other loads.

The .38 Special cartridge headspaces upon its rim, whether used in a revolver or an autoloader. Rim-thickness variations are generally far less than variations in case length. Yet variations in rim thickness can affect the consistency of primer ignition. If you want to eliminate this factor, take a piece of $1/8$-inch flat steel and very carefully file a T-shaped notch in it, which will slip over .38 case rims. Make two of these, one with the notch forming the arm of the "T" only .060-inch wide, the other with this dimension .055-inch. The one with the wider notch is your "go" gauge, and any case rim that passes through it and does *not* pass through the second, or "no-go," gauge should give consistent ignition. Any case that does not pass through the "go" gauge or will pass through the "no-go" gauge should be set aside for practice or plinking. Ideally, maximum uniformity of primer ignition will be obtained when all case rims are of exactly the same thickness—but it would be virtually impossible to achieve this condition. The .005-inch tolerance built into our gauges is about as close as you can hope to come. In fact, with some lots of cases, you may reject more than you pass. If you want to be really snooty about case-rim thickness, have some tool-maker acquaintance make you a fixture and dial indicator to measure the precise thickness of every rim. I think it's a waste of time, but it can be done.

The final operations in producing target-quality handloads are some-what misunderstood. The first is, of course, thorough cleaning to en-sure that no bullet lubricant or resizing lubricant remains on the sur-face. I do this with a large, long-napped bath towel moistened with lighter fluid or similar solvent. A couple of hundred loaded rounds are dumped in the middle of the towel, which is rolled up lengthwise, grabbed at each end and shuffled about vigorously until the solvent-moist nap has removed all traces of lubricant from the cartridges. A word of caution: Never get the towel actually *wet* with solvent. It's pos-sible for the solvent to penetrate the joint between primer and case, and if it does so it might possibly wet or contaminate the primer and cause poor ignition. After cleaning, cartridges should be carefully in-spected. Any visible defect, nick, dent, deformed primer, deformed crimp, etc., is justification for setting a cartridge aside to be used for plinking or rough practice.

The last operation (except for packaging and labeling) is to make sure the ammunition will actually work in the gun. Dents or slight de-formations not readily visible might interfere with proper chambering. The easiest way I know to check this is to use the chamber of the gun as a profile gauge. Simply hold barrel in one hand, cartridges in the other and drop each into the chamber. If it falls freely and the rim halts flush with the rear of the barrel tang, or very slightly below, the cartridges will chamber properly when the time comes to use it. Fac-tory-loaded ammunition is gauged in the same manner, though special fixtures do the job automatically. Considering that the most ammuni-tion fired in a given caliber in a particular match is probably 100 rounds, the pre-match profile gauging isn't going to take much time—certainly it doesn't cost any extra money. Most people overlook this, but the small amount of time that is spent upon it can represent a really worthwhile investment.

Another subject sometimes overlooked is bullet shape, at least in the .45 auto. Even a load that produces a recoil impulse within acceptable limits, used in a gun that is otherwise in perfect condition, may not feed correctly. Virtually all mid-range handloads utilize bullets that are lighter and therefore shorter than the 230-grain round-nose type for which the basic design was originally intended. When the bullet is re-duced in weight and length, it becomes necessary to deviate from the normal round-nose shape in order to maintain adequate bearing-sur-face length. This length is, of course, important to accuracy but is more important in securing the bullet properly in the case. Recoil and feed-

At left is a typical .45 ACP handloaded with a swaged 200-grain lead bullet seated to the proper depth. The one at right shows what happens to the bullet as a result of recoil and heat if it is not held tightly in the case mouth and supported by a slight ridge or cannelure.

ing can force the bullet backward into the case if it is not held tightly enough, and long bearing surface is necessary to a tight grip.

In selecting a bullet, choose one with near-standard bearing-surface length, and of the greatest overall length you can obtain within the desired weight range—assuming, that is, overall length will not exceed that of a standard 230-grain bullet. It is entirely possible that someone might come up with a weird shape that would actually be too long, even though lighter than standard. Bullets approximating shape and length of those used in factory-loaded match ammunition are generally quite good, though somewhat shorter than standard. Stay close to those shapes and you won't have any trouble. Every major manufacturer offers bullets of approximately this shape, in weights ranging from 185 to 210 grains, and all of them work quite well.

In the search for ultimate accuracy, bullet diameter should not be overlooked. Bullet diameter can be quite important—even critical—to accuracy in a particular gun. The standard .357-inch diameter of .38 caliber is obviously not perfectly matched to the fairly wide range of .38 Special barrel-groove diameters offered by different makers. This rẻ res from .354-inch in some Colt guns up to .357 or even .358 in some S&W guns. It has long been my opinion, based on experience, that the most practical bullet diameter ranges from precisely barrel-groove diameter upward to no more .0015-inch greater than groove diameter. I can produce no great stack of test records to substantiate this opinion, and I must admit that many near-perfect scores have been shot from .354-inch barrels with .357-inch bullets.

In .38 caliber you would be wise to begin with bullets of .357-inch diameter, and in .45 with bullets of .451- or .452-inch diameter. However, if accuracy isn't all you think it should be, and the other factors have all been checked out, a change in bullet diameter is worth investigating. Before doing this, carefully slug the bore and determine groove diameter. Then obtain a sizing die to produce bullets within the diameter range already indicated. Lubricating-sizing dies are not terribly expensive, and if a half-thousandth change improves accuracy the money

Here is a typical low-cost electric lead-melting pot for casting bullets. The example shown is made by Lee. The can of Marvelux flux is another great aid in producing perfect bullets.

will be well spent. However, before going to all this trouble, make certain you possess or have available the facilities and the expertise in marksmanship to determine whether the change is for better or worse. The Ransom machine rest mentioned in the chapter on testing is the ideal way to go, but if you know a solid master-class shooter, perhaps he can run the tests by hand. It should be readily apparent that a ¼-inch change in group size at 50 yards simply cannot be demonstrated by the typical handgunner, though it may be clearly visible with a machine rest or V-rest test gun. I readily admit that on my best days I would be hard put to identify even a ½-inch change in group size, and the amount produced by a change in bullet diameter will most likely be less than that.

Most target shooters are inclined to use relatively soft lead alloys for their bullets. I'm certain this comes mainly from the fact that factory-loaded target ammunition generally employs a very soft bullet. This is doubtless best for standard factory loads intended to be used in a wide range of gun makes and models—but is not necessarily true of a particular gun in the hands of a particular individual. The fact must also be considered that soft lead is more easily swaged into the desired bullet than a harder alloy. Certainly the manufacturers are concerned with cost, and the overall cost of swaging soft bullets is less than for hard. When it comes to casting, though—given a good mold, a good technique and a well-fluxed alloy—hard metal casts just as easily and cheaply as soft. It may require a bit more effort going through the lubricator-sizer, but certainly not enough to present any problem.

I suggest that you explore harder bullet alloys in the search for accuracy. Clean, well-fluxed linotype metal casts beautifully, though the bullets are a bit lighter than if cast of alloy with a higher lead content. Over the years, I've found that it's easier to obtain perfect bullets from linotype metal than from softer alloys. Linotype metal is getting scarce and more costly as printing technology changes, but I have always obtained just a tiny bit better accuracy from the harder bullets. This has been especially true of the .45 ACP with its relatively shallow rifling grooves. Hard alloys also seem to improve feeding in autoloaders because the bullet nose is less likely to be deformed or to stick as it strikes the feed ramp. You will also find that with a harder bullet alloy it becomes more desirable for bullet diameter to approach barrel-groove diameter. A *soft* .357-inch bullet will easily swage down in a .354-inch barrel; a hard linotype .357-inch bullet fired in the same barrel will cause pressures to be increased somewhat and will also cause them to fluctuate a bit more. The increase is by no means dangerous, but if such a hard bullet is sized to only very slightly over-groove diameter, this potential problem is eliminated and accuracy may be improved.

My personal preference for use in autoloaders is a bullet cast of linotype metal and sized precisely to barrel-groove diameter or only very, very slightly over. In revolvers, another problem arises in that the chamber throats in the cylinder are often substantially larger in diameter than the barrel grooves. This means that even if bullets are sized to groove diameter, they will upset to some degree under the initial shock of acceleration and will thus be oversize as they enter the barrel. If one is fortunate enough to have a revolver whose chamber throats are equal to groove diameter or only very slightly over, then hard groove-diameter bullets will perform quite well. But oversize throats (let's say more than .0015-inch) may not perform well with hard bullets of groove diameter. Light target loads simply may not produce sufficient upsetting of the hard bullet to fill the throat, so the bullet may fishtail in the oversize throat and enter the barrel at a slight angle—"skewed." If the bullet enters the barrel slightly tipped—with its center line not coincident to that of the bore—then the bullet's path will be more of a spiral and groups will be enlarged. A softer bullet will upset more under the acceleration of a light powder charge, so it will fill the

Handloading .38 and .45 Match Ammunition

This C-H canneluring tool is being used to roll a cannelure in a jacketed bullet so that the case can be crimped tightly on it. The tool is also used to cannelure cases in order to provide greater support for the bullet bases.

chamber throat and thus is more likely to be properly aligned with the bore as it enters the barrel.

The answer to all this confusion is to check not only the barrel-groove diameter, but all of the chamber-throat diameters and strike an average of the latter. Base both bullet diameter and hardness on throat diameter. If the throats are more than .0015-inch over groove diameter, use a soft bullet of throat diameter; if throats are under that size, use a hard bullet sized to groove diameter. If you should be so unfortunate as to obtain a revolver with chamber throats of *less* than barrel-groove diameter, I can only suggest that you have the condition corrected.

Some custom pistolsmiths regularly rebarrel revolvers with .358-inch groove diameter, and then hand-ream all chamber throats to the same diameter to ensure best accuracy. If the throats are too large to permit this, a replacement cylinder is installed. If I were building up a revolver to use my own lead-bullet handloads, this is the approach I would take to obtain maximum accuracy.

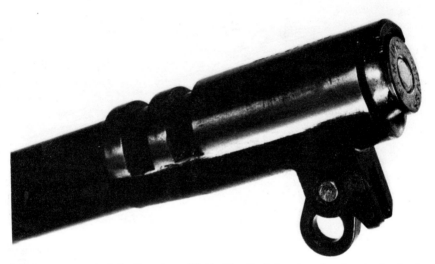

A sure, easy way to check the dimensions of finished handloads is to drop them into the chamber (or chambers) of the gun in which they will be used. Here, a .45 ACP load shows that it will chamber correctly in the barrel of a Colt autoloader.

It was established even before the turn of the century that deformation of the bullet nose does not necessarily cause any significant reduction in accuracy—while even very slight deformation of the base can cause accuracy to go to hell very quickly. The late, great Dr. F. W. Mann conducted extensive experiments along these lines, and they are covered in great detail in his book *The Bullet's Flight from Powder to Target.* Regardless of whether you buy bullets or cast your own, every reasonable effort should be made to ensure that the bases remain true. Plain-base, solid bullets normally have a sharply defined right-angle edge. Nicks or dents on this edge will cause a bullet to strike out of the group. Bevel-base bullets are less likely to become so damaged, but where the bevel breaks into the bearing surface is still subject to deformation. This will cause bullet flight to be less than perfect, but deformation where the bevel breaks into the base is not likely to cause any noticeable effect on accuracy unless they are very severe.

Much has been said about the effect of base-edge formation on accuracy, but seldom does anyone hear anything said about angular displacement of the entire bullet base. The effect is the same as base-edge formation, and of much greater magnitude. Accuracy is reduced because the deformed area begins to exit the muzzle before the entire base, and thus propellent gas under pressure exits there and tips the bullet slightly away from the location of the deformation. If a small dent on the base causes a bullet to tip away as it exits, think how much greater the effect will be if the entire base is slightly angled.

The incidence of slightly angled bullet bases is probably far greater in cast bullets than one would suspect. It can be caused by slight angular displacement of the bullet cavity, which I consider generally unlikely. More commonly, it can be caused by a bent or warped sprue cutter or by looseness in the sprue cutter or bending of the pivot screw. Sprue-cutter plates are often warped or bent by incorrect use (mainly use of a metal object to strike off) and thereafter simply cannot produce a perfectly square base. The angular relationship of the underside of the sprue plate determines whether the base will form a right angle in all directions to the centerline of the bullet. Anything that prevents the entire surface of the sprue plate, in contact with the bullet base, from being parallel to the top of mold blocks will cause angled bases. I have seen (and produced myself) bullets that were otherwise virtually perfect, yet when stood on their bases and examined closely, showed a clearly noticeable list to one side because of base angularity. Such bullets simply cannot produce the level of accuracy needed for competitive shooting.

Should you ever encounter the foregoing problem, look first at the sprue plate. Sighting across it from various angles in good light, you should be able to see any warps or bends. Look also for lead soldered to the underside of the plate or to the top of the mold blocks. A replacement sprue plate is easily installed, but if there is any indication of damage to the upper surface of the blocks, best send the entire outfit back to the manufacturer to have that surface ground flat and true, before a new plate is installed. A plate only slightly warped can sometimes be restored by simply rubbing its underside on abrasive cloth stretched tight over a perfectly flat surface. It can sometimes also be repaired by taking it to a machine shop and having the undersurface trued up on a surface grinder.

There are handloaders who can produce ammunition whose accuracy is much better than that of factory loads in certain *rifles,* and they make much of this accomplishment. They are justified, for their accomplishment indicates the high level to which advanced handloading has risen. The accuracy of almost any good rifle with the best factory ammunition can more often than not be exceeded by careful development and assembly of handloads matched very carefully to that particular gun. But this is seldom true for handguns.

Handgunners often expect that they will be able to show similar improvement over factory-load accuracy with handloads. My experience (and that of many acquaintances) does not indicate this is true. Advanced handloaders, using the best components, tools and techniques, can normally approach or equal the accuracy of match-grade factory ammunition in a good target handgun. But they are almost never able to do any better. At the other end of the scale, the product of the average handloader will usually be measurably less accurate in a given gun than factory match ammunition. The handgun is inherently far less mechanically accurate than the rifle, and the average handloader does not devote the care and attention to selection of components and assembly of ammunition that he would lavish on cartridges for a rifle, with its much greater accuracy capability.

Nevertheless, handloading is the way to go if you're to enjoy handgun target shooting to any great extent. It will enable you to shoot 10 times as much for the same money, or shoot the same amount for a tenth of the money. And if you're careful enough, you won't lose a thing in performance.

17
Care and Maintenance

Every shooter should not only learn the mechanical and functional characteristics of his guns but should become thoroughly familiar with all of the care and maintenance procedures and problems that will eventually arise. It's great to have a skilled armorer in a truck or tent a few hundred yards from the firing line, but when something starts going sour between strings there simply isn't time to get him there to do the work. The few moments between strings will allow you to make minor corrections that may well save the match. Afterwards, the armorer can do a more thorough job, but you are the only one instantly available. Moreover, you won't always have an armorer waiting on you, and to keep your guns in top operating condition, you'll have to give them proper care at home, between matches.

Relatively few tools and supplies are required for routine care and maintenance. Remember, I'm not talking about major repairs, just care, cleaning, preventive maintenance and perhaps some immediate action when prevention fails. Here's what you'll need:

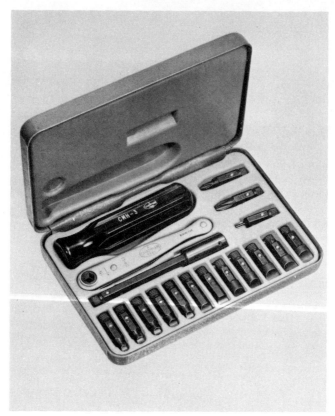

To maintain his handguns properly, the first thing a shooter needs is a set of good screwdrivers to fit every screw in all his guns. Because they can take up a lot of space, the author prefers a set like this one, made by Chapman, with a handle and a collection of bits of various sizes and types. But even a set like this won't fit every gun screw, so the author files and grinds extra bits, and fashions his own handles for them when necessary.

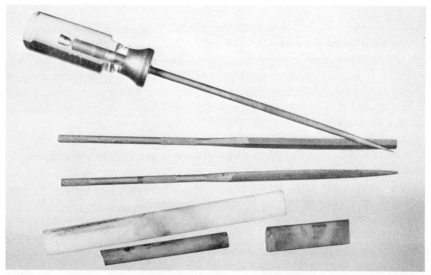

Needle files and stones will be needed for many repairs and touch-up jobs.

Stiff cleaning rods, close-fitting bore brushes and wool mops are essential for cleaning bores and chambers properly. For lubrication, the author prefers molybdenum disulfide, but it's often difficult to obtain and the Gunslick preparation shown here has earned an excellent reputation. So have a number of solvents, spray-lubricators and rust-preventive liquids. Perhaps no brand or type is perfect, but each has advantages and they are sufficiently inexpensive so that a gun enthusiast can have several on hand. Ordinary bristle brushes work well for some cleaning operations, but brass-wire brushes are needed to remove bore leading and chamber fouling, and are excellent for taking residue from the forcing cone or chamber throats. Pipe cleaners and cotton swabs are also useful, and several old toothbrushes may be even more useful than the commercial gun-cleaning implements shown here.

- Set of first-quality screwdrivers to fit all screws in your battery.

- Set of pin punches or drifts to fit all pins.

- Set of needle files.

- Small plastic hammer.

- Brass or bronze bristle brushes to fit all bores tightly.

- One-piece cleaning rods for all calibers.

- Wool or cotton bore mops.

- Bore-cleaning compound such as Hoppe's #9.

- Ordinary non-petroleum-base solvent (non-flammable).

- Special tools for all guns requiring them—barrel-bushing wrench, socket-screw wrenches, etc.

- Very fine steel wool and/or abrasive cloth.

- Bore-polishing compound such as J-B.

- A very tight-fitting brass chamber-cleaning brush.

- Lewis lead-removing tool for revolver-throat.

- Assortment of small plastic or soft-metal scrapers and probes.

- Assortment of small cleaning brushes (cut-down toothbrushes).

- Lubricants, greases and preservatives.

- Preservative-impregnated wiping cloth (silicone cloth).

- Touch-up bluing compound.

Most of the items are fairly common and of low cost, and they won't occupy much space. Except for the oils and greases, virtually everything on the list can be fitted neatly into a small cloth tool roll or carried in a plastic box that will occupy very little space.

Functional reliability demands cleanliness—proper gun cleaning. Most target guns are autoloaders these days, so let's look at them first. Centerfire autos are generally of the basic Browning type, with a tubular slide and mobile barrel. There are rather large rubbing areas where friction loads are fairly high and where an accumulation of dirt, grit or fouling can cause rapid wear that deteriorates the mechanical fit and eventually reduces accuracy. These surfaces require lubrication for proper functioning and friction reduction, and they accumulate dirt during firing. The grit forms an abrasive paste which not only wears away metal but increases friction, reducing functional reliability, especially with the lightest target loads. The main areas of this type are the guide grooves and ribs on slide and frame, barrel and barrel-bushing contact surfaces, and slide-breech areas that contact the barrel. Look closely and you'll see other rubbing areas.

Proper cleaning here begins with removal of the barrel and slide from the frame, and this first requires careful removal of the barrel bushing, utilizing whatever special tools (if any) are supplied with the gun. The bushing normally has a very tight fit in the slide and a very

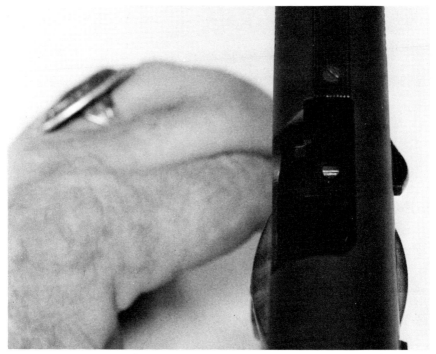

Fouling and unburned powder granules must be carefully removed from any area where they might interfere with functioning. In autoloaders, this applies especially to the extractor, its seat, and the breech area.

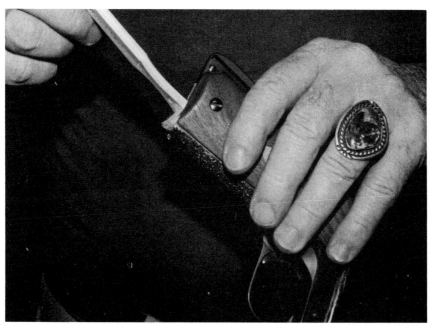

Be sure to clean the bottom of the magazine well, not just the top. Especially with light loads (and certain powders), fouling and unburned granules find their way down. Even if they don't, cleaning the upper end will drop bits of dirt down below.

With an autoloader, pay close attention to the part of the barrel that contacts the barrel bushing. Some bushings tend to turn up burrs or wear grooves, and powder fouling can accelerate this wear. The area should be kept clean, lubricated and (if necessary) deburred.

close fit over the barrel muzzle. Care should be taken not to gall the bushing or its seat in the slide. By the same token, too-frequent removal of the bushing will eventually make it loose in its seat, and this can cause accuracy to deteriorate slightly. With the bushing removed, it should be wiped or scrubbed clean both inside and out, then the outer surface where it engages the slide should be coated uniformly with a fairly thick-bodied grease. This grease not only makes subsequent removal easy without galling, but fills the uneven gaps between the two parts and makes for a more stable assembly.

With the slide removed from the frame and the barrel removed from it, all powder fouling and grit should be carefully cleaned from the breech face, underside and interior of the breech of the slide. This can be done with swabs and brushes—perhaps aided by scrapers and picks—but unless the debris is compacted, the easiest way I've found is simply to slosh the entire slide around in a can of solvent, using a cut-down toothbrush wherever the material doesn't come off easily. Look for debris—especially unburned powder granules—compacted in recesses such as the ejector slot, extractor cut, etc. This material should be removed with soft scrapers. Incidentally, the lighter the loads being fired, the more likely you are to encounter unburned powder compacted inside the slide.

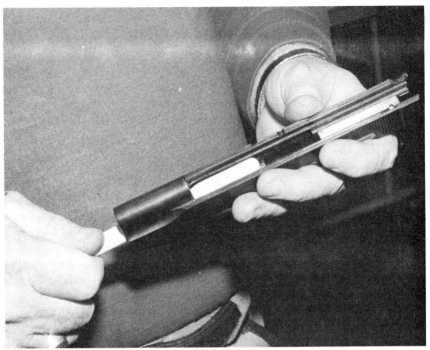

The slide's breech face must be clean for smooth, reliable feeding. Powder fouling piles up here, so you may need both a toothbrush and a brass-bristle brush.

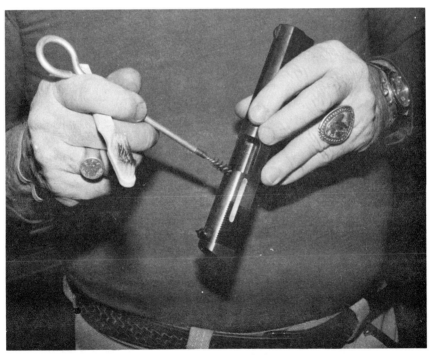

All of a slide's interior—but particularly the underside of the breech area—accumulates fouling. The whole thing should be cleaned thoroughly, and a toothbrush is again the best tool. It's especially handy for getting into the locking-lug recess.

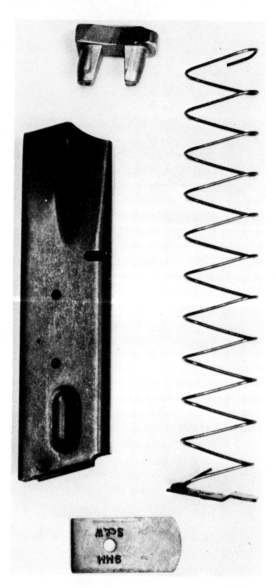

Magazines should get a thorough periodic cleaning and should be stored where they will be protected from airborne dirt. The best way to clean a magazine is to disassemble it and scrub all components with solvent.

With the slide thoroughly cleaned and dry, I prefer to apply molybdenum-disulphide dry lubricant, sparingly but uniformly, on all of the rubbing surfaces. This means the underside of the slide where it runs over the hammer and disconnector, the full length of the guide ribs and grooves, and those areas inside which contact the barrel. It will certainly do no harm to apply this material to the breech face to reduce friction as cartridge-case heads slide up over it during feeding. Molybdenum disulphide has a high affinity for non-ferrous metals, and after application literally cannot be removed short of damaging the surface. After the M-D has been applied, all surfaces should be wiped down with a cloth and a good grade of preservative. Don't use a thick,

Powder fouling and unburned granules will eventually seep under a revolver's extractor, and an accumulation can prevent the extractor from seating fully. This can cause the cartridge heads to protrude and bind against the recoil shield. Clean this area thoroughly.

heavy, petroleum-based oil for this; use one of the light, thin synthetic preservatives which will not gum up or oxidize and will not thicken or harden under extremes of temperature. Care should be taken to ensure that as little as possible of the preservative comes in contact with the rubbing areas already coated with M-D. The M-D, being a dry lubricant of superior performance, does not tend to catch and hold grit; thus, while grit may get onto the rubbing areas, it is not held there to form an abrasive paste as it is with a fluid lubricant. Eliminating that abrasive paste greatly reduces wear and this in turn greatly increases the accuracy life of the gun.

The barrel is next, and it is obvious that the bore should be spotlessly clean and smooth. Modern ammunition, including handloads, will not actually induce bore corrosion as was the case when primers left a hygroscopic residue. When lubricated lead bullets are being used, a very thin film of bullet lube is deposited on the surface of the bore, and while it is not a really good preservative, it does tend to reduce the probability that rust will form. When jacketed bullets are used, no such coating is left in the bore and it is somewhat more subject to light rust resulting from atmospheric moisture. For this reason, if the gun is not to be cleaned right away, a light coat of preservative should always be placed in the bore after each firing session. Both bore and chamber should be thoroughly cleaned and then examined in good light while perfectly dry. Looking at the bore and chamber when coated with oil presents a false picture; the coating reflects light and gives the impres-

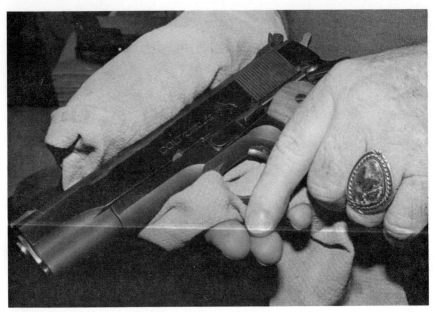

When the piece is put back together, wipe it down to remove the acid of fingerprints and leave a thin preservative coating. A silicone-impregnated cloth or mitt works very well, but so does a lightly oiled shop towel. Some shooters prefer the convenience of a silicone spray. It, too, is great if used sparingly. Overdoing it with a spray can flood the works and cause malfunctions.

sion of a smooth, glossy surface, even when it is not. Under normal conditions, a few passes through the bore with a bronze bristle brush will loosen normal fouling, after which the bore is wiped clean with a tight-fitting patch or mop, then coated lightly with preservative.

When jacketed bullets are being used, a very thin copper wash is normally deposited on the inside of the bore. I have not found it necessary to thoroughly remove this wash during normal cleaning. However, if it is patchy and of uneven thickness rather than uniform throughout, accuracy is probably best served by its complete removal. Ordinary scrubbing with a brass brush will not completely remove this material. It can be cleaned out quickly and easily by coating a tight-fitting patch or mop with JB Bore Polishing Compound and using this in full-length strokes, working from the breech and not allowing the patch to exit completely from the muzzle. Usually, only a few strokes are required to do the job. The residual compound should be washed out thoroughly with solvent, then the bore dried and coated with preservative.

Leading may also be encountered, but usually only if the bore is a bit rough to start with or if the bullet is too soft, poorly lubricated or oversize. In a bore that is otherwise in good condition, leading is accuracy's worst enemy. Light leading can be removed with bore-polishing compound, but this tends to produce very slight surface irregularities in the bore and I don't recommend it. The most practical method and one that works well on even the most extensive deposits is to coat the bore heavily with mercuric ointment, let it sit a few hours, and then scrub with a bristle brush. If the first effort does not remove all of the lead, repeat as needed.

Cleaning the chamber is another matter. Here you have no problem with copper wash or leading, but depending to a large extent on the powder used, a hard coating of powder fouling may accumulate. This tends to be thickest at the front of the chamber, tapering to virtually nothing at the rear. It not only reduces the diameter of the chamber and thus makes the case fit tighter, but its surface is hard, rough and abrasive. This causes a case to cling more tightly and thus increases extraction effort, which will reduce functional reliability, especially with the lighter loads. Normal cleaning methods will seldom remove this fouling completely, unless it exists only in a very minor degree. I've had the most success in removing it with a very tight-fitting brass brush rotated at slow speed in an electric drill. In a very bad case, it might be necessary to wrap fine steel wool around the brush; I've yet to find a fouled chamber that wouldn't yield to this treatment. Some individuals have advocated the use of an abrasive cloth to polish this fouling out, but I feel the risk of chamber damage and enlargement is too great. If some such treatment becomes absolutely necessary, I would suggest the bore-polishing compound mentioned above, applied to patches wrapped around a tight-fitting brush and spun very slowly by an electric drill. Some law-enforcement agencies have become so concerned with chamber fouling (especially in 9mm) that they specify the chambers to be hard-chrome-plated, which greatly reduces fouling adhesion. You might try this, though I see no need for it with light loads and proper periodic cleaning.

Naturally, all exterior surfaces of the barrel should be thoroughly freed of fouling, grit and abrasive paste, using soft scrapers if necessary. Particular attention should be paid to camming and locking surfaces so that an accumulation of debris there does not change the barrel-slide-frame relationship when the gun is in battery.

Also carefully examine that area of the barrel in contact with the barrel bushing (especially in the Colt Mark IV series) for any nicks or burrs produced by the bushing. If any exist, they should be very carefully removed with abrasive cloth or fine Arkansas stones. When doing this, be especially careful to remove *only* the burrs. These are seldom encountered except with the Colt Mark IV where the spring-fingers of the bushing tend to dig into the barrel, producing raised burrs and slight depressions. At the same time, examine the muzzle for any nicks

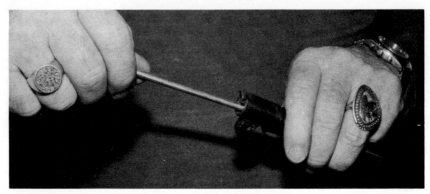

An auto barrel can—and should—be cleaned from the breech. Never try to save time by failing to remove the barrel and clean it this way. It prevents rifling damage from cleaning-rod wear at the muzzle and permits more thorough cleaning of the chamber.

or burrs intruding into the bore. Any that exist might damage the bullet slightly as it exits, and possibly reduce accuracy. Such burrs should be very carefully removed as described elsewhere. Should you be unfortunate enough to encounter a large bore intrusion, perhaps produced by the gun being dropped or by something being dropped on it, I strongly recommend that the barrel be re-crowned. Also check around the locking and camming surfaces and the chamber mouth for burrs and remove them if they exist.

If you discover light rust in the bore, first scrub it out thoroughly in the usual manner and then, if the damage appears to be nothing more then a very light frosting or etching of the surface, the barrel is worth an attempt at salvage. This is done by using JB Bore Polishing Compound on a very tight patch, working from the breech and polishing the surface smooth. Especially with jacketed bullets, a modest amount of polishing may get the barrel shooting as well as before. This remedy is well worth trying before condemning a costly barrel to the scrap heap simply because it looks as if its accuracy might be reduced. With the barrel thoroughly cleaned and checked, apply M-D to all the rubbing surfaces and then wipe the balance down with preservative.

The temptation may be great to completely dismantle the rest of the gun. It is by no means necessary, nor is it even recommended for normal cleaning and maintenance. The grips should be removed, however, and all the rubbing surfaces cleaned thoroughly as described for the slide. The interior of the magazine well, with the feed ramp, should be brushed clean of powder fouling and unburned powder, then coated lightly with preservative. If there is any significant buildup of lead or copper on the feed ramp (where the bullets strike initially) it should be removed with a twist of fine-grit abrasive cloth.

Care and Maintenance

If compressed air is available, and if the interior of the gun has been properly lubricated, dirt and grit that has filtered inside the frame can be blown out. It's unlikely you will have compressed air at home, but your favorite service station will have it, and a clean gun is well worth the trip. Just don't get reckless and wave the gun around so that some skittish attendant thinks you're going to rob the joint.

On the other hand, if fluid lubricants have been used inside the gun, it will no doubt require complete disassembly and thorough scrubbing in solvent. Then all contact and rubbing areas should be lubricated with M-D, the balance of the surfaces coated lightly with preservative, and reassembled. Thereafter, a shot of air now and then will keep it relatively grit-free.

It is unfortunate that magazines are seldom given much attention when a gun is cleaned. Functional reliability probably depends as much on the magazine as on any other mechanical factor. Powder fouling, unburned powder and other debris invariably enters the magazine through the top, as well as the counting holes in the sides. If allowed to accumulate, this will eventually produce feeding problems. If the magazine is not easily disassembled (an example is the Colt GM), then it should be sloshed vigorously in solvent, and a toothbrush used to scrub inside the feed lips with the follower depressed. However, if disassembly is practical, it should be done and the interior scrubbed thoroughly. The interior of magazines should not be oiled heavily, because oil will attract debris and form a thicker accumulation than if it is kept relatively dry. I prefer to check out and break-in a new magazine, fitting it to the gun as needed, and then have at least the interior lightly plated with hard chrome or coated with spray-on Teflon. This prevents rust and makes any lubrication or preservative unnecessary. It can be kept completely dry, and debris can be blown out at regular intervals.

Rimfire autloaders do not really present any different problems. Those of target types generally utilize a fixed barrel (attached rigidly to the frame, even though probably removable) and a small reciprocating breechblock rather than a long, heavy slide. Mechanically, then, proper cleaning of a rimfire autoloader is really much simpler because there are fewer areas of concern. Essentially, the same operations must be accomplished as already described—that is, removal of all residue and careful application of M-D on all rubbing and contact surfaces. In one respect, however, the rimfire auto presents a more difficult problem in that a greater amount of residue is generated by each shot. You not only have powder fouling and unburned powder granules, but—depending to a large degree on the make of ammunition—a fair amount of excess lubricant which is peeled off by the chamber mouth as the round is chambered. This builds up around the barrel breech and the

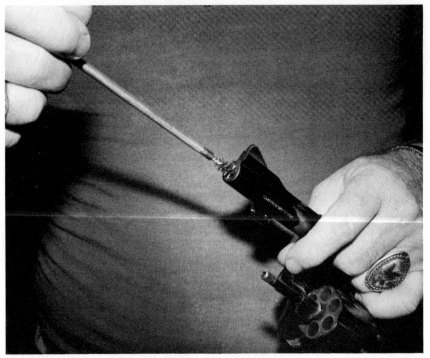

Unfortunately, a revolver bore has to be cleaned from the muzzle. Use a clean, stiff rod and make sure it doesn't rub on the muzzle and wear down the rifling.

slide face. With some lots of ammunition, this accumulation can build up very quickly until it interferes with extractor function or even with proper ignition. While most designs are self-cleaning to some extent—that is, the lubricant is forced out as rapidly as it accumulates past a certain point—this material should be removed as frequently as possible. Fortunately, disassembly is not generally necessary, so it's a simple operation. Just scrape off the accumulation, then wipe with a solvent-wet cloth.

The disassembly of autoloading pistols can present some problems. Too-frequent disassembly can cause looseness in critical areas and thus reduce accuracy. In this respect, too much cleaning is bad, perhaps worse than not enough. Provided one uses dry molybdenum disulphide as a lubricant wherever possible, the intervals between disassembly for cleaning can be greatly extended. The use of compressed air also prolongs cleaning intervals. Even the Colt GM can be blown free of most dirt and debris without any disassembly whatever—unless there is fluid lubricant to trap and hold this material. Simply open the breech, wipe out any debris, then blow all the loose gunk out with air.

Care and Maintenance

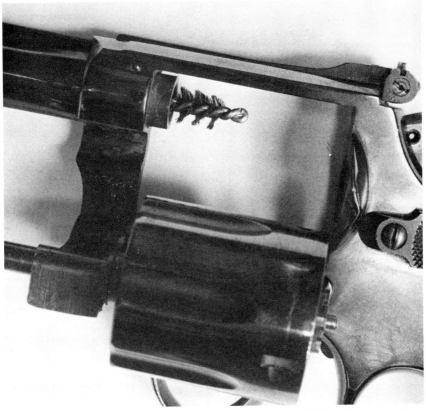

A stiff, oversize bore brush will expand to clean the forcing cone properly if rotated vigorously.

Cleaning without disassembly does preclude cleaning the bore and chamber from the breech. This presents no real problem if you take care to ensure that the cleaning rod does not rub upon the rifling at the muzzle. This can be easily avoided by making up a plastic bushing to fit over the cleaning rod, a flanged bushing that fits loosely into the muzzle for a very short distance and keeps the rod centered. Thorough cleaning of the chamber does require that the oversize brush be inserted from the breech, then a cleaning rod inserted from the muzzle and screwed to it, after which the rod may be chucked in an electric drill and spun as described before. When this is done, though, it is absolutely essential that the gun be examined very carefully for bits of wire thrown off by the brush in the chamber. Tiny wire fragments may find their way down into the action and cause later malfunctions. It is probably a better idea not to power-clean the chamber except on those occasions when the gun is disassembled.

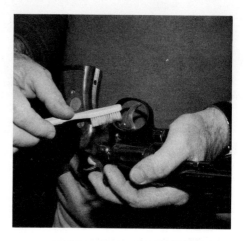

Revolvers—especially those with a separate sear or trigger-stop exposed behind the trigger—tend to accumulate dirt in this area. Brush around the trigger thoroughly but gently, watching for stray bristles that might invade the lockwork.

I don't wish to give the impression that frequent disassembly is at all necessary. I have known top-notch shooters to do a thorough disassembly and cleaning and lubrication job at the beginning of the season in early spring—and not disassemble the gun again until the close of the season at the end of summer. The scores of these shooters did not seem to suffer in the least from this prolonged disassembly-cleaning interval. On the other hand, I have known shooters who use copious amounts of fluid lubricants and find it necessary to disassemble the gun for cleaning about once a week, especially when shooting in the Southwest during the summer where there is often a great deal of sand and dust in the air. All that fluid lubricant soaks up grit and builds up large amounts of abrasive paste that must be scrubbed off frequently.

Revolvers present a few problems not encountered with autos, but then they are not plagued with many of the auto problems. After all, proper revolver functioning is not dependent on the recoil energy of the cartridge. Friction and the cleanliness of rubbing surfaces assume only relatively minor functional importance in revolvers.

Revolvers are most often used with lead-bullet ammunition. Therefore, leading of the chamber throats and the bore is much more common. Removal of lead in these areas is generally performed as described for autos, with one exception. The conical barrel throat, into which the bullet passes from the cylinder, often accumulates lead even when the bore does not. This can be removed by mercuric ointment, but if a tool known as a Lewis Lead Remover is used frequently, the accumulation will never be great enough to justify the time and effort of mercury treatment. The Lewis tool consists of a cleaning rod which is inserted down the bore from the muzzle, after which a piece of copper or brass gauze or screening is attached to the end of the rod. The

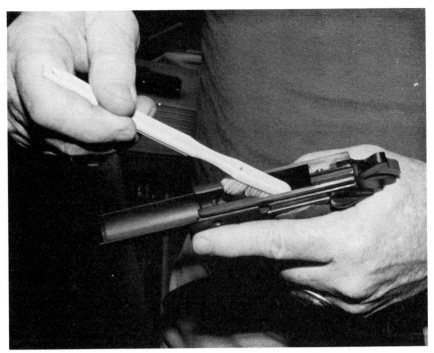

Fouling, unburned powder and even bullet lubricant can blow down onto the feed ramp and the magazine well. Use the toothbrush vigorously here.

In cleaning a revolver's chambers, you can work from the rear to avoid belling the chamber mouths. Use a tight brass brush and twist it as you push and pull, especially in the throats, where leading is likely to begin.

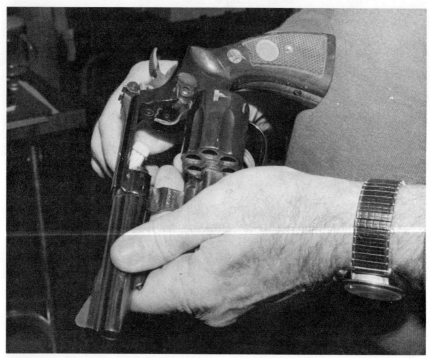

As a rule, a revolver's most neglected spot is the narrow space between the top-strap and the barrel tenon. Powder fouling accumulates rapidly here, together with oxidized bullet lubricant and microscopic fragments of lead and bullet-jacket metal. The mixture can become almost as hard as rock because of heat and powder gas. The way to prevent build-up and hardening is to clean the area thoroughly with a toothbrush—and a scraper if necessary.

rod is then rotated while pulling forward, and the screening scrapes the lead away from the conical throat. If this is done whenever lead becomes visible in the throat, no more difficult cleaning will ever be necessary.

Another cleaning problem peculiar to revolvers is removing the accumulation of unburned powder granules under the extractor star. It takes quite a while for enough of this material to accumulate to cause any functional problems, but it should be checked after every match. A small, stiff brush suffices to clear out the powder. If it accumulates, it will hold the extractor out of its seat a few thousandths of an inch. Then the firing-pin blow is cushioned, and ignition becomes somewhat erratic. This, of course, produces wide variations in velocity and great vertical stringing on target. I have seen powder granules accumulate to the point where case heads rubbed heavily against the recoil shield and interfered with functioning.

Care and Maintenance

Another spot often ignored is the bottom of the extractor seat, where fouling, brass shavings and powder granules can pack at the rear of the cylinder. This is another job for the toothbrush. But here and elsewhere, make sure no bristles get into the works.

Fouling also builds up around the ejector. If left unattended, it will drag on the slide during recoil movement.

Handgun Competition

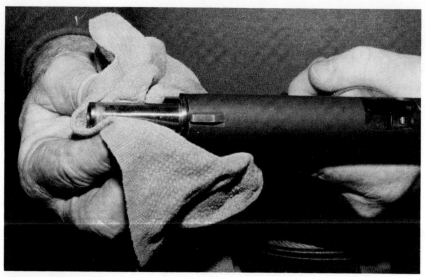

With some loads, fouling blow-back from the muzzle builds up on the barrel's bearing surface. If not removed, it will accelerate barrel-bushing wear.

Periodic revolver maintenance also requires that you check closely for tightness of the extractor rod. This is especially true of Smith & Wesson and some other revolvers where the front of the rod mates with a locking plunger. If the rod works loose from the shock of firing (and this often occurs), then the result may be a cylinder jammed in the closed position. When that jam occurs, you have no alternative but to very carefully tighten the rod by means of a pair of needlenose pliers applied to the knurled end. This is most likely to produce at least some marring of the finish, and if you aren't very cautious it may gouge the metal as well. In any event, tighten the rod only enough to allow the cylinder to be opened. Then remove the rod, degrease its threads and the threads in its seat, and reassemble with Loc-Tite. The only way to get this rod thoroughly tight is to wrap it with tape or thin leather and then apply pliers or a vise-grip tool to obtain sufficient purchase to wind it in all the way. Be careful that you don't grip it so tightly as to collapse the tube and that you don't mar or burr the external surface.

My preference for revolver cleaning is essentially the same as for autos—initially a complete disassembly and scrubbing, then application of molybdenum disulphide on all rubbing and bearing surfaces. After that, dirt and grit entering the action may be blown clear and the disassembly interval is prolonged almost indefinitely.

Disassembly of the lockwork of modern double-action revolvers is not as simple as with most good autoloaders. Take care to study exploded views and parts drawings, and thoroughly understand the mechanism before attempting disassembly and reassembly. If there is anything a gunsmith hates to get, it's a "shoe-box job" where the unhappy shooter brings in what he took apart but can't get back together and asks the 'smith to correct his mistakes.

Other routine maintenance operations are really quite simple. Front sights often become nicked, dented or burred from careless contact with another gun or hard object. Burrs should be carefully removed with a needle file, and then the bright surface coated with touch-up blue. Other areas of the gun might become nicked or marred, and require the same treatment. A certain amount of bluing wear will occur, sometimes accompanied by light surface rust caused by the acids in perspiration. The rust is most likely to occur on the front- and backstraps and trigger guard. These areas can be carefully polished smooth with fine abrasive cloth and then coated with touch-up blue.

Grips also become nicked, marred and splintered. A bit of sanding or trimming with a sharp knife, followed by a dab of stock finish, will make them look much better. A grip panel may also split from excessive tightening of its screws or from some other cause. If you keep a small tube of cyanoacrylate adhesive handy, a drop applied to the crack will make a permanent repair—just make damn sure the adhesive doesn't contact the frame, the screw or the other grip panel. If it does, you have a permanent assembly that can be removed only with a chisel.

After extensive shooting, burrs may be turned up on the face of the recoil shield or firing-pin bushing. If they protrude too far, they may interfere with cylinder rotation, or the primer cup may flow around them and lock the cylinder solidly. This is easily prevented by periodic inspection; as soon as burrs begin to rise, remove them with a needle file and polish lightly with abrasive cloth.

Sideplate or other screws may work loose from the shock and vibration of firing. They should not do so if properly tightened with a screwdriver that fits correctly, but sometimes excess oil or lubricant or worn threads make it impossible to keep them tight. When this occurs, you have two choices—replace with new screws (which isn't always successful since the problem may be in the holes) or simply degrease both screw and hole and use a sealing compound. The most common compound for this purpose is Loc-Tite. A single small drop should be applied to the threads of the screw, after which the screw is turned in quite tight. The Loc-Tite then sets up and holds the screw securely, yet it breaks loose with relative ease when you wish to remove the screw. I caution against attempting to use cyanoacrylate adhesive for this purpose. This compound may well hold the screw so tightly that the head splits when you attempt to remove it later.

Of course, if there has been any carelessness with the screws—and especially if improper drivers have been used—the screw heads will look a bit ragged. If you're careful, you can smooth them up, removing the burrs with a needle file and then polishing the heads smooth with abrasive cloth. Once this has been done, touch-up blue will give them color, and then they can easily be re-installed properly.

If the various procedures described here are followed with regularity, you'll be assured not only of maximum accuracy, but of the functional reliability that becomes so important in most matches.

18
Range Facilities

Whether the arms being used are BB guns, rimfire pistols or high-powered rifles, the ability of the projectile to cause serious injury or death makes safety the primary consideration. Where land is still relatively cheap, safety can be achieved without too much difficulty by simply fencing off a parcel of land adequate in length and breadth to provide a safety zone, or impact area, beyond which bullets fired in the general direction of the targets cannot travel even when they ricochet. With such an area established and adequately fenced, shooting may be conducted in safety without the necessity of additional barriers and backstops.

Unfortunately, sufficient land at low enough price is usually not available within reasonable reach of heavy concentrations of handgun shooters. It is generally essential to use less land in combination with assorted barriers. This type of construction reaches maximum cost and complexity in the case of an indoor range—a bullet-proof building that may be located in the heart of a city.

There exist basic rules for range construction. Military requirements for small-arms ranges (without barriers) specify a safety zone shaped like a fan. From the firing line, the right and left boundaries are splayed outward at an angle of 15 degrees to the direction of fire.

Handgun Competition

There are many types of bullet traps for indoor ranges. This one, made by Caswell, is convenient on large ranges. It can be adapted to either rifle or handgun use by changing the target hangers and locations.

Experience has indicated that this angle will contain most inadvertent shots, but it will not contain shots negligently fired at a greater angle. The assumption is made that the range officers and safety officers will be sufficiently sharp enough of eye to ensure that all shots will be fired within this 30-degree fan. The length of the safety zone is calculated at 50 percent more than the established maximum range of the gun and ammunition to be used. This maximum range, published in various references, is first calculated from ballistic tables, then verified by test firing, assuming an angle of departure (angle of the gun barrel above the horizontal) of 30 degrees. Inasmuch as military pistol ranges are employed almost exclusively with the .45-caliber autoloading pistol, the length of such ranges is based on the 1,700 yard range of that cartridge. That distance, plus the 50 percent safety factor, establishes a fan length of 2,550 yards. Because of that safety margin, such military ranges are generally considered safe with .38 and 9mm guns which have, in some loadings, a somewhat greater maximum range.

This is all very well for a single range whose firing line is of reasonable length. However, where multiple ranges are involved and different activities may be going on simultaneously, adjacent ranges are separated by earth barriers, or "burns," running parallel to the direction of fire. These burns are loose earth piled up by dozers, high enough to stop stray bullets wandering off to the flanks. Any bullet that does clear

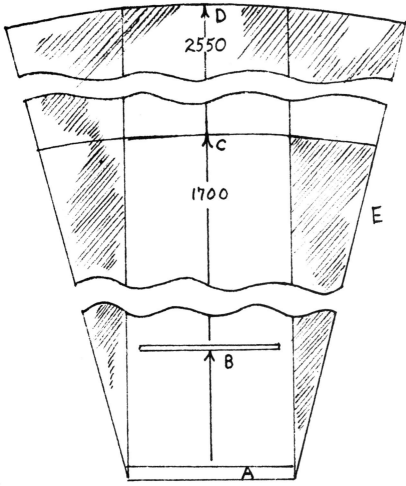

Here's a typical fan-shaped layout for a range on flat ground. The firing line is at A; the target frames are at B; C marks the maximum range of the arms to be used; D is the downrange safety zone; and E—the shaded area angling out from the firing line—is the safety zone at each side. The diagram is not drawn to scale (for lack of space on a book page) but the angles on each side are correct.

the top of the burn will pass well over the heads of any people who might be downrange scoring or changing targets on an adjacent range. Such multiple ranges are enclosed in the typical 30-degree fan whose length is calculated on the maximum range of the longest-range gun and ammunition to be used on any of the ranges in the complex.

The foregoing applies only to open ranges with a single direction of fire. It is quite adequate for NRA-type and International-type matches, as well as PPC matches and variations thereof. In all of those, competitors stand shoulder to shoulder and fire at an angle of approximately 90 degrees to the firing line and line of targets. However, in combat matches and the field-type matches of the National Shooters League, the individual competitor must fire in several directions, sometimes covering a fan of as much as 90 degrees.

Several NRA-type ranges exist here, side by side but separated by earth barriers. The ridge in the background forms an excellent backstop. The lower, closer, flat-topped ridge extending across the photo is an earth barrier between the pictured range and a neighboring one. The portable target frames can be moved from one target line to another and set into sockets at the required distance for a given course of fire.

Also, shooters in this type of match move from one firing point to another, generally advancing forward, and this has the effect of enlarging the fan through which bullets will travel. On level ground, a barricaded range for a National Shooters League Match would require a fan covering roughly 90 degrees and would use up nearly two square miles of land. An open range on flat land for IPSC shooting would require about the same amount of space for safety. And there would be, in addition, the cost of fencing or patrolling or both, to keep people from wandering into the danger area.

Even where land is cheapest, an open, flat-landed range would be prohibitively expensive. Barricaded ranges are the only logical choice. Depending on the nature of the terrain chosen, either natural or artificial barricading can be used. The former is far less costly. A combat-type range where the individual contestant shoots in different directions from different firing points (whether it be IPSC or NSL competition) is best situated in a depression surrounded by hills, cliffs or banks, with a box canyon being ideal. Careful choice of setting, and laying out the course of fire to take maximum advantage of terrain features, will often allow such a range to be installed without requiring any artificial barricades. The requirements for both IPSC and NSL ranges are sufficiently flexible so that many arroyos, stream beds or fairly deep, narrow valleys and canyons can eliminate the need for all but the most rudimentary artificial barriers.

Lacking such a natural barrier system, artificial barriers can be kept to a minimum by centering the range against a steep hill, cliff or stream bank and then adjusting the firing points and the directions of fire so that the majority of bullets fired will strike this natural backstop. It remains necessary only to construct wing barriers extending outward

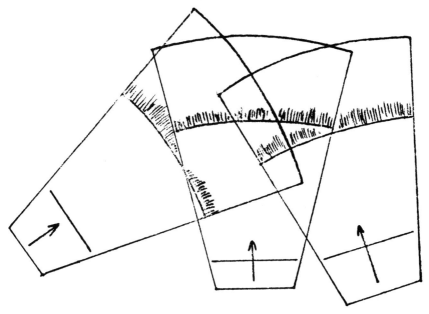

Space requirements for more than one firing line can be reduced by laying out the angles of fire to use the same impact areas and safety zones or at least to overlap them, as shown here.

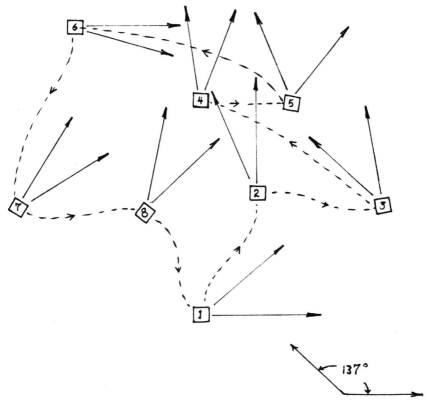

This diagram represents a field- or combat-type range where shooting is at different angles and where the several firing points require a large area. This example (by no means an extreme one) has a 137-degree arc of fire; with 30 degrees added for safety, 167 degrees would be needed. On flat terrain and without barricades, such an arrangement would require almost three square miles of land—one of the chief problems to be overcome in laying out ranges for matches of this kind.

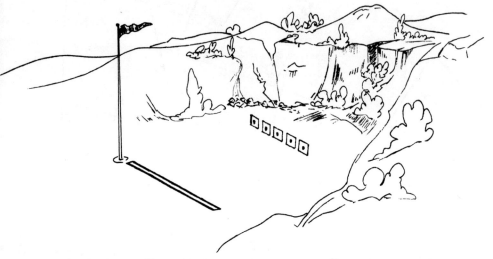

An adequate area with a semicircular natural barrier—a ridge, cliff or small box canyon, for instance—surrounding a reasonably level floor forms an ideal location for a low-cost range.

from the natural one. Of course, direction of fire should be generally north for best light, and natural barriers may not always allow this.

In thickly settled areas, this is usually not possible even if desirable terrain exists. The terrain may not be accessible, and nearby property owners usually object strenuously to shooting in their area, even after it is shown that they are entirely safe from stray bullets. There is often a great deal of objection to the mere noise of firing. In such areas, the only practical range for shooting of this sort is the barricaded type. A completely enclosed indoor range might sound feasible, but any building large enough for a combat-type range (unless the course were greatly reduced in distance and scope) would be prohibitively expensive.

The simplest approach is to lay out the course of fire so that the shortest possible U-shaped earth barricade can enclose all firing positions and targets. Earth barricades are by far the the simplest, least expensive, and fastest to build. They also have the advantage of appearing massive and impenetrable. A non-shooter can look at a 10-foot high, 15-foot wide (at the base) earth barrier and have the comfort of certainty that there is no possibility whatever of a bullet penetrating it to cause harm outside the range. Show that same person a six-inch reinforced concrete barrier or an equal-thickness wall of green-oak planks and he'll worry about "one of those big Magnums punching through it."

On flat terrain, the best use can be made of the least land at the least cost by pushing up three earth barricades to form a U-shaped backstop enclosing both targets and firing line. (This also deadens noise somewhat.) The barricades can then be made higher by an extension of upright planks (A) or a poured-concrete wall (B).

No matter how high such surrounding barriers may be, it's always possible for someone to let off an inadvertent shot at a sufficiently high angle to pass over them. This is certain to produce a strongly adverse reaction, even if it does no harm. Depending on the amount of fill material available, it is sometimes possible to build the earth barriers high enough so that the surrounding populace won't object. Another advantage to high barriers is that they tend to reduce the intensity of sound by deflecting the sound waves upward. There is, though, a practical limit to the height of earth barricades, and it may be advisable to extend them by topping them with a wall of green-oak planks or concrete. This begins to get very expensive, though, and it still won't satisfy a few of the nearby residents who visualize some negligent shooter letting off a round over even the highest barricade.

A better solution is an overhead barricade construction of thick planks, preferably green oak or similar hardwood, situated over the firing points in such a manner that any bullet fired at a sufficiently high angle to clear the lateral barricades would be caught by it. In its simplest form, the overhead barricade consists of one or a series of wide, thick planks (baffles) suspended horizontally between shooter and targets, with their widest face toward the shooter. Their height and spac-

Overhead plank baffles, when properly dimensioned and placed, will prevent any inadvertently high shots from escaping over the backstop.

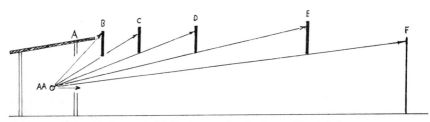

Here's how overhead baffles work. In this diagram, the shooting position is designated AA. Even an extremely high shot that clears the front of the firing-line roof (A) will strike the first baffle (B). If it passes under B, it will strike C— and so on. Any bullet with a low enough path to clear the bottoms of all baffles must strike the backstop (F) even if it misses the target.

ing is regulated so that from the shooter's position they mask all open space above the lateral earth barricades. Properly positioned, they also mask the space between one another, so that from the shooter's position no bullet can escape upward unless fired almost vertically between the individual baffles. With a range or firing point properly baffled, bullets are prevented from leaving the range overhead just as surely as if it were covered by a bullet-proof roof. And baffles are a lot cheaper than a complete building, or even a roof.

Where there are fixed firing points in a single row, as in NRA-type shooting, overhead barricading is relatively simple and all points can be accommodated by a single set of baffles. However, in a combat-type range, where one shooter at a time moves through several firing points and fires in different directions, the baffling becomes a bit more com-

This IPSC combat-pistol range shows typical use of overhead timber baffles supported on steel I-beams. A natural ridge backs the targets, and bulldozed earth barriers form the flanks. This is a very safe range, yet it consumes very little space. The bullet holes in the lower part of the nearest baffle testify to its effectiveness.

plex and expensive. The principle of basic baffle design remains the same, but separate installations must be used (unless the entire range is covered with baffles) for each firing point-and-target combination. Firing points, targets and baffles must be laid out so that the baffles for one firing point do not obstruct the line of fire for another. It is not uncommon in an open range of this sort for lines of fire from different points to intersect, and if everything isn't thought out carefully beforehand, a baffle might block a line of fire, especially if the range is laid out on rolling ground where vertical angles of fire differ substantially.

The ideal baffle material is hard, tough wood of a thickness sufficient to stop any bullet that might legally be fired on the range. Rough-sawn green oak offers considerable resistance to bullet penetration and will not throw off fragments of wood or bullet material to present a safety hazard. Planks of sufficient thickness to stop .45-caliber and Magnum bullets are quite heavy and require very strong supporting posts bedded deeply in concrete, and they must be strongly bolted to those posts.

If no full-charge Magnum loads are to be fired on the range, a four-inch thickness of oak will stop almost any bullet that might strike it. However, it would be impractical to use single planks of that thickness because of their weight and the fact that they would have to be joined edge-to-edge—and the joint extending completely through might permit bullets to escape. This would be particularly true after weathering, aging and warping caused the joints to gap open here and there. A safer method is to utilize thinner planks, around two inches, assembled in two layers with their joints offset so that at no point can there be a gap completely through the baffle. An even better (and more expensive) form of baffle construction utilizes a layer of ⅛-inch steel plate sandwiched between two-inch or thicker layers of oak. When bullets strike this sandwiched construction, even though they might break up against the steel center, the fibrous texture of the facing layer of oak will prevent any fragments from bouncing back toward the shooter or out the top. And, of course, the layer of steel greatly increases the baffles' resistance to bullet penetration and makes a thinner (overall) baffle adequate. Even the most full-charge Magnum loads will be stopped by such a sandwich of oak and steel. Softer woods can be used, but greater thickness is then required.

Other forms of baffle construction have been utilized, but what they offer in simplicity and economy can result in excessive maintenance and erratic performance. Old railroad ties make satisfactory baffles, but this is economically feasible only when one has access to very cheap or free ties. Because of their relatively short length, ties require a much greater number of closely spaced uprights, and this adds to the cost and complexity.

Just in case you ever run across a few hundred ties to be picked up for the work of hauling them away, remember that they can be made into excellent lateral barriers and backstops as well. I've seen many a small range whose backstop consisted mainly of old ties stacked parallel to the line of fire, so that all bullets strike the end grain. A fence of closely-spaced ties sunk into the ground for a third of their length makes a good substitute for an earth barrier as well. One range I encountered a number of years ago had extended the height of its earth barriers by sinking a row of railroad ties vertically in their tops.

The firing points should be slightly elevated above the surrounding earth, and should be smooth, solid and well-drained. Concrete firing points are desirable, but they are by no means necessary. Well-compacted, medium-size gravel held in place by two-by-four boards or similar lumber will do very nicely. Constructed in this way, single firing points should be at least 24 inches square. A long, continuous strip containing several firing points should be at least 36 inches wide. For shooting of the NRA type, each firing point should be supplied with a sturdy stand upon which guns and ammunition, sporting scope, etc., may be placed. A simple 18-inch square of heavy plywood nailed securely to the top of a post at about waist height will be adequate, but a continuous bench serving several adjacent points will be sturdier and provide more room for relatively little extra work and money.

A roof over the firing points is especially desirable. It intensifies the muzzle blast, but ear protectors eliminate this problem. While the roof is certainly protection from rain, its greatest advantage is keeping the shooters from the direct rays of the sun. If wide enough, it also keeps the sights in shadow, which permits sharper definition. In some areas where wind isn't a great problem, otherwise unprotected firing points are adequate. Where stiff winds are the rule, some form of windbreak is particularly desirable. This need be nothing more than canvas tacked to the posts supporting the firing-line roof with occasional openings for entrance and exit. Canvas is relatively cheap, but if it is left up for months on end it will suffer damage from sun and wind and may not be all the bargain that it appears. Light wood walls or fences are probably more economical in the long run, and they eliminate the labor of installation and removal for each shooting season.

Each organization that governs particular types of competitive handgun shooting publishes its own range specifications and drawings. Generally these specifications don't say a great deal about actual construction, but all the dimensions and prescribed or recommended layouts are shown clearly. The National Rifle Association offers the greatest amount of this material, covering its own type of shooting as well as International ranges and those required for modern police courses. Anyone anticipating or planning range construction of any type will find the pertinent NRA publications of great help, even though they might not apply directly to the particular range in question.

Much of the printed material supplied by the various shooting organizations depicts target setups that are a bit too ambitious or costly for the average club, and are certainly so for most individuals. They depict the ideal target installation. A much less sophisticated layout will be perfectly adequate for all purposes except actual conduct of high-level sanctioned matches.

Generally, the difference between economical and sophisticated, expensive target mechanisms is the difference between fixed and rotating targets. In both NRA and International matches, all but slow-fire is normally shot on precisely timed turning targets. The hydraulic, electric or compressed-air systems for turning an entire bank of targets through 90 degrees, and the electronic timing systems for establishing the proper firing times are very costly.

Simple, fixed target frames are the cheapest answer. They need be nothing more than rectangles nailed together from one-inch or two-inch lumber, with legs shaped so that they can be inserted in lengths of two-inch pipe buried vertically and flush with the ground. By fitting them into buried pipes, they may be removed easily for repair or replacement, and can be stored out of the weather when not in use. This type of installation also makes it possible to use the same frames for both short- and long-range shooting by simply moving them from one row of pipes to another. The frames need only be wide enough to accommodate standard-size paper targets, and high enough to place the center of the target at shoulder to eye level of the average shooter. Actually, target centers can be located as much as a foot lower than that without causing any problems, but the line of fire should not be at a significant downward angle. On level ground, placing the center of the target 4½ feet or so above ground level seems to be a good compromise. If the terrain slopes sharply, then the height of the frames should be adjusted to keep target centers reasonably close to eye level. I've shot on upward-sloping ranges in a canyon where the targets were right down on the ground in order to maintain an adequate level.

Since the tagboard material from which targets are made is rather brittle and easily torn or broken, the target proper should be backed by heavy cardboard. Target manufacturers supply thick, sturdy board almost ¼-inch thick for this purpose, but it is needlessly expensive. Panels cut from ordinary, corrugated-board cartons work quite well. Simply cut large squares of cardboard and staple them to the target frames. Targets may then be stapled or taped to the cardboard, and you're in business. The cardboard also tends to stiffen flimsy frames, and if they aren't to be used too heavily, this will allow the use of cheaper wood. Eventually, the centers of the cardboard panels will be shot away, and they must be replaced. It's easy to staple a second or third layer over the original, but beyond that all the damaged cardboard should be stripped off before replacement, or the frame becomes too bulky and unwieldy. An excess amount of cardboard will also absorb a great deal of moisture during showers and high humidity, and in some climates may never dry out thoroughly. In the long run, sticking to a single layer of cardboard is probably best.

Wood frames are highly perishable. A few hits—especially from wadcutter bullets—will splinter them badly. It's a good idea to keep several spares ready to go, because it upsets a shooter to have his target fall down in the middle of a string. If you can afford a bit more money and have available someone equipped and experienced for welding, better frames can be made from scrap water pipe or electrical conduit. The metal members, scarcely an inch in diameter, will be hit by stray bullets far less often than four-inch widths of lumber, so they will usually last a great deal longer. When made from pipe or conduit, frames may be either the two-legged, H-shaped type already described, or shaped as an open square, welded to the top of a single upright. This latter T-shaped arrangement is easier and cheaper to make and handle but is less stable in wind, and not often used in fixed installations for this

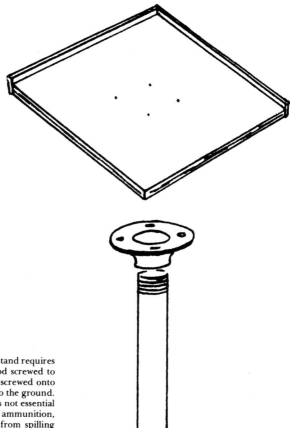

A simple, inexpensive shooting stand requires only a square of ¾-inch plywood screwed to a pipe flange which, in turn, is screwed onto a length of one-inch pipe set into the ground. A thin lip around the plywood is not essential but very helpful in preventing ammunition, magazines or small accessories from spilling off.

reason. Since cardboard can't be stapled directly to the conduit or pipe, sheet-metal strips are usually shaped into U-shaped clips and brazed or welded to the inside of the frame, then the cardboard is simply bent and snapped into the channels thus formed. If you want to keep it even simpler and cheaper, dispense with the sheet-metal brackets and simply tape the cardboard over the frame.

The T-type frames are easily adapted to manual rotation. To do so, a supporting flange should be welded on the leg to rest on top of the pipe buried in the ground, and the leg should be closely fitted in the pipe. The flange need be nothing more than a big washer. Then you need only add a crossbar just above the flange, with two light lines or strong cords extending back toward the firing line. A helper can stand or sit behind the shooter and turn the target—"edge and face" it—for whatever course is being fired. An individual practicing any type of

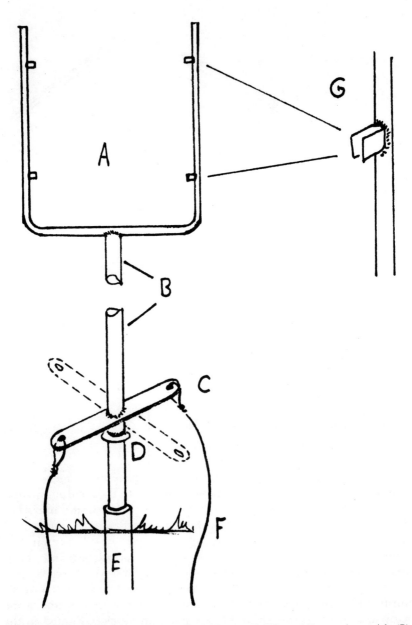

A simple holder for a turning target consists of a bent-conduit frame (A) on a pipe upright (B). A cross-arm (C) on the pipe allows ropes (F) to rotate the frame. A pipe flange (D) rests on a large pipe (E) which is sunk into the ground so that the smaller pipe can turn in the larger one. Stakes can be driven into the ground to halt cross-arm rotation at the proper point and thus limit target movement. Target-holding clips (G) are brazed to the frame.

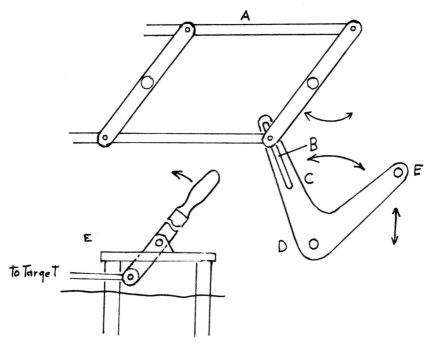

Several turning targets can be linked together by a rod (A)—or better yet, two rods. A crank (C), working through a long slot (B) turns the entire bank of targets. The crank turns on a pivot (D) and is hooked to a rod-and lever system (E) for remote manual control. The lever should be at or behind the firing line and is connected to the crank by a long, light but stiff rod.

rapid-fire or the International Center-Fire Course (with the single exception of International Rapid-Fire, where five targets are required) can get quite good practice this way if he can persuade someone to man the target ropes. Target timing won't be as precise as with electronic timers and power operation, but that detracts very little from the value of such practice.

If more than one turning target (operating in unison) is desired, it becomes a question of beefing up the frames and their pipes in the ground, and then connecting a bank of, say, five targets, by means of a lateral rod pivoted to a single-arm crank welded to each upright. Turning one target by means of ropes will then turn them all simultaneously. Of course, turning several targets requires a good deal more effort, so it might be advisable to use a rod and a long lever that can be set up to multiply the force exerted and to allow more than one person to work it.

When using manually turned targets, it's a good idea to have a separate individual with a whistle and stop-watch indicate the time intervals.

The parties operating the ropes or levers have enough to do without trying to watch a clock face.

Assuming the targets and linkages are solidly built, it really isn't very costly to substitute a surplus double-action hydraulic cylinder and a compatible power-driven pump for the lever, and thus obtain powered operation of the targets. As a matter of fact, some clubs (and mechanically adept individuals) have used surplus hydraulics and electronics that are available cheaply to home-build sophisticated turning-target set-ups that are fully as good as commercial units offered for many thousands of dollars.

These days, with tool-rental establishments on almost every corner and every home a do-it-yourself shop, any club or individual can have good target installations. A very high percentage of the cost of the commerically manufactured powered units represents labor; certainly there is plenty of free or low-cost labor at home, and that can be coupled with surplus components and native ingenuity to construct a home-built target installation that will serve every purpose currently known to organized handgun competition.

Appendix 1

Handgun Glossary

ACCURIZE: To modify a gun in various ways in order to produce maximum accuracy.

BACK-STRAP: Rear portion of that part of a handgun frame to which the stocks are attached; not always present.

BACK-THRUST: Force exerted rearward on the breech face when a cartridge is fired; may be calculated by multiplying chamber pressure by case-head area.

BARREL BUSHING: Barrel support in the slide muzzle of an auto pistol; may be fixed (Browning) or removable (Colt).

BARREL CAM: Cam in the barrel or frame which serves to lock and unlock the breech.

BARREL-TO-CYLINDER GAP: Space between barrel and cylinder of a revolver, essential to smooth operation; normally about .006-inch.

BARREL EXTENSION: In a short-recoil autoloader, a tubular member attached to the rear of the barrel, containing the breech bolt, and movable upon the frame. (Not common but found in Parabellum, Mauser M96 and Auto Mag pistols.)

BARREL LINK: Short, pivoted bar which raises and lowers an autoloader's barrel to lock and unlock in Colt-Browning designs.

BARREL LUG: Protrusion on the barrel for attachment of accessories or to house other parts.

BARREL TANG (HOOD): Projection at the upper rear of an auto barrel which controls relative longitudinal positions of barrel and slide when in battery; also aids feeding.

BARREL TRAVEL: Distance traveled by the barrel in locking and unlocking in a recoil-operated auto pistol.

BOLT (CYLINDER STOP): Movable stud protruding through a revolver frame into a notch in the cylinder to hold the cylinder in alignment with the barrel.

BOSS: Protrusion on a part, to house other parts or maintain alignment with related parts.

BREECH FACE: Portion of a revolver frame or autoloader slide which supports the cartridge head upon firing.

CALIBER: Bore or groove diameter, expressed in decimals of an inch or in millimeters; frequently combines a name, initials or a second number to indicate powder capacity of cartridge case, date of adoption, case length, proprietor, etc., as in .357 S&W Magnum, .22 Rem. Jet, .38-40 Winchester. (Often misleading, as in .38 Special, which has actual diameter of .357-.358 inch.)

CAP GROOVE: In a percussion revolver, clearance cuts in the recoil shield to allow easy application of caps and provide clearance for fired caps.

CAPLOCK: Muzzle-loading ignition system employing a percussion cap, a small metal primer cup containing a detonating mixture.

CHAMBER: That part of the bore (or cylinder, in a revolver) at the breech, formed to accept the cartridge.

CHAMBER INDICATOR: A pin, button or lever forced outward when a cartridge is chambered in an autoloader to indicate that the gun is fully loaded; may be a separate part or a design function of the extractor.

CLICK: Increment of adjustment in adjustable sights; provided by a spring or ball detent engaging notches in the adjustment screw. (Of no established value, though normally producing less than a one inch change at 50 yards.)

CLIP: Detachable magazine. (Originally, this term designated a metal strip for feeding cartridges into a magazine well.)

COMBAT CONVERSION: Shortened, lightened handgun intended for law enforcement.

COMBAT GUARD: Trigger guard reshaped at the front to provide a secure seat for the off-hand forefinger in two-handed shooting.

COMBAT SIGHT: General term referring to sights of low profile and minimum bulk.

CONVERSION UNIT: Parts to be assembled to change a gun's caliber or configuration.

CRANE (YOKE):   In a solid-frame, side-swing revolver, that part which is pivoted to the frame (receiver) and carries the cylinder.

CRIMP: Inward bending of the case mouth to grip and hold the bullet.

CROWN: Radiused, recessed portion of a barrel muzzle which protects the edge of the bore from impact damage.

CYLINDER: In a revolver, rotating magazine-and-chamber unit, containing several parallel cartridge chambers (most often five, six or nine) each of which aligns, in turn, with the barrel as the cylinder is turned upon cocking or by other means.

CYLINDER LATCH: A part, usually actuated by the thumb, to disengage a revolver cylinder so it may be opened for extraction of fired cases and for loading and unloading.

CYLINDER STOP: See "Bolt".

DEHORN: To cut off the hammer spur and other non-essential projections to facilitate rapid handling.

DISCONNECTOR (INTERRUPTOR):   Device in an autoloader to prevent more than one shot from being fired by a single trigger pull; usually functions by breaking connection between trigger and sear as breech opens, and reconnecting when breech closes fully.

DOUBLE-ACE: Trade name for an unusual device which allows cocking of the Colt Government Model pistol by squeezing a lever at the rear of the grip. Manufactured by Caraville Arms.

DOUBLE-ACTION: The capability of cocking and firing from the uncocked position by trigger movement alone.

EJECTOR: Device(s) at the barrel breech or within the action to expel fired case from the gun.

EJECTOR ROD: Rod, protruding under a revolver barrel, which is pressed rearward to extract and eject cases from the cylinder.

END PLAY: In a revolver, undesirable fore and aft motion of the cylinder.

ESCUTCHEON: Metal or plastic insert in grips to provide a more secure seat for screws. (Sometimes also applied to trade-mark emblems inletted into grips.)

EXTRACTOR: Device that removes or partially removes fired cartridge cases from the chamber.

FEED LIPS: Upper edges of a magazine which position and guide cartridges during feeding from magazine to chamber.

FEED RAMP: Portion of the barrel and/or frame which guides cartridges from magazine to chamber.

FIRING PIN: Part of the action, actuated by a spring or separate hammer, which strikes the primer and fires the cartridge.

FIRING-PIN BLOCK: Mechanical stop or interlock which prevents a firing pin from reaching the primer until it is disengaged by linkage with the sear, hammer or trigger at the instant of firing. (In the Walther design, it is a vertical plunger engaging the firing pin and displaced by the sear at hammer release.)

FIRING-PIN BUSHING: Hardened steel bushing let into the breech face of a revolver or auto and containing the firing-pin hole; usually also functions to limit firing-pin protrusion.

FIRING-PIN STOP: Device for retaining a firing pin in an auto pistol while allowing easy removal of the pin.

FLUTES: Semi-circular lightening channels cut between chambers in the outer surface of a revolver cylinder; may also be any long lightening cut elsewhere.

FLY: Spring-loaded leg (generally) attached to a revolver hammer; allows hammer to be raised and dropped by a single pull of the trigger in double-action.

FOLLOWER: Platform in a magazine that pushes the cartridges upward at the proper angle for feeding into the chamber.

FORCING CONE: Funneled area at the rear of a revolver barrel where bullets pass into it from the cylinder.

FRAME LUG: Protrusion which engages the rear of a revolver cylinder when open to keep it properly aligned for subsequent closing.

GRIP ADAPTOR: Curved block fitting between a revolver trigger guard and butt as a filler to allow a better hold.

GRIP SAFETY: Manual safety on the grip or stocks which must be depressed before the gun can be fired.

HALF-JACKET: Type of handgun bullet in which a thin, soft copper-alloy jacket covers only the surface in contact with the bore.

HAMMER: Part of the action which drives the firing pin against the primer, thus igniting the powder charge.

HAMMER BLOCK: Device which interrupts hammer travel to prevent the firing pin from being struck unless the trigger is deliberately pulled.

HAMMERLESS ACTION: In an auto, a straight-line, striker-type firing mechanism which does not contain a pivoted hammer; in a revolver and a few autos, a design which merely encloses or conceals a pivoted hammer.

HAND: Finger-like part, attached to hammer or trigger, to rotate the cylinder of a revolver when the arm is cocked.

INERTIA FIRING PIN: Firing pin shorter than the recess which contains it, and dependent upon its own momentum for igniting the primer.

JUMP: Upward movement of the muzzle, due to recoil, which occurs before the bullet leaves the barrel.

LEADING: Accumulation of lead-alloy bullet metal in a barrel; usually due to too-soft alloy, inadequate lubrication or rough bore surface.

LOADING GATE: Pivoted part which swings outward to expose the chamber(s) of a solid-frame revolver's cylinder for loading.

LOADING LEVER: In a percussion revolver, the pivoted lever under the barrel by which balls or bullets are seated in the chamber.

MAGAZINE: Device or reservoir to hold extra cartridges, of many types and names.

MAGAZINE CATCH (RELEASE): Device which retains the magazine in an auto pistol and which is actuated to release the magazine for removal.

MAGAZINE EJECTOR: Spring device (only rarely encountered) which ejects the magazine forcibly from an auto pistol when the magazine catch is actuated.

MAGAZINE LOADER: Device for mechanically depressing the follower and spring to facilitate placing cartridges in the magazine. Important in use of large-capacity magazines equipped with heavy springs.

MAGAZINE SAFETY: Mechanical interlock which prevents firing when the magazine is removed from an auto pistol.

MAINSPRING: Spring which drives the hammer, striker or firing pin to provide energy for primer ignition.

MUZZLE BRAKE: Device attached to or machined into a barrel muzzle for deflecting gas outward or upward and rearward through slots to reduce recoil and jump.

NIPPLE: Small, metal cone at the rear of the barrel (or cylinder) on a muzzle-loader, through which flame from the percussion cap passes to ignite the powder charge.

PATRIDGE SIGHT: Standard form of handgun sight with rectangular front element and rear notch as viewed by shooter.

PEENING: Method of moving metal by hammering it lightly, causing it to flow laterally away from the hammer blow; done cold, and comparable to forging except in degree.

PERCUSSION CAP: Small, metallic cup containing primer material for a muzzle-loader.

QUICK-LOADER (SPEED-LOADER): Device for carrying revolver cartridges in a group of five or six, properly held for simultaneous insertion into the cylinder.

RATCHET: Notched ring centered in the rear of a cylinder and engaged by the revolver's hand to rotate the cylinder and align each chamber with the barrel in sequence.

REBOUNDING FIRING PIN: Firing pin fitted with a retracting spring or mechanical device which automatically withdraws it inside the breech after firing.

REBOUNDING HAMMER: Hammer which is moved slightly rearward after firing by springs or cams; present in all modern DA revolvers except those utilizing a transfer bar.

REBOUND SLIDE (LEVER): Part of a revolver action which withdraws the hammer slightly after the firing pin has struck the primer.

RECOIL BUFFER: Device installed in an auto pistol to reduce impact of the slide coming to rest at the end of recoil.

RECOIL LENGTH: Distance traveled by the slide of an auto pistol.

RECOIL SHIELD: Portion of a revolver frame which supports the heads of the cartridges to prevent their moving out of the cylinder.

RECOIL SPRING: In an auto pistol, the spring(s) compressed during recoil to provide energy for closing the breech and feeding cartridges.

RECOIL-SPRING GUIDE: Rod or tube inside the recoil spring to prevent its kinking or rubbing on other surfaces.

SAFETY LEVER (BLOCK):   In modern revolvers, a part that moves to prevent the hammer from going fully forward unless the trigger is deliberately pulled fully to the rear.

SHORT ACTION: Revolver action in which hammer travel has been reduced to the minimum.

SHORT RECOIL: Locked-breech system in which an auto's slide and barrel recoil a short distance together, then unlock and the barrel halts but the slide continues rearward. Also an auto-pistol malfunction in which the breech does not open fully and thus fails to eject or feed, sometimes also fails to extract or cock.

SIDE PLATE: Plate fitted into the side of a handgun frame, removable for access to the lockwork; found generally only in modern DA revolvers.

SINGLE-ACTION: Action, or method of firing, in which the hammer is cocked manually before firing by trigger movement.

SLIDE-STOP: Part of an autoloader which engages the slide to hold it rearward; may be manually operated or activated by the follower when the last round has been fired—or both, which is the most common form.

SMOKESTACK (STOVEPIPE):   In an auto, a malfunction in which the fired case is not ejected but is caught vertically, mouth up, between slide and barrel breech.

SPITTING: In a revolver, the throwing off of bullet material to one or both sides as a consequence of poor cylinder-to-barrel alignment.

STIRRUP: Short link connecting the hammer and mainspring of a revolver.

STRAIN SCREW: In a revolver, a screw used to vary mainspring compression.

STRESS RAISER: Any irregularity, recess or sharp corner in a part which causes concentration of stress under load; can greatly increase probability of parts failure.

STUD: Pin or axle threaded or swaged into a frame to support other parts.

SWAGE: To form metal cold under pressure in a die, as when a bullet is formed and assembled in a press or when an oversize bullet is squeezed down upon entering a barrel.

TAKEDOWN LEVER (LATCH): In auto pistols, a part actuated to disconnect slide, barrel and frame to permit disassembly; may be separate as in the Walther P38 or a function of the slide-stop or other part as in Colt-Browning designs.

TARGET HAMMER: Hammer with wider-than-normal spur, deeply checkered and shaped especially for rapid and easy manual cocking.

TARGET TRIGGER: Trigger with fingerpiece wider than normal to provide more positive control and to give a lighter feel.

THROAT: In a revolver, that portion of the cylinder's chambers ahead of the cartridge case; in an autoloader, that portion ahead of the chamber leading the bullet into the rifling.

THUMB REST: Curved ledge in a grip or stock to aid in positioning the thumb.

TOP-STRAP: Top portion of a revolver frame passing over the cylinder.

TRANSFER LEVER (BAR): In modern revolvers, a bar struck by the hammer and driven against the firing pin to fire the cartridge; arranged so that the bar is withdrawn except at the instant of firing and thus prevents the hammer from contacting the firing pin at any other time.

TRIGGER SHOE: Accessory attached to a trigger to provide wider or longer finger engagement.

TRIGGER-STOP: Device for halting trigger movement at the instant the hammer or striker is released; prevents trigger over-travel.

UNDERLUG: On S&W revolvers, an integral protrusion of the barrel which houses the forward portion of the cylinder-locking mechanism; on Colt revolvers, it merely houses the ejector rod.

WRAP-AROUND GRIPS: Grips or stocks which cover the front-strap and/or back-strap and meet along its centerline.

Appendix 2

Cartridge-Interchangeability Table

Many cartridges are the same in dimensions and performance but have more than one name. Names and designations often differ in the U.S., England, various European nations and the Soviet Bloc. In addition, revolvers chambered for one cartridge will often fire others safely. This table will be useful in sorting out such problems.

U.S.	ENGLISH	EUROPEAN
.22 Long Rifle	———	5.56mm LFB
.25 ACP	———	6.35mm Pistol
———	———	6.35mm Browning
.32 ACP	.32 Colt Auto Pistol	7.65mm Pistol
———	———	7.65mm Browning
.30 Luger	———	7.65mm Parabellum
.30 Mauser	———	7.63mm Mauser
.357 Magnum	.357 Magnum	.357 Magnum
.380 ACP	.380 Colt Auto	9mm Kurz
———	———	9mm Corto
———	———	9mm Browning Short

.38 ACP (Super)	.38 Colt Auto	9mm Colt
9mm Luger	9mm Luger	9mm Parabellum
9mm Ultra	———	9mm Ultra
.38 S&W	.380 Revolver	9.25x20.3mm S&W
.38 Special	.38 Special	.38 Special
.38-40 Winchester	———	10.1x33mm Winchester
.44-40 Winchester	.44 Winchester	10.75x33.5mm Winchester
.45 ACP	.45 Colt Auto	11.25 mm Colt

CHAMBERED FOR (REV. ONLY)	WILL ALSO FIRE
.32 S&W Long	.32 Long Colt, .32 Short Colt, .32 S&W
.38 Long Colt	.38 Short Colt
.38 Special	.38 Short Colt, .38 Long Colt, .38-44
.357 Magnum	.38 Short Colt, .38 Long Colt, .38 Special, .38-44
.38 S&W	.380 Revolver, .38 Short Colt
.41 Long Colt	.41 Short Colt
.44 Special	.44 Russian
.44 Magnum	.44 Russian, .44 Special
.45 Colt	.45 S&W, .455 Webley, .455 Colt, .450 Revolver
.45 ACP	.45 Auto-Rim, .455 Webley if rim is bent down slightly
.455 Webley	.455 Colt, .450 Revolver
7.62mm Soviet M30 (auto pistol)	.30/7.65mm Mauser

Index

Index